Revive
My
Heart

Revive My Heart

A YEAR OF DAILY REFLECTIONS

Nancy DeMoss Wolgemuth

MOODY PUBLISHERS
CHICAGO

Devotionals are adapted from the following with permission:
Adorned: Living Out the Beauty of the Gospel Together ©2017 Nancy DeMoss Wolgemuth
Brokenness: The Heart God Revives ©2002, 2005 Nancy Leigh DeMoss
Choosing Forgiveness: Moving from Hurt to Hope ©2022 Nancy DeMoss Wolgemuth
Choosing Gratitude: Your Journey to Joy ©2009 Revived Hearts Foundation
Heaven Rules: Take courage. Take comfort. Our God is in control. ©2022 Revived Hearts Foundation
Holiness: The Heart God Purifies ©2004, 2005 Revived Hearts Foundation
Lies Women Believe: And the Truth that Sets Them Free ©2001 Nancy Leigh DeMoss ©Revived Hearts Foundation
The Lord's Prayer: A Thirty Day Devotional ©2016 Revive Our Hearts
My Personal Petitions Prayer Journal ©2016 Nancy DeMoss Wolgemuth
A Place of Quiet Rest: Finding Intimacy with God through a Daily Devotional Life ©2000 Nancy Leigh DeMoss
Portrait of a Woman Used by God: Lessons from the Life of Mary of Nazareth ©2016 Nancy DeMoss Wolgemuth
The Power of Words ©2003 Nancy Leigh DeMoss
Seeking Him: Experiencing the Joy of Personal Revival ©2009 Life Action Ministries
Singled Out for Him: Embracing the Gift, the Blessings, and the Challenges of Singleness ©2023 Nancy DeMoss Wolgemuth
Choosing Forgiveness: Moving from Hurt to Hope ©2022 Nancy Leigh DeMoss
The Wonder of His Name: 32 Life-Changing Names of Jesus ©2014 Revive Our Hearts
Worries, Woes & Worship: Moving from Fear to Faith ©2007 Revive Our Hearts
You Can Trust God to Write Your Story: Embracing the Mysteries of Providence ©2019 Revived Hearts Foundation and Robert D. Wolgemuth

Edited by Erin Davis, Tim Grissom, Mindy Kroesche, and Mindi Stearns
Interior design: Brandi Davis
Cover design: Brittany Schrock
Cover art of olive branch copyright © 2023 by Evgeniya/Adobe Stock (255072739). All rights reserved.
Author photo credit: Claire Thomas

ISBN: 978-0-8024-3376-3

Originally delivered by fleets of horse-drawn wagons, the affordable paperbacks from D. L. Moody's publishing house resourced the church and served everyday people. Now, after more than 125 years of publishing and ministry, Moody Publishers' mission remains the same—even if our delivery systems have changed a bit. For more information on other books (and resources) created from a biblical perspective, go to www.moodypublishers.com or write to:

Moody Publishers
820 N. LaSalle Boulevard
Chicago, IL 60610

1 3 5 7 9 10 8 6 4 2

Printed in the United States of America

From Nancy's Heart

Dear friend,

How's your heart today? Contented and at peace, or anxious and unsettled? Enjoying and resting in Christ, or harried and hassled?

All too often, I find that the state of my heart is subject to pressures or challenges at home or at work, or how others are treating me, or the latest news headlines. But in the midst of all of that and more, God wants to *revive my heart*. And He wants to do the same for you.

When God revives your heart, He'll restore your delight in Him. You'll have a fresh preoccupation with Christ and find in Him the grace to deal with stubborn sin . . . for those days when you feel you're just going through the motions of being a Christian . . . for those seasons when you're running on "empty" spiritually in the press of everyday demands.

Day after day, no matter what's happening in your world—or in the whole wide world—Jesus is waiting to revive you, to bring you hope and healing, peace and joy. But your relationship with Him won't grow without intentional effort—seeking Him through His Word and reflecting on Him each day. As you do, His truth will cut through your busyness, calm your frayed emotions, and help you align with His agenda for your life.

It's my hope that this collection of daily reflections will provide a fresh infusion of grace and perspective for whatever you may face throughout this year. And that with the dawn of each new day and the turn of each new page, the promise of Psalm 69:32 (ESV) will become more real to you:

You who seek God, let your hearts revive.

Seeking Him with you,

Nancy DeMoss Wolgemuth

The Spoken Word of God

Then God said, "Let there be light," and there was light.
—GENESIS 1:3

There are many natural wonders on our planet. And man has designed and produced many scientific and technological marvels. But none comes close to equaling the wonder of those three words found in Genesis 1: "Then God said . . ."

The eternal God and Creator of the universe, the One who holds all the bodies of water on the earth in the palm of His hand, the One who uses the continents as His footstool, the One who measures the span of the universe with the width of His hand—that God has spoken to *us*.

In the spiritual realm, God has given us many marvelous gifts—divine wonders that make us stand in awe of His greatness, His power, and His love. The creation of the world, the incarnation of the Lord Jesus, the miracle of the new birth—each of these marvels is inextricably linked to the *Word of God*.

When God *said*, "Let there be light," there *was* light. The mere spoken Word of God brought into being our entire universe.

Make It Personal

*Make a list of some of God's divine wonders—
and thank Him for His glory.*

The Master Storyteller

All my days were written in your book and
planned before a single one of them began.

—PSALM 139:16

No one likes a dull story. We want it to have intrigue, action, conflict, and twists and turns.

But when it comes to our lives, we think differently. We want our story and the stories of those we love to have predictable endings where everything gets tied up neatly, the good people live happily ever after, and the bad people go away. So, when the unexpected, unwanted twist or turn happens, we may feel disappointed, betrayed, or even devastated.

But God rarely writes neat, tidy, sanitized stories. In fact, many of the accounts we find in Scripture are pretty messy.

This is no less true in our lives. Situations that seem confusing and chaotic to us are actually plot threads He is weaving together to create a story—a beautiful, compelling work of art. Incidents and events that make no sense at all now will one day make perfect sense—if not in this life, then in heaven—as we see the masterpiece He had in mind all along.

 Make It Personal

How can you start to view the events in your life
as part of the backdrop of God's ultimate story?

Surrender Issues

You are not your own, for you were bought at a price.
So glorify God with your body.

—1 CORINTHIANS 6:19–20

S ome people claim to be surrendered to God, and may even believe they are, but they're actually justifying attitudes or behaviors contrary to God's Word. It may sound like this: *The stuff I watch on TV isn't that bad.* Or, *I admit I have a chronic struggle with overeating and with controlling my temper. But none of us will be perfect until we get to heaven.*

If you claim to be a follower of Christ while living in denial about areas of your life that aren't pleasing to Him, you're not living a fully surrendered life—no matter how many people may think you're a "good Christian."

To some extent, we all find ourselves in this deceived condition. We may feel that compared to the world's standards we're doing fine. In fact, writing this has forced me to deal with several matters in my own life that I had been overlooking, tolerating, or excusing that are really surrender issues at heart. I challenge you to do the same.

 Make It Personal

Are there any areas in your life where you're living in denial?
Ask the Lord to help you have a fully surrendered life.

Choice Silver

The tongue of the righteous is pure silver.
—PROVERBS 10:20

The book of Proverbs refers to the tongue more than one hundred times, and twelve of those instances connect "tongue" with "heart." Godly people speak out of the overflow of a godly heart. They are spiritually minded and don't just speak about spiritual things on Sundays. They are restrained and think before they speak.

So, how do people get tongues of righteousness? Their hearts are connected to the Source of wisdom and grace—the One who reveals Himself in Scripture. I want to be a wise, godly woman, but I don't always want to pay the price for a heart of wisdom. It takes discipline and effort to fill our hearts with God's Word—and to have a tongue that is choice silver. Silver, of course, is a prized metal. The tongue of the righteous is excellent, superior, worthy—it has been carefully refined and is of the highest possible quality.

A heart that is rooted in the Word and character of God will bring forth words that are of superior quality. Those words will be of great value to those who hear them.

Make It Personal

*Ask the Lord to help your words
be of superior quality today.*

The Priority of Praise

[Jesus] was praying in a certain place, and when he finished,
one of his disciples said to him, "Lord, teach us to pray."

—LUKE 11:1

The Lord's Prayer is much more than a way to pray. Jesus was teaching the way to live and think.

The prayer begins with, "Our Father in heaven" (Matt. 6:9). It starts with worship. In this model prayer, Jesus taught that praise should precede petition. This is the pattern of prayers all through Scripture. Prayer before petition; worship before asking.

Only after focusing on God and His glory did Jesus move on to His requests. There are no personal pronouns in this first part of the Lord's Prayer because it's all ultimately about our heavenly Father—His name, His kingdom, His will.

Before we pray for our own needs and concerns, we need to pray for God's concerns. Our instinct is to start with requests that are urgent or foremost in our hearts. But according to the way Jesus taught, there's a better starting place. No matter how urgent or desperate our petition, the starting place is our Father.

Make It Personal

What does your prayer life say about your priorities?

The Reason Why

"You have not heard his voice at any time, and you haven't seen his form. You don't have his word residing in you."
—JOHN 5:37-38

The Pharisees were renowned for their knowledge of the Old Testament Scriptures. Yet one day Jesus looked them in the eye and said, "You have not heard [the Father's] voice."

I can just see those indignant, bedecked Bible scholars turning red in the face and spluttering, "He's just a blue-collar worker! He's never even been to seminary! And *he's* telling *us* that we have never heard God speak? Why, we've spent our whole lives mastering the Bible!"

But Jesus wasn't finished. He went on, "You pore over the Scriptures because you think you have eternal life in them, and yet they testify about me. But you are not willing to come to me so that you may have life" (John 5:39–40).

The purpose of getting into God's Word is to meet Jesus. He *is* the Word! If we master the Bible but don't end up knowing, loving, worshiping, serving, and being like Jesus, we're really no better than the Pharisees.

 Make It Personal

Before you read your Bible today,
ask the Lord to help you truly meet with Him.

Reflecting His Beauty

So that they may adorn the teaching
of God our Savior in everything.

—TITUS 2:10

I've never considered myself to be particularly beautiful. It's not that I think I'm unattractive. Instead, I've tried to focus on cultivating beauty of character and the heart. Yet I still remember the first time Robert told me I was beautiful.

Robert kept telling me I was beautiful—and he really seemed to mean it. Gradually I began to believe that he truly saw me that way. Our courtship and marriage have helped me realize in a new and deeper way that when we're adorned with another's love, we develop a greater capacity to reflect love and beauty to others.

God has placed us here on earth as ambassadors of the gospel. Our calling as His followers is to make His love and truth visible and believable—and beautiful—to skeptical observers.

Because they see it in *us*. Because they see it *changing* us. His love is making us beautiful. Adorning us. And, through us, adorning His gospel.

 Make It Personal

Think about someone you know whose life adorns the gospel. What is it about them that helps make Christ's love and truth believable?

Breaking the Silence

No creature is hidden from him, but all things are naked and exposed to the eyes of him to whom we must give an account.

—HEBREWS 4:13

It is for our good and by God's mercy that God reveals the truth about us, no matter how shameful that truth may be. The reason God discloses our thoughts, actions, and motives is to bring us peace.

God is not a bully; He is a Savior. He cannot be soft on sin. His justice requires holiness that we, in our humanity, do not have the capacity for. The demands of God's justice have been satisfied through the sacrificial, substitutionary death of Christ on the cross. However, we must come clean; we must confess. Silence only condemns by keeping us guilty. Confessing our sin and breaking the silence ushers in the forgiveness and cleansing of God.

So, why hide? Why remain silent? Is there something in your life that you know is displeasing to God, some attitude or past behavior? Are you trying to hide it from God hoping He'll overlook it? God is calling you to break the silence today.

 Make It Personal

Come clean to the Lord about any sin in your life.

We Need It All

All Scripture is inspired by God and is profitable for teaching,
for rebuking, for correcting, for training in righteousness.

—2 TIMOTHY 3:16

It's true that not all parts of the Bible are equally easy to digest. This week I have been reading in 1 Chronicles and Ezekiel. Unlike the succulent passages we might discover in 1 Peter or the Gospel of John, there are some passages in those books that seem particularly tedious and even unnecessary. Even the great Puritan pastor John Bunyan admitted, "I have sometimes seen more in a line of the Bible than I could well tell how to stand under and yet at another time the whole Bible hath been to me as dry as a stick."[1]

Yes, we need the Psalms and the Epistles. But we also need the Books of the Law, the Historical Books, the Prophets, and the Gospels. We need the whole of God's Word.

It was for this reason that Paul reminded Timothy that "all Scripture is inspired by God and is profitable" (2 Tim. 3:16). That means we need a diet that includes *all* of God's Word.

 Make It Personal

Are you reading all of God's Word, or are there sections you avoid?

Not What You Ordered

Do not fear, for I am with you; do not be afraid, for I am
your God. I will strengthen you; I will help you.

—ISAIAH 41:10

Not long ago, Robert and I were invited to eat at an up-
scale restaurant. When our entrées arrived, they were
served on plates covered with shiny domes. At precisely the
same moment, the silver covers were lifted, revealing exactly
what we had ordered.

The problem is, when it comes to real life, what's on our
plates is often something we didn't order and might not even
want. We'd prefer to choose what looks good and then have the
server return, lift the silver dome, and—voilà!—exactly what
we wanted. Occasionally that may be the case. But often it's
not. God's divinely apportioned sovereignty is usually a surprise to us mortals.

Yet imagine the peace, comfort, and hope that would be
ours if we really believed God knows and sees everything that
lies before us—and that He has already provided whatever we
will need when we get there! What freedom from fear, anxiety,
and dread that should give us.

 Make It Personal

*Take time to thank God for His providence and
ask Him to help you trust His working in your life.*

The Promise of Forgiveness

As far as the east is from the west,
so far has he removed our transgressions from us.

—PSALM 103:12

Forgiveness is a promise to never bring up that sin against that person again. It is a deliberate decision to deal with another's sin by doing away with it, pressing the delete button, wiping it off our slate. With the promise of forgiveness, we relinquish our "right" to punish the offender or to make him pay. His record has been cleared.

Sometimes a woman will come up to me and say, "I've forgiven my husband" or "I've forgiven so-and-so"—and then she'll begin listing all the hurtful things that person has done to her. While I can applaud her for recognizing what she needs to do, her own words reveal that she hasn't fully forgiven—because forgiveness is a promise.

It's a promise God has made to us. Yes, what we did to Him was real. What we *continue* to do against Him is real. But by the atoning blood of His Son, God has chosen not to remember our offenses. He has put them behind His back.

 Make It Personal

*Ask God to search your heart regarding those
who have hurt you. Are you keeping the promise
of forgiveness in your relationships with them?*

The Benefits of Scripture Memory

Set your minds on things above, not on earthly things.
—COLOSSIANS 3:2

A valuable aid to meditating on Scripture is memorization. In fact, when I encounter someone who is battling discouragement or depression, I often ask, "Are you memorizing Scripture?" It can change our perspective and attitude.

"But I can't memorize," some will respond. Don Whitney points out that the issue is not so much our *ability* to memorize as our *motivation*: "What if I offered you one thousand dollars for every verse you memorize in the next seven days? Do you think your ability to memorize would improve? Any financial reward would be minimal compared to the value of the treasure of God's Word deposited within your mind."[2]

Scripture memory will bring about many benefits, including cleansing and renewing your mind; keeping you from sin; providing direction; strengthening your spirit; combating the attacks of the enemy; stimulating spiritual desires; and fixing your mind and affections on the Lord.

Make It Personal

*Choose a section of Scripture to memorize
and start learning it today.*

Keep Your Heart for the Lord

Guard your heart above all else, for it is the source of life.
—PROVERBS 4:23

In our fallen, sinful condition, before we come to faith in Christ, Scripture says our hearts are foolish, desperately wicked, and bent on sinning. Praise God, when we receive Christ as our Savior, God gives us a new heart!

But as long as we're in this fallen world, our hearts are vulnerable to being influenced by the world around us, by our flesh, and by indwelling sin. That sin won't be fully removed until we see Jesus and become like Him. That's why it's so important that our redeemed hearts be protected, guarded, and kept for God.

So, how do we guard our hearts? First, we need to watch out for negative influences that can corrupt our hearts. Second, we need to fill our hearts each day with the Word and by prayer and meditation on God's ways.

May these practices never become routine to us—may we see them as a way to get to know God personally and allow Him to keep our hearts clean and fresh.

Make It Personal

What does your heart specifically need to be protected from in this season? What practical steps can you take today to help guard it?

Blessed Are the Beggars

"Blessed are the poor in spirit."

—MATTHEW 5:3

Jesus' first recorded sermon was about how to experience true joy—how to be happy. It begins, He explained, by being poor. In today's world, if we were asked to suggest ways to be blessed, I'm not sure we would have started there. We don't generally think of poverty as a blessing. But Jesus came to introduce a radically different way of thinking about life.

In the original language, Jesus could have chosen two words to speak of someone being "poor." The first option suggests someone who lives just below the poverty line, someone who barely makes it. That isn't the word He chose. He used another word that means a beggar—a person who has no hope of surviving unless somebody reaches out a hand and pulls him up.

What is Jesus saying? Blessed are *the beggars*—those who recognize they have no chance of survival apart from God's intervening mercy and grace. Because of their need, they reach out to Him. Because they reach out to Him, He responds by lavishing them with the riches of His kingdom and reviving their hearts.

 Make It Personal

Are you a beggar? Take time to praise the Lord for
rescuing you and for the glorious riches that He gives.

Growth Takes Time

There are some things hard to understand in [Paul's letters]. The untaught and unstable will twist them to their own destruction.

—2 PETER 3:16

As meaningful as Scripture has been to me, not every day or portion has been a spiritual feast, any more than every meal I eat is a scrumptious banquet. Some passages have tasted more like cardboard than honey! Some days, I've felt like I was trudging through mud rather than "walking on the King's highway."

However, the value and impact of the Word in our lives cannot necessarily be seen in one day's or one week's intake. When a child is growing up, you don't usually see evidence of physical growth on a daily basis. But gradually you realize that his pants are getting shorter and his arms are protruding out of his shirtsleeves. At the end of the year, you're amazed to realize how much he has grown.

Likewise, the value of a balanced, nutritious diet is not generally experienced in one day or one week; rather the cumulative benefits of eating right will be experienced over an extended period of time.

 Make It Personal

How did you grow in your relationship with the Lord last year? Make a list and keep it to compare to next year!

Every Believer's Goal

For he chose us in him, before the foundation of the world,
to be holy and blameless in love before him.

—EPHESIANS 1:4

God's goal in saving you was not just to make your few years on planet Earth easier or more enjoyable. He had an eternal end in view. His intent was to make you holy, as He is holy, that you might perfectly glorify Him, that you might bring Him pleasure, and that you might enjoy intimate fellowship with Him for all eternity.

Your holiness is not secondary to whatever other goals you may have for your life—it is God's supreme purpose for you. It is something He desired, planned, and made provision for before He even created the world.

To be holy is your created purpose. It is our destiny. And it will be the outcome for every true child of God and for the entire body of Christ, according to that wonderful promise in 1 John 3:2: "We know that when he appears, we will be like him because we will see him as he is."

 Make It Personal

Do you share the Lord's goal for your life?
Are you pursuing His eternal purpose to make you holy?

All I Need?

His divine power has given us everything
required for life and godliness.
—2 PETER 1:3

"Christ is all I need, all that I need." It's one thing to sing that little chorus when we're sitting in a church service. But when we walk out the church doors and into the rough-and-tumble world, do we really believe He is *all* we need?

When it comes down to it, we often don't believe God's Word is truly sufficient to deal with our problems. Oh, it can deal with everyone else's problems; but it doesn't speak to *my* needs, *my* relationships, *my* situation. The way we live reveals what we really believe.

I need God's Word *plus* these eight books from the Christian bookstore; I need God's Word *plus* conferences and counselors.

Sure, I need God. But I need Him *plus* close friends; I need Him *plus* good health; I need Him *plus* a husband; I need Him *plus* a job that pays enough.

The truth is God is enough. If you have Him, you have all you need. Do you believe it?

 Make It Personal

*What difficulties are you facing right now? Ask God
for His help and then trust that He is truly all you need.*

Wrestling with God

Are you not from eternity, LORD my God?
—HABAKKUK 1:12

What comes to mind when you think of wrestling? You probably picture muscular athletes grappling in a gymnasium or stadium. The Bible presents a different image—one that takes even more strength and courage.

The name Habakkuk means "One Who Wrestles." We don't know what Habakkuk's parents were thinking when they named their child, but their choice turned out to be appropriate. An Old Testament prophet, Habakkuk wrestled with God in candid conversation. He wrestled over unanswered prayer and injustice. He looked at his violent world situation and wasn't sure he trusted God's plan.

It could be that you're staring across the ring at some challenges like doubt, confusion, guilt, unanswered prayer—all strong opponents in daily life.

Sometimes in the Christian world we act as if it's wrong to have questions, and we should just put our minds to sleep. In contrast, Habakkuk says, "I've got honest questions. And I'm going to go to the One who can give me honest answers."

Make It Personal

Are you wrestling with unanswered prayer and injustices today? Take your honest questions to the only Source of honest answers.

A Family Prayer

We who are many are one body in Christ
and individually members of one another.

—ROMANS 12:5

Throughout the Lord's Prayer, we don't see the words "me," "my," or "I." Instead, nine times we read "our," "us," and "we." This is not a self-centered prayer. When we pray the Lord's Prayer, we're praying in communion and relationship with all other believers in Christ. He is *our* Father. We may pray alone or with other people, but we're never approaching God alone.

So, as we come to God, we want to not only be mindful of how something affects us. We can't express our own concerns, needs, or desires to God apart from consideration of our brothers' and sisters' needs.

That gives a whole new scope and magnitude to prayer. We're lifting up our own needs to the Lord as well as the needs of believers all over the world. We may not know who they are or what they're going through, but God knows, and we're coming together to His throne through prayer.

 Make It Personal

*How should knowing that each time you come
before God you're praying with other believers
around the world affect your prayer life?*

Supernatural Aid

Make your ways known to me, LORD;
teach me your paths.

—PSALM 25:4

God has been gracious to make the Word come alive to me as I take time to pray each morning with my Bible open. As I pray His Word back to Him, I'm acknowledging that this isn't an ordinary book I'm reading but a *supernatural* one, and, therefore, I need the assistance of its Author.

Jesus told His disciples He was going to send His Holy Spirit as a Helper to teach them and to guide them into all truth (John 14:26). First Corinthians 2:14 tells us the natural man cannot understand the things of God. Only the Spirit of God can open them up to us. James says, "If any of you lacks wisdom, he should ask God—who gives to all generously and ungrudgingly" (1:5).

"Even the Bible," Samuel Taylor Coleridge is attributed as saying, "without the Holy Spirit, is like a sundial by moonlight."[3] We need the Holy Spirit, who inspired this book, to give us wisdom and understanding, to be our teacher, and to shed divine light on the Word.

 Make It Personal

Ask the Holy Spirit to give you wisdom and
understanding as you read God's Word.

The Birds of the Air

"Consider the birds of the sky: They don't sow or reap or
gather into barns, yet your heavenly Father feeds them.
Aren't you worth more than they?"

—MATTHEW 6:26

There are thousands of birds in my neighborhood, ranging from tiny yellow goldfinches to massive hawks, herons, and bald eagles. And early in the morning, my husband, Robert, will refill the bird feeders, just to be sure our little feathered friends have breakfast.

However, none of these creatures needs Robert in order to survive. Our good, wise, sovereign God cares for and meets all their needs. That doesn't mean they never have problems. But Jesus assured us that even common, ordinary sparrows cannot fall to the ground and die apart from the "Father's consent" (Matt. 10:29).

God does a more than adequate job of feeding birds. So, what does that mean for you? It means you have a God who cares deeply about you and who will meet your needs. He doesn't just watch the birds eat. He is personally involved with their feeding. And what He does for these, He will do for you.

 Make It Personal

*Try to watch some birds today and give God thanks for
His care for these small creatures . . . and His care for you.*

A Soft Answer

A gentle answer turns away anger,
but a harsh word stirs up wrath.
—PROVERBS 15:1

When you watch a TV show and listen to the way people speak to each other, you're likely to hear a lot of harsh, angry words. A soft or gentle answer can defuse a tense situation, but fighting words generally produce a fight!

This doesn't mean you avoid speaking the truth, however. Ephesians 4:15 commands us to speak "the truth in love." Sometimes it's not so much our words as the *spirit* in which they're said.

The men of Ephraim were easily angered and offended (Judg. 8:1–3). Yet Gideon defused their anger with a humble word. Likewise, we can create a calm climate in our homes by the way we respond to those around us, even if they're not acting as they should.

Soft, gentle words minister grace, strength, and encouragement. Try saying some of these gentle words to those around you today: *I love you. . . . I'm praying for you. . . . I'm so proud of you. . . . I'm sorry I treated you that way. . . . Would you please forgive me. . . . I appreciate you. . . . You're such a blessing!*

 Make It Personal

Ask the Lord to help you use soft, gentle words with family, friends, coworkers, and anyone you interact with today.

God's Final Word

Your word is a lamp for my feet
and a light on my path.
—PSALM 119:105

Jesus Christ, the living Word, was active in creation, and He holds together the world He created. The Word is active in redemption and in illumination. He is the one who shines light on our steps.

Jesus is the eternal Word of the eternal God, the full and final revelation of God to all people. He didn't come just to give us the Word of God—He is the Word of God. When Jesus speaks, God speaks.

Jesus reveals the way to the Father. He is God's final Word. Are we listening? Are we filling our mind with novels, TV shows, and music, or are we filling our mind with Jesus?

Because of Jesus, we can know the Father. But we'll never know the will of God, the thoughts of God, the mind of God, or the heart of God any better than we know His Son. If you want to know God, you must know Jesus. If you want direction for your life, listen to Jesus. Let Him speak to you through His Word.

 Make It Personal

How are you getting to know God through His Son?
Is there anything you need to get rid of to make room for Jesus?

Being Honest

If we say, "We have fellowship with him," and yet we walk
in darkness, we are lying and are not practicing the truth.

—1 JOHN 1:6

The apostle John had known the joy of deep fellowship with God through Christ, and he wanted his readers to experience it too. He reminds us that when we cover up or refuse to acknowledge sin in our lives, we deceive ourselves and cannot enjoy full fellowship with God or with each other.

In fact, the person who habitually covers his sin has no basis for assurance that he is a child of God at all! The willingness to be honest and confess our sin is evidence of genuine salvation and is vital to experiencing God's forgiveness and restored fellowship when we sin as believers.

God wants to experience intimate fellowship with His children. That's possible only if we're honest with Him about the true condition of our heart as He knows it to be. No matter what you may have done, you can experience God's great love and amazing grace.

Make It Personal

*Pour out your heart to the Lord, being honest about your sin,
and ask that you might experience intimate fellowship with Him.*

A Great Tapestry

How can a young man keep his way pure?
By keeping your word.
—PSALM 119:9

This past year I've read through the Bible three times in order to get a bird's-eye view of the panoramic plan of God. The view was magnificent—much like the spectacular vista from a mountain peak. There are themes that run like rivers from Genesis to Revelation—at points they are just a trickle; at other places they become a powerful, gushing force.

Like threads in a great tapestry, those themes are woven together to form the matchless story of Redemption. God's plan to create and redeem a race for Himself; His unending love, mercy, and grace; His long-suffering toward sinners and yet His righteous judgment against those who refuse to repent; the wiles and persistent hatred and rebellion of Satan against God; Satan's never-ending attempts to persuade man to join him in his sedition; God's ultimate, decisive triumph over Satan and His eternal rule over heaven and earth and hell—these are some of the overarching views that have filled my vision as I have looked at the Scripture as a whole.

 Make It Personal

*What's one of your favorite themes that
you see woven throughout Scripture?*

Filled with His Love

"As the Father has loved me, I have also loved you.
Remain in my love."

—JOHN 15:9

There are hundreds of commandments in the Old Testament, but when Jesus was asked to choose the greatest, He said, "Love the Lord your God with all your heart, with all your soul, with all your mind, and with all your strength" (Mark 12:30). Then He listed the second: "Love your neighbor as yourself" (v. 31).

But we can't love God or others the way we're supposed to. The fact is we love *ourselves* first and foremost. If we want to truly love God and others, we need His help. We can't love God—or our family and friends (not to speak of enemies)—without God's love filling us and flowing through us.

We need to put our roots down deep into the soil of the love of God we've received through Christ. As He pours His love into us, we can become channels through whom He can love others. What will draw people to Christ more than all our arguments, books, and conferences is when they see us really love one another.

 Make It Personal

What would it look like for you to really love others as He loves you? Whom do you find difficult to love that way?

A Great and Precious Gift

My God will supply all your needs according
to his riches in glory in Christ Jesus.
—PHILIPPIANS 4:19

God's providence. The word describes His care and guidance of all things, but it also speaks to His wise, sovereign rule over every detail of His creation. Now, this is admittedly a subject that can stir up animated arguments. But there are basically two options.

Either God sovereignly causes and/or permits everything that happens in our lives and in this world or He stands by and watches passively and powerlessly, unwilling or unable to do anything about what happens.

I choose door number one. Where would we be without the certain knowledge that "He's got the whole world in His hands" and that every detail of our lives and days is ordered by our all-wise, all-knowing, loving God? Far from being a crushing burden to be borne or diminishing our value, the providence of God is a great and precious gift. To be helpless victims of chance, tossed about on the storms of life—that would be forever disconcerting and tragic. Thank God it is not the case.

Make It Personal

How have you seen God's providence at work in your life?
How does knowing He's in control help when things are difficult?

Waving the White Flag

Therefore, submit to God.

−JAMES 4:7

We all begin life as members of a rebellious race, fighting our own personal war against the sovereign King of the universe. For most, that resistance unfolds into a lifelong story that could be titled *No Surrender*.

Some express their resistance overtly, perhaps through a lifestyle of unbridled lust and perversion. Others are more subtle—they are upstanding citizens and community leaders; they may even be active in church work. But beneath the surface, every human being has an inborn determination to run his own life and an unwillingness to be mastered by Christ, the King of Kings.

The decision to give up the fight is no small matter, especially after years of resistance. Surrender means nothing less than a radically altered lifestyle. Surrender to Christ as Savior and Lord is life changing. Whether we first wave the white flag at the age of eight or eighty-eight, that surrender involves a transfer of allegiance and a transformation of perspective that ought to affect every aspect of our lives.

Make It Personal

How are you surrendering to Christ today?

Why Be Holy?

Be holy, because I am holy.

—1 PETER 1:16

There are moments when I think, *It's so hard to have to "be holy" all the time! Why can't I just relax sometimes?*

To be honest, don't you find it easier to go with the flow of your natural desires than to deny your flesh and choose the pathway of holiness—every moment of every day for the rest of your life? Why make the tough, daily choices that holiness requires:

- To get out of bed in the morning and spend time in God's Word before you jump into your to-do list?
- To turn off that suggestive program or to put down that novel that glamorizes sensuality?
- To admit you have sinned and seek forgiveness for speaking roughly to that family member or being critical of that fellow church member?
- To eat and sleep and dress and go to work and play and give and pray and go to church—all for the glory of God?

One reason suffices—because you want to please the Lord.

 Make It Personal

What are the daily areas of your life where you need to make a conscious decision to choose holiness rather than going with the flow?

Power of the Word

This is my comfort in my affliction:
Your promise has given me life.

—PSALM 119:50

The Word of God has power to keep us from sin (Ps. 119:9, 11), to strengthen us when we are grieving (v. 28), to comfort us when we are suffering (vv. 50, 52), to grant us freedom (v. 45), to give us understanding and light for our path (v. 105), and to give us peace and keep us from stumbling (v. 165).

The Word of God will light your way; help you make right choices; heal your wounds and settle your heart; warn you of danger; protect and cleanse you from sin; lead you; make you wise. It is bread; water; a counselor; life. It is satisfying; sufficient; supreme; supernatural. The hymn writer put it this way:

Holy Bible, book divine, precious treasure, thou art mine. . . .
Mine to show by living faith, man can triumph over death.
Mine to tell of joys to come, and the rebel sinner's doom;
O thou Holy Book divine, precious treasure, thou art mine.[4]

 Make It Personal

How has the Word been a valuable treasure
during times of trouble or stress in your life?

A Great Benefits Package

My soul, bless the LORD,
and do not forget all his benefits.

—PSALM 103:2

I once interviewed a woman for *Revive Our Hearts* who had faithfully memorized and meditated on Scripture for more than fifty years. She talked about the many benefits she received as a result of hiding God's Word in her heart.

I was amazed when she mentioned that she had never really been depressed. She explained that whenever she finds herself becoming a bit down or blue, she begins to quote Psalm 103. At that point in the interview, she proceeded to recite the entire psalm from memory, thoughtfully, with heartfelt expression.

It was a moving experience for all who were in the room. When she finished, there was a holy hush. My first thought was, *How in the world could I ever give in to discouragement, if all these blessings are ours—and they are!*

As we recognize and identify the specific blessings we have received from God, we discover countless reasons for expressing gratitude. The psalmist took time to bless the Lord for specific benefits—he didn't want to forget even one!

 Make It Personal

Ask God to reveal today just how great your "benefits package" in Him really is. Then take time to give thanks.

Take Every Opportunity

I offer thanks and praise to you, God of my ancestors,
because you have given me wisdom and power.

—DANIEL 2:23

For gratitude to become a true joy-maker in our hearts, it must be expressed everywhere, at every opportunity, both privately before God and publicly before others. Gratitude occupied the prophet Daniel's private and his public life.

After praying for God to show him the interpretation to Nebuchadnezzar's dream, Daniel reacted to God's supernatural revelation—not by rushing out to tell the king, thereby anchoring his position as the number-one wise man in the kingdom—but first by pausing to thank God for the answer.

Once again, in the well-known affair of Darius' decree that all petitions for favor were to be directed toward the king alone for thirty days—the set-up that landed Daniel in the lions' den—his response revealed the pattern of his life: he prayed and gave thanks, "as he had done before" (Dan. 6:10). Nothing could deter Daniel from his established practice of offering prayer and thanksgiving—even in the face of great danger.

 Make It Personal

*How can you make it a point to thank God today
in every opportunity that's presented to you?*

We Need to Be Broken

Humble yourselves before the Lord, and he will exalt you.
—JAMES 4:10

In God's economy, the way up is down. You and I will never meet God in revival until we first meet Him in brokenness. Our families will never be whole until spouses, parents, and young people have been broken. Our churches will never be the vibrant witness God intended them to be in the world until their members have experienced true brokenness.

This is a message people are not eager to hear. Most of us don't walk into a Christian bookstore and say, "Can you help me find a book on how to mourn and weep?" We want to know how to be happy and whole, how to improve our self-esteem, how to feel better about ourselves and our lives. We think our problem is that we are gloomy and depressed and we need someone to make us happy. But God's Word says, "No, before you can get close to God, you have to find the highway of lowliness." We want to lift ourselves up. He says, "Humble yourself, and I will lift you up."

 Make It Personal

Take time to pray today, humbling yourself before God and asking Him to help you experience true brokenness.

Free to Choose?

"God knows that when you eat it your eyes will be opened
and you will be like God, knowing good and evil."

—GENESIS 3:5

Over and over, Scripture teaches that God's laws are for our good and our protection. Obedience is the pathway to freedom.

But Satan places in our minds the idea that God's laws are burdensome, unreasonable, and unfair, and that if we obey Him we will be miserable. In the garden, he caused Eve to focus on the one limitation God had placed on her. The deceiver's motto is "Have it your way: no one has the right to tell you what you can or cannot do."

So, we throw off the restrictions, determined to "have it our way." We're free to choose our own way, just as Eve was free to eat the forbidden fruit. But there's one thing we are not free to choose, and that's the consequences.

Believing and acting on a lie will ultimately lead to bondage. But when we discover the truth that true freedom comes from obedience, and when we act on that truth, our bondage is shattered.

 Make It Personal

*What lies have you believed about God? What consequences
have you experienced as a result of believing them?*

From Our Heart

The heart of a wise person instructs his mouth;
it adds learning to his speech.

—PROVERBS 16:23

Do you sometimes trivialize your words by saying things like, "I didn't mean that. It just came out"? Unfortunately, the truth is that we really do mean what we say—our words reveal what's in our heart.

I think about careless or hurtful words I have said to family members, coworkers, and friends—words I regret and wish I could take back. But I can't take back my words.

According to God's Word, all of us sin with our tongues (James 3:2); we need to confess our sin and turn from it. We need to take responsibility for our words, agree with God about what our words reveal about our hearts, and ask the Lord to change our hearts so we can speak words that heal.

Today, may we allow God to transform our hearts by the power of His Holy Spirit. When our hearts are filled with Him and with His wisdom and grace, we will speak wise, gracious words that bless and instruct others.

Make It Personal

Ask the Lord to transform your heart and help you speak words that are wise, gracious, and helpful to instruct others.

Son of Man

"The Son of Man did not come to be served, but to serve,
and to give his life as a ransom for many."

—MATTHEW 20:28

Have you ever considered that Jesus had a favorite title for Himself? Scripture seems to indicate that He did: "Son of Man." We find it eighty-four times in the Gospels alone, and the title shows us much about our Savior.

First, it shows us His humanity. Jesus had a physical body, which means He experienced hunger, thirst, weariness, grief, and temptation.

It also shows us His humility. We want people to know us by our most impressive title, yet Jesus chose His lowliest. The title speaks to us of why Jesus came: to seek, to save, to serve, and to give His life as a substitute for sinful man.

As children of God, we are being made like Christ our brother. Slowly but surely, we are taking on our eternal family resemblance. Our lives are increasingly marked by character-istics that were true of Jesus—humility, a heart to serve, and a willingness to suffer on behalf of others, as He suffered for us.

Make It Personal

What lessons can you glean from Jesus' example of humility for your interactions with others at home? At work? At church?

Cure for the Blues

Why, my soul, are you so dejected?
Why are you in such turmoil? Put your hope in God.

—PSALM 43:5

I have spoken with many people who are chronically unhappy, down, or depressed. The details and reasons vary, of course. But I've become increasingly convinced that one of the chief reasons behind a pervasive sense of blues and blah-ness is a failure to be thankful.

Ungrateful people tend to hold tightly to their rights. And when others fail to perform the way they expect, they feel justified in making demands and retaliating emotionally.

It's the opposite of what we see in the life of Ruth in the Old Testament who, having lost home and husband and finding herself alone with a bitter mother-in-law in Bethlehem, chose to accept whatever God provided and expressed gratitude for the simple kindness of Boaz. She never forgot she was a foreigner, undeserving of favor from anyone.

As Matthew Henry said, "When we have no other answer to the suggestions of grief and fear, we may have recourse to this: 'I thank Thee, O Father.'"[5] What a difference gratitude makes.

 Make It Personal

How could giving thanks to God for all that
He has provided in your life affect your mood today?

When We Won't Forgive

"Blessed are the merciful, for they will be shown mercy."
—MATTHEW 5:7

I have met many believers who find it difficult to accept and experience God's love and forgiveness. One of the biggest reasons is that they refuse to forgive others. Jesus' words on the subject of unforgiveness are so stark and direct. Yet we who are saved by grace but unforgiving in our hearts find ourselves looking for loopholes, trying to convince ourselves that He must have meant something less exacting. Certainly, He who knows how deep our hurt goes couldn't possibly expect full forgiveness from us!

Yet in reality we find nowhere to hide. "Blessed are the merciful," He said, "for they will be shown mercy," implying, we can assume, that those of us who are *not* merciful toward others shouldn't expect to find ourselves on the receiving end of that promise.

When we refuse to forgive, something is blocked in our relationship with the Father. The Scripture affirms what our own experience confirms—a clear connection between our willingness to extend forgiveness to others and our ability to appropriate and experience His forgiveness for our sins.

 Make It Personal

Is there someone you need to forgive in order to enjoy the full, sweet taste of His compassion and mercy?

Our Relationship with Our Father

"Father, the hour has come."

—JOHN 17:1

Throughout the Old Testament, God is referred to as Father only fourteen times, always regarding the nation of Israel. Jews in Jesus' day understood that God was the Father of their nation collectively, but they had never dared to call God "our Father" personally. He was too high and holy for that.

But then Jesus taught His disciples to pray "Our Father." He used the Aramaic word for father—*abba*—which is tender, familiar, and warm. To the people of this time, it was amazing that anyone would have the audacity to talk to God in this way.

But Jesus revealed to those startled people a relationship with God they had never experienced.

Not everyone can pray, "Our Father"—only those who are His children through faith in Jesus Christ. Through His death on the cross, Christ opened the way for us to have a relationship with God as our Father, giving us the freedom and boldness to approach God with our requests.

 Make It Personal

Do you approach God as your Abba, Father, or do you approach Him as someone who is distant?

Giving Thanks Publicly

I will praise you in the great assembly;
I will exalt you among many people.

—PSALM 35:18

How quick are you to give thanks to God when everyone is looking? How much space does gratitude take up in your everyday interactions with others? Gratitude is not just for private consumption but for public conversation.

Have you ever been in one of those church services or small-group settings, for example, when the pastor or leader asks for testimonies of praise concerning God's goodness and the room suddenly falls silent, as if everyone's too embarrassed to lead out or (perhaps) it's the first time the thought has crossed anyone's mind all week? We are often quick to share our concerns with others but reticent to share our expressions of gratitude.

Yet David in the Old Testament was irrepressible when it came to public thanksgiving. "I will praise you, Lord, among the peoples; I will sing praises to you among the nations" (Ps. 57:9).

Give thanks privately to the Lord and also *publicly*, where others can hear and be reminded of God's goodness.

 Make It Personal

As you give thanks to the Lord privately today,
also take advantage of any opportunities you
have to give Him thanks publicly.

Relinquishing Control

"For whoever wants to save his life will lose it,
but whoever loses his life because of me will find it."
—MATTHEW 16:25

I assume that most who are reading this devotional have come to that initial point of surrender that the Bible identifies as being born again. You've placed your faith in Christ's sacrifice for your sin, relinquished control of your life to Him, and been converted into the kingdom (the control) of God. My hope is you will grow in your understanding of what it means to live out the implications of that surrender on a daily basis.

However, some of you may have never come to that point. You may have long considered yourself a Christian, but you have never waved the white flag of surrender to Christ; you have never relinquished the right to run your own life.

My appeal to you is to recognize the foolishness and futility of further resistance and to believe and obey the gospel that Jesus is Lord. The war is over . . . it's time to hand over your sword to the King of Kings!

 Make It Personal

Have you relinquished the right to run your own life to Jesus?
If not, stop right now, pray, and surrender everything to Him.

Casual Infidelity

"You have played the whore with many lovers;
and would you return to me? declares the LORD."

—JEREMIAH 3:1 ESV

I magine your spouse casually saying, "Honey, I've been carrying on an affair with a woman at work. Nothing serious. We've slept together a few times, but I want you to know I still love you, and I hope you'll stay with me and keep meeting my needs."

Worse yet, imagine if he refused to break off the relationship but continued to sleep with his girlfriend once or twice a week, month after month, year after year, all the while insisting he really loved you and wanted to keep living with you.

How long would it take for you to say, "*No!* You can't have her and me! You've got to make a choice."

As revolting as such scenarios are, they give us an inkling of what we're doing to our heavenly Husband when we persist in "sleeping" with our sin while claiming to be committed to our relationship with Him. Oh, may we choose to forsake our sin and be loyal to the One who gave His life for us!

 Make It Personal

*Ask God to show you if there are any ways
you've been unfaithful to Him, then ask for His
help in protecting you against future infidelity.*

Kiss the Son

Kiss the Son, lest he be angry, and you perish in the way,
for his wrath is quickly kindled.

—PSALM 2:12 ESV

The "Son" in Psalm 2 is none other than the Son of God—the King whom God has appointed to reign over the world. In the ancient Orient, kissing the king's hand or robe was a way to show homage. So, to kiss the Son is a sign of subjection. It means to give Him our wholehearted allegiance. To kiss the Son is also a token of friendship. It is to draw near to Him and offer our worship, love, and affection.

Jesus came to earth the first time as the humble Son of Man, but when He comes the second time, He will come as God's instrument of judgment. Everyone who has refused to kiss the Son will perish eternally.

Psalm 2 ends with a word of resounding hope: "Blessed are all who take refuge in him" (v. 12 ESV). As you place your trust in Jesus, you can know that you are forgiven, and you can look forward to His return with great joy.

Make It Personal

*How can you "kiss the Son" today and give Him
your sincere, heartfelt homage, your wholehearted allegiance,
your respect, your honor, your submission?*

Even the Little Things

Giving thanks always for everything to God the Father
in the name of our Lord Jesus Christ.

—EPHESIANS 5:20

As we grow in our Christian faith, I hope we become more alert to the many reasons we have to be grateful. But I'm reminded of that visual illustration about the jar filled with rocks. The speaker asks, "Would you say this jar is full?" Yes. But by continuing to add smaller pieces of rock and sand, we soon discover there was more room inside than we realized.

I remember hearing a friend tell how, while brushing his teeth and meditating on Ephesians 5:20–21, he was struck by the word "everything."

He was reminded of the importance of thanking God for even those "little things" we often overlook. It made him pause and be thankful for, well . . . his toothbrush. And his toothpaste. And while he was at it, he thanked God for his teeth, probably for the first time in his life.

My friend told me he also asked himself, "If tomorrow's supply depended on today's thanksgiving, how much would I have tomorrow?" Something to think about!

 Make It Personal

What little things can you thank God for right now?

Wrestling Match

Jacob was left alone, and a man
wrestled with him until daybreak.
—GENESIS 32:24

J acob was a man with a godly heritage and a future bright
with God's promises. But he was also a man who wanted
it his way. In spite of momentary glimpses of God, he always
seemed to be kicking against the boundaries.

One day he came to a wall he couldn't move. In a matter
of hours, he would have to face his twin brother, whom he
had cheated years earlier and who was now coming to meet
him accompanied by an army. For the first time, Jacob couldn't
manipulate his way around or out of a problem—which was
exactly where God wanted him.

In the middle of the night, he finally got alone with the One
who had been silently engineering all the circumstances of his
life. In the stillness of that long night, Jacob wrestled for all he
was worth, until finally exhausted, he realized he would never
be able to control God. His will broken, his hip out of joint,
his name changed, Jacob emerged from that divine encounter
a new man.

 Make It Personal

*Take time to acknowledge God as your Lord and yourself
as His servant—and submit to His authority in your life.*

Never Impossible

"With God all things are possible."
—MATTHEW 19:26

Do you have a situation where forgiveness seems impossible? Perhaps you're thinking you just can't forgive that person for what she did to you. She hurt you too deeply.

But is there a threshold of pain beyond which we're not required to forgive, one perhaps where it's *impossible* to forgive?

Scripture reminds us that God has "cast all our sins into the depths of the sea" (Mic. 7:19). This is the same God who "sweep[s] away your transgressions" and who will "remember your sins no more" (Isa. 43:25), who found us "dead in our trespasses" and made us "alive with Christ" because of His "great love" for us (Eph. 2:4–5).

You may not feel any natural "great love" toward the one who brought such shipwreck into your life—no one would expect you to. But the power—and the beauty—of the Christian life is that "it is God who is working in you both to will and to work according to his good purpose" (Phil. 2:13).

 Make It Personal

Is there someone in your life whom it seems impossible to forgive? Ask the Lord to make that "impossible" situation possible today.

Stand Still

"Fear not, stand firm, and see the salvation
of the Lord. . . . The Lord will fight for you."
—EXODUS 14:13–14 ESV

O ne of the most dramatic examples of God's providence in the Old Testament was when the Israelites were finally released from their Egyptian captors. They came to a massive body of water, with no way over or around it, and a ferocious army bearing down on them.

Yet in spite of watching Yahweh perform one miracle after another on their behalf, they feared for their lives. Undaunted, Moses challenged them to stand still and trust God.

Not only did God provide a path through the water, He went on to lead the Israelites through the wilderness, providing food, water, protection, and more until they finally reached the land He had promised them.

When things seem to be falling apart, it's natural to freak out, give in to fear, anger, or despair, or try to wrestle the problems down. But this moment in your life is part of a bigger story He's writing in and through you. Remember the Red Sea. Stand still. See the salvation of the Lord.

 Make It Personal

*In what areas of life is God asking you to stand still
and trust Him to fight for you right now?*

Breaking Ground

Break up your unplowed ground.
It is time to seek the LORD.

—HOSEA 10:12

G od's pattern through the Bible is to restore His wayward people. Consider, for example, the prophet Hosea.

God sent Hosea to prophesy to the nation of Israel. Though they were God's chosen people, the nation was in a sad state of spiritual and moral decline. For years they had enjoyed God's blessings—material bounty, military strength, peaceful relations with neighboring nations—yet they still turned away from Him.

They stopped viewing God as the source of their blessings and chose instead to credit themselves. They put off worshiping God. They ceased loving Him. They replaced Him with idols, worldly pursuits, and earthly wealth.

It was to these confused fellow countrymen that Hosea delivered repeated rebukes and appeals. If they did not return to the Lord, he warned, judgment would surely come. Look at the essence of Hosea's message in Hosea 10:12. If we want to return to God, we must be prepared to break up the hard, barren ground of our spiritual lives. When? Now.

 Make It Personal

*Ask God to help you break up any hard ground
in your spiritual life—and do it today!*

Mighty to Save

For a child will be born for us, a son will be given to us. . . .
He will be named . . . Mighty God.

—ISAIAH 9:6

The opening chapters of Isaiah's prophecy paint a dark and gloomy picture, but then comes a dramatic transformation. This promised child would be a powerful warrior. Christ is the fulfillment of this prophecy. He is the God who conquers and prevails.

He is omnipotent. He's able to bring joy and gladness and to transform anguish into joy. He is able to free His people from their oppressors. He has all the strength needed to intervene, to redeem, to deliver, and to save.

He "breaks the power of canceled sin" in our lives. His power enables us to say no to sin and yes to God. It sets us free from the shame, guilt, and bondage of past sin. Jesus is mighty to preserve us from sin and Satan and self.

Nothing is too hard for Him. There is no one Jesus can't save. There is no heart so hard He can't change it. He is the Mighty God!

 Make It Personal

Do you trust Him as the Mighty God?
How can you affirm His power over all areas of your life?

Balanced Prayers

First of all, then, I urge that petitions, prayers,
intercessions, and thanksgivings be made for everyone.

—1 TIMOTHY 2:1

There's nothing wrong with being totally honest with God, imploring Him to help and heal. But prayer is more than asking. It is a vehicle of worship and gratitude.

Think about the overall makeup of your prayers. Are they out of balance in favor of asking and seeking? Are they top-heavy with complaints about your current circumstances? Or do your prayers include expressions of gratitude?

These are important questions to ask of ourselves, not to discourage honesty or to deny reality but to help train our hearts to see all that concerns us within the context of God's goodness and blessing. We must not forget His benefits while dealing with our problems. Even before His answer is in sight, thank Him—for being there, for listening, for working all things according to His will.

As surely as our "supplications" and "intercessions" are specific, heartfelt, and time-consuming, so should our "thanksgivings" be. Pave the way with gratitude, and see if prayer "without ceasing" doesn't become your experience instead of your exception.

 Make It Personal

*Challenge yourself to include as much gratitude
in your prayer life as you do supplication.*

Belief and Behavior

You are to proclaim things consistent with sound teaching.

—TITUS 2:1

My friend Holly Elliff is a pastor's wife, mother of eight, and has a vibrant ministry. But there was a time when her experience of the abundant Christian life was hindered by a case of bad doctrine.

Holly had picked up the belief that if she did her best to be a good Christian, if she prayed and read her Bible, then God would place her in a no-trouble zone. You can imagine how Holly's world was shaken when trouble started.

After giving birth to two children, she had a miscarriage. Her next child had a birth injury requiring months of therapy. Then a loud faction began stirring up dissent in their church and targeting her husband.

If you came from the doctrinal standpoint Holly had embraced, what would your response be?

This whole experience challenged Holly to build a solid foundation for her life by getting into the Word and getting to really know God. The fruit of that resolve has been extraordinary and beautiful.

 Make It Personal

Like Nancy's friend Holly, have you believed any wrong doctrine? What was it, and how did it affect the way you lived?

Heaven Rules

Your kingdom will be restored to you as soon
as you acknowledge that Heaven rules.

—DANIEL 4:26

Heaven rules. No phrase pulses more frequently in my mind and heart than this one. It's on the screensaver photo of my phone. It's printed on the mug I use each morning. It's featured on artwork hanging in my study.

"Heaven rules" is a right-sizing truth putting our view of God, ourselves, and our problems in proper perspective.

I love being surrounded by reminders of this simple but profound truth. It has become foundational to how I view all of Scripture and all of life. When I have found myself in tumultuous waters, it has been both an anchor and a life preserver for my soul.

My hope is that the promise and the perspective contained in the phrase will become deeply ingrained in the fabric of your being, that it will bring you comfort and courage in every painful season of your life, and that it will become your reflexive, trusting response to every troubling development in our upside-down world.

 Make It Personal

*How can having a "Heaven rules" perspective change the way
you are currently thinking about a situation in your life?*

A Secure "Ladder"

"Everyone who hears these words of mine and acts on them
will be like a wise man who built his house on the rock."

—MATTHEW 7:24

My husband has a self-admitted fear of heights. Put him on a ladder, and his knees turn to Jell-O. Robert is also a gifted handyman. Over the years, some of his projects have required him to do his work up high.

How does he deal with his fear? "That's easy," he says. "I never climb a ladder until I'm certain I have taken the time to level the legs on a perfectly solid place."

That's a perfect metaphor for my desire to be adorned with the gospel. I hope that's your desire too. But the starting point might not be what you expect.

You may be tempted to skip ahead, looking for practical tools to help you become a more godly person. But you first need to secure your "ladder"—by addressing doctrine before laying out specifics of your practice.

Doctrine—what we believe—is foundational to how we live. If you miss it, you'll never get to where you want to be.

 Make It Personal

Why do you think doctrine matters so much?
What steps can you take to make sure your doctrine is "secure"?

Filled with the Spirit

"The Spirit is the one who gives life."
—JOHN 6:63

If you're a child of God, the Holy Spirit lives in you. He wants to fill every part of you with Himself—your words, your actions, your attitudes, your day, your night, your everything!

As we're dependent upon the Spirit, Christ's supernatural power will be manifested in and through our lives. We cannot do what God has called us to do apart from being filled with His Spirit. It's an ongoing way of life.

In the Corrie ten Boom Museum in Holland, this quote is written on a sign: "Trying to do the Lord's work in your own strength is the most confusing, exhausting, and tedious of all work. But when you are filled with the Holy Spirit, then the ministry of Jesus just flows out of you."

To be filled with the Spirit doesn't mean you have some amazing emotional experience or a visible manifestation. We're filled by faith, the same way we come to Christ and receive Him. As you ask God to fill you with His Spirit, by faith believe that He is doing so.

 Make It Personal

How can you depend on the power of the Holy Spirit (and not your own abilities) to live the Christian life and serve Him?

Rescued by Gratitude

Though the fig tree does not bud and there is no fruit
on the vines . . . yet I will celebrate in the Lord.

—HABAKKUK 3:17–18

O ver the years I've sought to make gratitude a way of life. However, if I'm not ceaselessly vigilant about choosing gratitude, I easily get sucked into the undertow of life in a fallen world. My life starts to feel hard, wearisome, and overwhelming.

But in those moments when I've felt I was going under, I've discovered that gratitude is my life preserver. Even in the most turbulent waters, choosing gratitude rescues me from my runaway emotions. It buoys me on the grace of God and keeps me from drowning in what otherwise would be my natural bent toward doubts, discouragement, and anxiety.

Over time, choosing gratitude means choosing joy. But that choice doesn't come without effort and intentionality. It's a choice that requires constantly renewing my *mind* with the truth of God's Word, setting my *heart* to savor God and His gifts, and disciplining my *tongue* to speak words that reflect His goodness and grace—until a grateful spirit becomes my reflexive response to all of life.

 Make It Personal

*How can you be intentional about choosing gratitude today—
in both the good things and the hard things?*

Hiding from God

For [God's] eyes watch over a man's ways,
and he observes all his steps.

—JOB 34:21

Adam and Eve were the first to make a futile attempt to conceal their sin.

After partaking of that which God had forbidden, they lost their innocence and discovered their guilt—and their nakedness. Immediately they went into concealment mode, looking for ways to blend into the landscape.

Have you ever thought how ridiculous it was for them to hope a tree or shrub would hide them from God? Have you ever thought how ridiculous it is for us to believe that by keeping silent about our sin we can throw God off the trail?

Of course, God knew exactly where Adam and Eve were—He had seen the whole thing. He knew what they had done, and He knew where they were hiding.

God faithfully gives His straying children opportunities to repent. He wants us to break the silence and admit our wrongdoing. However God chooses to get our attention, the best response to Him is an honest one. Honesty is liberating.

 Make It Personal

How can being honest about your sin open the door
for you to experience God's amazing grace?

The Opposite of Brokenness

Draw near to God, and he will draw near to you.

—JAMES 4:8

I believe one of the reasons many believers are afraid of the idea of brokenness is that they have misconceptions about what brokenness really means. As is true in so many other areas, our idea of brokenness and God's idea of brokenness are usually quite different.

Some people think of brokenness as always being sad or gloomy. They assume it means having a downcast countenance. They imagine that broken people never smile or laugh. In reality, brokenness brings a release, which produces a deep sense of joy and peace.

Others think of brokenness as being morbidly introspective: "Oh, woe is me! I've confessed every sin I can possibly think of, but surely there must be something I've missed. Oh, what a worm I am!" This kind of "confession" can lead to false humility, wherein people are quick to put themselves down and cannot receive genuine affirmation or encouragement. False humility and morbid introspection are, in fact, the opposite of brokenness, as they reveal a preoccupation with self rather than Christ.

 Make It Personal

*Ask the Lord to help you experience
true brokenness in your life.*

A Bride-in-the-Making

He did this to present the church to himself in splendor, without
spot or wrinkle or anything like that, but holy and blameless.

—EPHESIANS 5:27

As an earthly groom eagerly anticipates the moment when his bride walks down the aisle to meet him, beautifully arrayed in a spotless, white wedding dress, so the Lord Jesus anticipates the day when we will appear before Him, free from all defilement, clothed in His righteousness, to be His holy bride forever.

As an engaged woman eagerly, lovingly prepares for her wedding, desirous to be her most beautiful for her groom, so the thought of being wedded to our holy Groom should motivate us to spend our lives here on earth in pursuit of the holiness that we know is our ultimate end and His great desire for His bride.

When I consider my created purpose and my ultimate destiny—when I remember that I am a splendid, pure bride-in-the-making—I am inspired to be intentional about pursuing holiness, in anticipation of that glorious day when I will finally be holy through and through.

 Make It Personal

How does knowing that someday soon you will
stand before your Groom affect your choices today?
How can you pursue holiness right now?

No Shortcuts

Make yourself an example of good works
with integrity and dignity in your teaching.

—TITUS 2:7

Becoming a godly older woman has been one of my goals for as long as I remember. Even as a teen I realized the choices I was making then would contribute to my life as a college student and a young adult and a middle-aged woman and, eventually, a little old lady.

However, I realize that there are no shortcuts to acquiring the traits of a godly, older woman. They must be cultivated over time and slowly seasoned to acquire their taste and savor.

Here's the truth of it: the most amazing, godly older women you know likely were serious about being godly *younger* women.

So, the message of Titus 2 is for all of us, older and younger. When we dig more deeply into its treasures, we see how older women in the church thrive by staying attached to the younger and how younger women can find a compelling vision for their long-term character and fruitfulness in the lives and faces of their older spiritual sisters.

 Make It Personal

*How did the choices you made as a younger
person affect who you are today?*

Because of Grace

"Greetings, favored woman! The Lord is with you."
But she was deeply troubled by this statement,
wondering what kind of greeting this could be.

—LUKE 1:28–29

Repeatedly in Scripture, we see that God chooses to use people who are undeserving. For example, when God chose Mary to be the mother of Jesus, He didn't look down from heaven and say, "I see a woman who has something to offer Me; I think I'll use her."

Mary didn't deserve to be used by God; to the contrary, she marveled at God's grace in choosing her. She wasn't chosen to be Jesus' mother because she was worthy of the honor. The angel said to Mary, "Greetings, favored woman!" That phrase could be translated, "you who are graciously accepted." If any of us is to be accepted by God, it will be because of grace—not because of anything we have done.

The moment we cease to see ourselves as undeserving instruments, chances are we will cease to be useful in the hand of God.

 Make It Personal

Are you trying to make yourself worthy to be used by God?
Thank God that we're accepted solely because of His grace.

Which Will You Choose?

These people are discontented grumblers,
living according to their desires.

—JUDE 1:16

D o you consider yourself to be grateful or ungrateful? It's the difference between squandering life and sharing life, between being blinded to glory and "To God Be the Glory," between assured bitterness and "Blessed Assurance."

It's a difference you can see lived out in every daily decision. It's a choice you make—almost with every breath.

We pay an incalculable price for our ingratitude. After decades of ministry to hurting people, I've come to believe that a failure to give thanks is at the heart of much of the sense of gloom, despair, and despondency that's so pervasive even among believers today. I believe many of the sins plaguing and devastating our society can be traced back to that persistent root of unthankfulness that often goes undetected.

This "attitude of gratitude" is something that desperately needs to be cultivated in our hearts and homes. Its presence brings a host of other blessings in its train, but its absence has profound repercussions.

Make It Personal

How could being unthankful have an impact on every area of your life? How can you choose an attitude of gratitude today?

He Loves Us

God proves his own love for us in that while
we were still sinners, Christ died for us.

—ROMANS 5:8

It's no small matter to give in to the lie that "God doesn't love me." The implications affect every other area of our lives and relationships. Tiny little seeds, allowed to take root in our minds, grow up to produce a great harvest.

The truth is God *does* love us. Whether or not we feel loved, regardless of what we've done or where we have come from, He loves us with an infinite, incomprehensible love.

God loves me—because He *is* love. His love for me is not based on anything I have ever done or ever could do for Him. It's not based on my performance. I don't deserve His love and could never earn it.

The Scripture says that when I was His enemy, *He loved me.* He loved me in eternity past; He will love me for all of eternity future. There's nothing I could do to make Him love me any less; there's nothing I could do to make Him love me any more.

Make It Personal

*How does knowing that God loves you
no matter what impact your life?*

Friend of Sinners

The Pharisees and scribes were complaining,
"This man welcomes sinners and eats with them."
—LUKE 15:2

Ironically, "Friend of sinners" is a name given to Jesus by His enemies (Matt. 11:19). Who were these sinners with whom Jesus ate? They were outcasts in Jewish society—the ceremonially unclean, money lenders, prostitutes, and those who made their living by ill-gotten gain.

The Pharisees were shocked that Jesus would associate with people who didn't live by the rules. Jesus offered a powerful response: "It is not those who are well who need a doctor, but those who are sick. I didn't come to call the righteous, but sinners" (Mark 2:17). Jesus came to heal those who were spiritually sick with sin. The Pharisees didn't realize they were just as needy of spiritual healing as the sinners they avoided.

Through the Gospels we see that Jesus welcomed sinners and reached out to them, and sinners welcomed Jesus and responded to Him. That's an amazing picture of redemption. It foreshadows the day when a multitude from every nation will sit together and eat with Him at the marriage supper of the Lamb.

 Make It Personal

What does it mean to you that Jesus is the Friend of sinners?
How has He healed you from the disease of sin?

Immediate Access

Since we have boldness to enter the sanctuary
through the blood of Jesus . . . let us draw near
with a true heart in full assurance of faith.

—HEBREWS 10:19, 22

If you or I were to walk up to the White House, there's no way we could get in to see the president. But when we approach the throne room of the God of the universe, we have immediate access. If you're a child of God, you have access to God through Christ's death on the cross.

To be able to call Him our Father means that when we approach Him, we don't have to cower in fear. We can come in confidence and walk right up to Him. Through faith in Christ, we're made children of God. Then we can be confident He will do as we ask in any matter that He has declared to be His will.

That doesn't mean He will give us everything we ask for. But it does mean He will grant us anything that's in accordance with His character, His will, and for our good.

 Make It Personal

How do you approach God when you go before Him?

Ruler Over All

The LORD has established his throne in heaven,
and his kingdom rules over all.

—PSALM 103:19

When I use the phrase "Heaven rules," I mean "God rules." He rules over every tide of history, over every king and kingdom, over every part of His creation. It's a truth meant to instill healthy fear within every proud heart that aims to be its own ruler and that believes we humans can determine our own direction.

God is kind, not cruel, in reminding us who's in charge and in doing it at whatever cost He knows is necessary to get our distracted attention.

But this same truth that corrects us is also intended to comfort us. To reassure and free us. "Heaven rules" means He is sovereign over everything that touches us, that nothing comes to us unbidden by His desire to use it for our good and for His glory and for the greater things He created us to be part of. He is ruler over every diagnosis and prognosis, over all incomes and outcomes, over the most daunting challenges as well as the most seemingly trivial details of our lives.

 Make It Personal

How can knowing that God is ruler over everything bring you comfort in the difficult situations you're facing today?

A Story to Share

Older men are to be . . . sound in faith, love, and endurance.

—TITUS 2:2

Sound in faith" means to be sound in *the* faith—grounded in the truth of God's Word and able to affirm from experience the trustworthiness of God's promises.

I think of Joshua, standing before the people of Israel near the end of his life, declaring, "I am now going the way of the whole earth, and you know with all your heart and all your soul that none of the good promises the LORD your God made to you has failed" (Josh. 23:14).

Joshua's words reveal an unshakable confidence in God and His Word. He wasn't merely speaking of something he'd heard but testifying to something he knew firsthand.

What you have gleaned of God's nature and ways throughout your life, however inadequate you may feel, is worth passing on to others, particularly to those following behind you. Wherever you've seen God prove Himself faithful, wherever His Word has sustained you and provided needed direction, and yes, even wherever you have experienced the consequences of *failing* to walk according to His Word—there's your story to share.

 Make It Personal

How has God proven Himself faithful throughout your life?
How can you pass that knowledge to others around you?

Full-Time Christian

Not that I have already obtained this or am already perfect,
but I press on to make it my own, because Christ Jesus
has made me his own.

—PHILIPPIANS 3:12 ESV

Years ago, a Communist leader said, "We must train men and women who will devote to the revolution not merely their spare evenings but the whole of their lives." The cause of Christ is far greater than any social or political revolution. The idea of an eight-hour workday, with "the rest of the time for myself," ought to be foreign to a Christian.

This doesn't mean that someone who is devoted to Christ never relaxes. It does mean that the whole of his or her life belongs to Christ and is devoted to pleasing Him. The older I get, the more I find myself evaluating every aspect of my life in light of the price it will bring in eternity. From time to time, I sense the Lord directing me to cut back on, or eliminate, certain legitimate activities that are robbing me of time to pursue Him and to make an eternal investment in the lives of people.

Make It Personal

*Does your use of leisure time and choice of activities
reveal a commitment to Christ and His kingdom?
Is there anything you need to change?*

No Laughing Matter

A gossip goes around revealing a secret,
but a trustworthy person keeps a confidence.

—PROVERBS 11:13

I chuckled as I watched an old episode of *I Love Lucy*, in which Lucy hung up from talking to Ethel on the phone and Ricky asked Lucy, "Were you gossiping?"

Lucy answered, "*Who me? Gossiping?* I prefer to think of it as a 'mutual exchange of vital information.' Anyway, *she* was gossiping; I was just listening."

Although we find Lucy entertaining, gossip is no laughing matter. Scripture tells us that a gossip cannot be trusted and betrays confidential information. Before repeating information, ask yourself, "Would the person who originally shared the information (or prayer request) give me permission to repeat it?"

Proverbs 17:4 says, "A wicked person listens to malicious talk; a liar pays attention to a destructive tongue." It's not only wrong to gossip, but it's also wrong to listen to gossip.

When we spread gossip or slander about a fellow believer, we are actually sinning against our own body—for as Christians, we are all part of the body of Christ.

 Make It Personal

Ask the Lord to help you be aware of what you say and listen to today—that you will avoid gossip in all forms.

The Problem with Justice

There is no one righteous, not even one.

—ROMANS 3:10

Have you ever become angry over receiving bad service while traveling? Some of Jesus' disciples did. They were on their way to Jerusalem, and a Samaritan village refused to let them enter. James and John asked Jesus, "Do you want us to call down fire from heaven to consume them?" The Bible says Jesus "turned and rebuked them" (Luke 9:51–55).

This incident follows an argument among the disciples over which of them was the greatest. They were guilty of pride and selfish ambition, yet they were quick to call out for justice when they perceived sin in others.

You and I, like Jesus' disciples, are sinners. We can easily drift into the kind of vindictive, unloving reactions that caused James and John so much trouble.

If God gave everyone what they deserved, the disciples would have been consumed along with the Samaritan village. You and I would be destroyed in God's just wrath.

God is the only One fit to judge, because only God is perfect.

 Make It Personal

Are you seeking justice from the Lord today?
Ask Him to help you have an attitude of humility and love.

The Mighty God

Who is this King of glory?
The LORD, strong and mighty,
the LORD, mighty in battle.
—PSALM 24:8

It is astonishing that the Mighty God humbled Himself and became a helpless baby. He took on flesh and dwelt among us, and during this time He pulled back the curtain to show His might. He stilled storms, forgave sins, and healed diseases. He fed thousands with a boy's lunch. He raised the dead.

Later, on the cross, Jesus conquered sin, Satan, and hell and accomplished the mighty work of redemption. Then He threw off the shackles of death. He walked out of the tomb because He is the Mighty God!

That same Mighty God bears our burdens, supports us in our afflictions, and enables us to resist the power of temptation. He has delivered us from the penalty of sin and continues to deliver us from its power. And one day He will deliver us from its presence. He gives us strength to serve Him when we're weak and weary. He gives us the desire and power to obey Him when we're pulled by the world. He is the Mighty God!

 Make It Personal

How does knowing that He is the Mighty God make a difference in the circumstances and difficulties you face today?

In Your Right Mind

As an overseer of God's household, he must be . . . hospitable,
loving what is good, sensible, righteous, holy, self-controlled.

—TITUS 1:7–8

"Self-controlled" comes from the Greek word *sophron*, which
derives from two words, one meaning "saved" or "sound," and
the other meaning "mind." To be self-controlled is to operate from
a "saved mind," a "sound mind"—to be living in one's right mind.

Interestingly, the last portion of the word—*phron*—is related
to the modern Greek word for car brakes. The self-controlled
person knows how to curb her desires and impulses. She's
self-restrained under the control of the Holy Spirit. She gov-
erns herself and disciplines her mind, her passions, her affections, her behavior.

There are no shortcuts to acquiring this trait. Each of us
knows from hard experience how insistent and resistant our
human wills can be. We naturally resist not only others' attempts
to manage and direct us, but our own efforts as well. That's why
younger people need older models who have experienced the
challenge of becoming *sophron*, but who can also show by their
lives what this quality looks like and how it's cultivated.

Make It Personal

*Ask God to help you live under the control of the Holy Spirit
and that your life would be an example of self-control to others.*

Devotions vs. Devotion

These people approach me with their speeches to honor me
with lip-service, yet their hearts are far from me.

—ISAIAH 29:13

Some of us have had *devotions*, but we've not had *devotion*.
We may have gone through the motions of reading our
Bibles and saying our prayers, but we haven't been cultivating
a love relationship with God. We know a lot *about* Him, but
we don't really know *Him*. We're active in a multitude of spiritual activities, but we've lost perspective of who we're serving—and why.

The result is seen in the way we respond to pressure. So
many Christians are chronically stressed out. Everywhere I go,
I see it in people's eyes, I hear it in their voices, and too often
I see it when I look in the mirror. I know what it is to respond
out of weariness with an impatient, demanding spirit. I know
what it is to contend with God Himself, even as my eyes fill
up with tears of frustration with myself.

I also know there's only one place where that angry, reactive,
overwhelmed self can be transformed—at the feet of Jesus.

 Make It Personal

How do "devotions" and "devotion" look different in your life?
How can you choose today to sit at the feet of Jesus?

Give God Time

"Joseph, son of David, don't be afraid to take Mary
as your wife, because what has been conceived
in her is from the Holy Spirit."

—MATTHEW 1:20

When Mary explained to Joseph what the angel had said, apparently he didn't believe her. But Mary knew how to trust God. She gave Him time to work in Joseph's heart.

Sometimes we as believers are sensitive to perceive spiritual truth before others in our lives do. The natural tendency is to think we must convince them of the rightness or the importance of the insight we've received.

Mary didn't have that spirit. She didn't feel it was her responsibility to convince Joseph. She didn't manipulate or control. She simply waited on the Lord and trusted Him to fulfill His purposes. And in His time, God sent an angel to reveal to Joseph what he needed to know.

You may be tired of waiting for God to speak to your spouse or pastor or another spiritual authority. Don't try to take matters into your own hands. Wait on the Lord. Trust Him. He will accomplish His purposes in His time and in His way.

 Make It Personal

*Ask God to help you wait on Him and trust Him
to fulfill His purposes in your life and circumstances.*

Where We Begin

For the grace of God has appeared . . . instructing us
to deny godlessness and worldly lusts and to live in a
sensible, righteous, and godly way in the present age.

—TITUS 2:11–12

Titus 2 was originally written by Paul to a young pastor named Titus, who was struggling to lead a church on the island of Crete. The Roman Empire, which ruled Crete, was just coming under the reign of the ruthless emperor Nero. Just imagine what Nero's threats felt like to the churches of his day.

We may not live in Nero's Rome, but we do live in a decadent, deceptive culture that threatens the Church with its allure as well as its attacks. We need help to see how our lives can portray the gospel so that others are drawn to follow Christ. And we need help keeping His gospel attractive enough to *ourselves* that we will trust Him, obey Him, and experience His power, peace, and joy.

The more we let the gospel define our lives, the more lovely Christ will be to us—and the more clearly the beauty of His gospel will shine through us.

 Make It Personal

*How could living by the principles of Titus 2
let the beauty of the gospel shine through you?*

God Is Light

This is the message we have heard from him and declare to you:
God is light, and there is absolutely no darkness in him.

—1 JOHN 1:5

The apostle John had known the joy of deep fellowship with God through Christ, and he wanted his readers to experience it too. He reminds us that "God is light" and that when we cover up or refuse to acknowledge sin in our lives, we deceive ourselves and we cannot enjoy full fellowship with God or with each other. In fact, the person who habitually covers his sin has no basis for assurance that he is a child of God at all.

Therefore, the willingness to be honest and confess our sin is an evidence of genuine salvation and is vital to experiencing God's forgiveness and restored fellowship when we sin as believers. God wants to experience intimate fellowship with His children. That is possible only if we are honest with Him about the true condition of our heart as He knows it to be. No matter what you may have done, you can experience God's great love and amazing grace.

 Make It Personal

Pour out your heart to God in honest confession.

A Bigger Story

God is greater than our hearts, and he knows all things.

—1 JOHN 3:20

God is writing a Story—the Story of redemption. It is grander and greater than anything we can imagine. And there are some important things we need to remind ourselves often about His Story and how it relates to the story He is writing in and through each of our lives.

First, our individual stories are part of a much bigger Story. At times, we will experience heartache, loss, disappointment, and unfulfilled longings. But He is weaving all of that into a Story that will have us lost in wonder and worship when we get to the end.

Ultimately, this Story is not about us but about Him. We are bit players in His Story. We are not the stars. He is.

Finally, perspective makes all the difference. God sees the beginning and the end and everything in between; we only see this present moment. He has a wide-angle lens and sees the whole mural He is painting in all of history. We see only the little speck of time and space we occupy at this moment.

 Make It Personal

Take time to thank God that He sees the beginning and the end and everything in between—and ask Him to help you trust His perspective.

A Forgiving Spirit

"Do not condemn, and you will not be condemned.
Forgive, and you will be forgiven."

—LUKE 6:37

In the verses that follow directly after the Lord's Prayer, we hear Jesus saying, "If you forgive others their offenses, your heavenly Father will forgive you as well. But if you don't forgive others, your Father will not forgive your offenses" (Matt. 6:14–15).

Jesus' words challenge us to examine our hearts to see if we have ever truly been forgiven. As John Piper said, "If we hold fast to an unforgiving spirit, we will not be forgiven by God. If we continue on in that way, then we will not go to heaven, because heaven is the dwelling place of forgiven people."[6]

The point isn't that a forgiving spirit causes us to merit God's forgiveness but simply that forgiven people forgive others and that those who persistently refuse to forgive others have no basis to claim to have been forgiven by God.

Make It Personal

*Are you holding fast to any unforgiveness in your heart?
Ask God to help you truly forgive those who have hurt you.*

A Fixed Pitch

"Everyone who is of the truth listens to my voice."

—JOHN 18:37

As I listen to my piano tuner at work, adjusting each note to a fixed pitch, I can't help but think how a fixed standard of truth has been largely discarded in our day. People tune their lives to whatever pitch they happen to like, and the result is confusion and chaos.

It's become increasingly difficult to convince people that Jesus is the absolute, unchanging standard of truth. But that's what He claimed to be. And that's what He is.

God is true to His Word and His promises. He is faithful, reliable, and trustworthy. There is no deception or hypocrisy in God. He is the fixed standard of truth.

That truthful character of God establishes the standard for all of mankind. It's an absolute standard, one from which there is no deviation, and it's absolutely required for anyone who wants to have fellowship with Him. If we're off pitch, then we cannot walk in one accord with God. But if we walk with Jesus, we can be "in tune" with Him.

Make It Personal

What can you do today in order to live in a way that's "in tune" with God's truth?

Take Courage

For his dominion is an everlasting dominion,
and his kingdom is from generation to generation.

—DANIEL 4:34

Heaven rules. This truth that is powerful enough to take down the great is also powerful enough to bear up the least of us, both in our private ordeals and as we face the world that seems to be imploding around us. We can take comfort as we walk on this earth because of our Father's rule from heaven. Comfort and courage—for "Heaven rules" does not call for a passive acceptance of fate; it comes with the promise of grace for the battle.

When we feel we just can't withstand any more pressure, problems, or pain, the awareness of God's rule infuses us with supernatural strength. It enables us to live with contented, cemented clarity through the chaos and the ugly fallout of a fallen world, through struggles and circumstances that make us want to run away in panic or curl up in despair. We find the courage to patiently, even joyfully, persevere in the assurance that Heaven rules.

 Make It Personal

*Ask God to give you courage in the situations you face today,
remembering the truth that Heaven rules.*

Knowing God

The LORD would speak with Moses face to face,
just as a man speaks with his friend.

—EXODUS 33:11

We see in Moses a man who was always yearning for a deeper, more intimate fellowship with God. In one of his most intimate recorded conversations with God, Moses pleaded, "If I have indeed found favor with you, please teach me your ways, and I will know you" (Ex. 33:13). This is the prayer of a man who didn't just want to know more *about* God. He wanted to *know* God.

As you meet with God in your daily devotional time, don't forget that the ultimate purpose isn't simply to gain more knowledge about God or His Word but to know Him and to enjoy intimate communion with Him. You may be a seasoned student of the Word. You may even be a Bible study leader. But if your study of the Word doesn't lead you to know God, you've missed the whole purpose.

 Make It Personal

*How can you design your daily devotional
to be a time when you get to really know God?*

Desperate for Doctrine

They are ruining entire households
by teaching what they shouldn't.

—TITUS 1:11

The culture in first-century Crete, where Titus was a pastor, was the furthest thing from good or godly. Paul described unbelievers there as "unfit for any good work" (Titus 1:16).

As is invariably the case, rampant false teaching went hand in hand with the irreverent lifestyle prevalent in Crete. That unsound doctrine was causing great upheaval for entire Christian families.

So, what were those first-century believers to do? And what are we to do in similar circumstances?

"But you," Paul said to Pastor Titus, "are to proclaim things consistent with sound teaching" (2:1).

That's it. That is God's plan—truth and light overcoming deception and darkness.

The Cretan culture was in desperate need of believers who valued right doctrine. Our culture has the same need. Because where such doctrine is taught, believed, and put into practice, the gospel of Christ is put on display; it is proclaimed with power and becomes believable.

 Make It Personal

Why can sound doctrine have that much of an impact on society?

Outposts of Grace

"By this everyone will know that you are my disciples,
if you love one another."
—JOHN 13:35

You may be concerned about the moral disintegration around us. Our reflexive reaction is to think the solution will be found in better laws. It's tempting to think that different elected officials or better social programs will make the difference.

But what Paul argues in the book of Titus is that what we need are disciples who know and live in accord with sound doctrine. People who are grounded in the Scripture and who live out what they believe. Believers who are godly, wise, good, and kind.

Our best arguments will never persuade the world about God's existence, Christ's uniqueness, the way to salvation, or anything else. They're more likely to be persuaded as they see the gospel lived out in our lives and relationships.

You, your family, and your church may be tiny islands of godliness in a vast sea of wickedness. But don't underestimate what God can do to make the gospel desirable to lost souls through those outposts of grace and beauty. That's how His kingdom spreads.

Make It Personal

What steps could you take to deepen your grasp of God's Word and to saturate your mind, heart, and life with sound doctrine?

Not Just Lip Service

Bow down to him, for he is your lord.

—PSALM 45:11

There is a huge difference between giving lip service to Jesus as "Lord" and truly knowing Him as Lord. Jesus said, "Not everyone who says to me, 'Lord, Lord,' will enter the kingdom of heaven" (Matt. 7:21).

On another occasion, He said, "Why do you call me 'Lord, Lord,' and don't do the things I say?" (Luke 6:46). Jesus then paints a picture of the destruction that comes upon those who don't submit to His lordship. You can claim to know Jesus, but that's not necessarily proof of genuine faith. True faith will always be demonstrated in a life that desires to obey God.

If Jesus is God (and He is), then He must be Lord. He is supreme. We are not our own; we belong to Him. That's the truth about Jesus as Lord. But we're not talking about some onerous obligation. There is infinite grace wrapped up in His lordship! He is a compassionate Lord. He always does what's best for His subjects. We can surrender our lives to Him without fear.

 Make It Personal

Are there any areas where you're reserving the right to be your own lord? What would it look like to surrender them to Jesus' control?

In Heaven

The LORD looks down from heaven.... He gazes on
all the inhabitants of the earth from his dwelling place.
—PSALM 33:13–14

Heaven is understood in Scripture as the place of all authority, power, and greatness. It speaks of the exalted position of God. So, when we pray, "Our Father in *heaven*," we're praying to a Father who is high above everything going on here.

This doesn't mean God doesn't care or isn't involved. He came to earth to deal with these issues and has identified with us in our suffering, but He exists in a realm all His own.

Because God is in heaven, He has a different perspective. As He looks down on us, He knows our hearts, issues, and struggles. And He knows how everything fits together in His grand, redemptive plan. Because He is our Father in heaven, He has the power to help us when we pray.

This God in heaven is also here in our world, in our home, in our situations, seeing our tears, knowing our struggles, knowing the issues we face. He's a very present help in times of trouble (Ps. 46:1).

 Make It Personal

*How does knowing God is in heaven affect
how you approach Him in prayer? How does it
help you in the circumstances you face today?*

On Asking Why

Why do you force me to look at injustice?
Why do you tolerate wrongdoing?
—HABAKKUK 1:3

"Why, God?" Every generation has asked this question in some form.

Habakkuk had some questions for God as well. He wondered why God allowed sin to flourish among His people and why it seemed God wasn't listening. He joined others who questioned God in the pages of Scripture.

After losing his property, children, and health, Job asked, "Why was I not stillborn; why didn't I die as I came from the womb?" (Job 3:11).

When his mission did not seem to be going well, Moses wondered, "Lord . . . why did you ever send me?" (Ex. 5:22).

One psalmist wanted to know, "Lord, why do you stand so far away? Why do you hide in times of trouble?" (Ps. 10:1).

When my family suffered the loss of my younger brother, we were comforted by a family friend who made this helpful statement: "It's all right to ask God 'why?' as long as you're asking not with a clenched fist but with a searching heart."

Make It Personal

Are you asking God "why" today? Ask Him to help you have the attitude of a searching heart rather than a clenched fist.

A Present Help in Trouble

God is our refuge and strength,
a very present help in trouble.

—PSALM 46:1 ESV

Life is hard. We live in a fallen world. Even those who have been redeemed live in earthly bodies and have to deal with the realities of temptation, sin, disease, loss, pain, and death.

Becoming a Christian—even being a mature, godly Christian—doesn't wrap us up in some sort of celestial cocoon where we're immune to pain. Not until God makes a new heaven and a new earth will we be totally free from the ravages of sin. Until then, there will be tears, sorrows, pressures, and problems.

But—and here's the good news—God isn't removed or detached from our problems. He doesn't just sit up in heaven and watch to see if we will manage to survive. No, the God of the Bible is "a very present help in trouble." That doesn't mean He waves a magic wand and makes all our problems disappear; it does mean He uses pressures and problems to mold and shape our lives and to make us like Jesus, who "learned obedience from what he suffered" (Heb. 5:8).

Make It Personal

How has God used (and is currently using) your problems to change you and reveal His grace and power to the world?

Living Stones

You yourselves, as living stones, a spiritual house,
are being built to be a holy priesthood to offer spiritual
sacrifices acceptable to God through Jesus Christ.

—1 PETER 2:5

Through faith in Christ, we become living stones built on Him. We get a new identity. We are no longer defined by the failures of our past. Our identity is not found in our performance, our gifts, or our abilities. We are chosen ones, precious to God, just as Jesus is. In Christ we're joined into a holy construction project—the building of a temple for God. This gives us hope when we're struggling to overcome a particular sin or trial.

The weight of the Church rests on Jesus and His finished work on the cross. Aren't you glad your salvation doesn't rest on you? He's the One who joins the whole building together. One day, when it's all finished, there will be a glorious, holy dwelling place for God. And in the meantime, we, as living stones, are safe and secure because we rest on Christ, our Cornerstone.

 Make It Personal

*Today, how can you choose to listen to God's voice and know
that if you're in Christ, you are chosen and precious?*

He Is Faithful

Because of the LORD's faithful love we do not perish,
for his mercies never end.
They are new every morning;
great is your faithfulness!
—LAMENTATIONS 3:22-23

Less than five years after Robert and I said "I do," the Lord led us into a major opportunity to experience and embrace His sovereign rule in our lives. Just as the world was being upended by the global pandemic, my otherwise healthy husband, over the course of just a handful of months, received diagnoses of two different unrelated cancers.

Looking back, we can see clearly that God had been preparing us for this journey. In 2019, Robert and I coauthored a book called *You Can Trust God to Write Your Story*. We reflected on God's providences—some painful, some beautiful, but all good—in our own story. And while we didn't know then (and still don't!) what rocky paths we may yet be called to travel, we know He has been faithful in each chapter thus far. And we know that He will be faithful in each one yet to come, that His grace will be sufficient for wherever He leads us.

 Make It Personal

How has God been faithful in each chapter of your life?
How does that help you to trust Him for the future?

The Gift of Sound Doctrine

Preach the word . . . correct, rebuke, and
encourage with great patience and teaching.

—2 TIMOTHY 4:2

In 2 Timothy, Paul pointed Timothy toward the solution for drifting away from sound doctrine. Pastors and elders are responsible for providing spiritual *direction* and *protection* for the flock of God. An unswerving commitment to sound doctrine is central to that calling.

If the pastors and leaders of your church love, live, and teach sound doctrine, you've been given a huge gift. If you're looking for a church home, make sure to choose one where you'll find a steady diet of solid, biblical teaching that encourages you to live out the implications of sound doctrine.

And if your church is searching for a new pastor, pray that God will bring a man who will "proclaim things consistent with sound teaching" (Titus 2:1). He doesn't have to be a spellbinding orator or a superb administrator. But he does need to be able to preach the Word—to "encourage and rebuke with all authority" (v. 15).

 Make It Personal

*Take time to pray for your church's pastors and leaders today,
thanking God for them, and asking that He would help
them teach sound doctrine.*

Loss of Intimacy

They hid from the LORD God.
—GENESIS 3:8

Adam and Eve were the first of God's creatures to experience a remarkable relationship with Him. Nowhere do we see God seeking out a relationship with any of His creation—except for man.

Only to Adam and Eve did God reveal Himself. The pair responded in wonder, love, and obedience. There was no fear or shame because they delighted to know and do the will of God. Communion with Him was the reason for their existence.

Perhaps you've experienced that kind of relationship with God.

Do you also know what it is to lose that intimacy? To make a choice that creates distance where there was once nearness, fear where there was once trust, and shame where there was once freedom?

Even though Adam and Eve made the choice to sin—and as a result lost that intimacy with God—He never stopped loving them, communicating, seeking, or initiating. Just as He never stops loving and seeking you and me.

 Make It Personal

*Ask the Lord to search your heart and to do whatever
it takes to restore any lost intimacy with Him.*

Beauty in Holiness

Worship the LORD in the splendor of his holiness.
—PSALM 96:9

Holiness may not be at the top of our list of things to talk about, but those in heaven never stop talking about it! We need to "reclaim" true holiness—to see it in all its beauty as it is revealed in God's Word.

In Jonathan Edwards' memoirs, he spoke of his fascination for holiness: "It appeared to me, that there was nothing in it but what was ravishingly lovely; the highest beauty and ami-ableness—a *divine* beauty; far purer than anything here upon earth; and that everything else was like mire and defilement in comparison of it."[7]

Likewise, A. W. Tozer challenged the misconceptions often associated with holiness: "Holiness in the Bible means moral wholeness—a positive quality which actually includes kindness, mercy, purity, moral blamelessness and godliness. It is always to be thought of in a positive, white intensity of degree."[8]

If we really understood holiness and could see how beautiful and splendid it is, we would make it a high priority for our lives.

Make It Personal

How have you seen holiness shine through someone else? How can you reclaim the beautiful image of true holiness in your own life?

Purpose in the Trial

Pursue peace with everyone, and holiness—
without it no one will see the Lord.

—HEBREWS 12:14

God has a purpose in every trial you're in right now. You can trust Him. In fact, His willingness to become involved in your life—even as the disciplining Father—gives evidence not of His disapproval but of His love.

When received with a tender, submissive heart, God's chastening reassures us that we are in relationship with Him, that we belong to Him. That gives great encouragement and stamina to persevere. Instead of resenting the people He uses as instruments in our discipline or responding sinfully to the problems we face, we are challenged to "pursue peace with everyone" (Heb. 12:14).

The author of Hebrews reminds us of God's provision for dealing with life's painful circumstances, as well as what will happen if we don't receive and appropriate that provision: "Make sure that no one falls short of the grace of God and that no root of bitterness springs up, causing trouble and defiling many" (Heb. 12:15).

 Make It Personal

*Ask the Lord to help you see His purpose in any
difficult circumstances you're currently facing
and to protect you from bitterness.*

Walking by Faith

We walk by faith, not by sight.

−2 CORINTHIANS 5:7

We see a contrast throughout God's Word and in our Christian lives between things that are seen and things that are unseen. The things that are seen—things of this material world—are temporal. But faith takes us into the realm of things not seen, things you cannot know with your natural senses, things that are eternal.

Most people spend the majority of their lives in the realm of the natural. But as followers of Christ, we're called to walk by faith—to trust the heart and hand of God, even when we can't see where He's leading. It's walking by faith that will help us endure when the storms assail us, because we're building our lives on the Rock of Jesus Christ.

When we walk by faith, we don't live for the "here and now," but for the "there and then." When we face affliction, we see it has eternal purpose. Walking by faith helps us keep our eyes on the finish line, where one day we will see our Savior face to face and our faith will be rewarded.

 Make It Personal

How are you being tempted to follow your feelings,
emotions, or circumstances rather than the Word of God?

A Heart for Home

Every wise woman builds her house.

—PROVERBS 14:1

It wasn't anything fancy—but what a sweet gift it was.

My husband and I joined our friends "Gretchen" and "Alex," along with their family, for an evening in their home. We gathered around their table to feast on soup and bread. We talked, laughed, and played a board game. Then we closed the evening with a time of prayer.

Gretchen, a generous-hearted wife and mom, is pulled in many directions these days—juggling the needs of her husband, homeschooled children, aging parents, a disabled sister who has come to live with them temporarily . . . yet she intentionally makes her home a place of outreach and welcome.

She doesn't typically offer gourmet meals. What she does offer is extravagant love, warmth, acceptance, conversation, and smiles. Her home isn't an idol or an end in itself. It's a tool, a means of putting the gospel and the grace of God on display.

My friend is giving those who come through the front door a taste of heaven. Because she—like all true Titus 2 women—has developed a heart for home.

Make It Personal

Think of someone who has graciously opened their home to you.
How did their hospitality put God's grace on display?

Dual Dangers

"Are you a teacher of Israel and don't know these things?"

—JOHN 3:10

When it comes to doctrine, there are two dangers to avoid. The first is *life without sound doctrine*. The second is having *doctrine without life*.

This was Nicodemus' problem when he first came to Jesus. He had his doctrine down, but he didn't have life. He was a prime example that it's possible to *know* right and *do* right and yet not *be* right.

Further, doctrine that produces self-righteous, critical defenders of truth isn't in accord with the heart and character of God. It's not truly sound—because sound doctrine is true and right and also beautiful and good.

We may have the right answers to hard questions, but do we exhibit tenderness as we share those answers? We may have mastered God's Word, but is it evident that our hearts are moved by the wonder of what we know?

As we live out His truth, our lives are made more beautiful. And that truth becomes more compelling and irresistible in the eyes of those around us.

 Make It Personal

Which of the two dangers do you tend more toward:
living without sound doctrine or doctrine without life?

Bread of Life

"I am the bread of life.... No one who comes to me
will ever be hungry, and no one who believes
in me will ever be thirsty again."

—JOHN 6:35

In ancient times, bread was vital for life. In Scripture, bread is an object lesson for our basic spiritual needs; it also points to God's presence to fill and sustain us.

In John 6, Jesus performed a miracle with bread, feeding a hungry crowd from just five barley loaves and two fish. Afterward, there were twelve baskets of bread left over. The next day Jesus told the crowd, "You are looking for me, not because you saw the signs, but because you ate the loaves and were filled" (v. 26).

Those people were following Jesus for miracles. They were impressed with Jesus but not ready to invest their lives in Him. They wanted Jesus for what they could get from Him.

Where do you turn for fulfillment? Earthly things—even good things—don't last. Oh, that we would cease seeking fullness in things that can't give us life! Christ is the Bread from heaven—the One who eternally satisfies our souls.

 Make It Personal

How has Jesus, the Bread of Life, sustained you in the past?
How can you increase your hunger for Him?

Several Steps Ahead

"Go to the sea, cast in a fishhook, and take the first fish that
you catch. When you open its mouth you'll find a coin."
—MATTHEW 17:27

Few people enjoy thinking about taxes, so it was a challenging day for Peter. The disciple was reminded that he and his Master, Jesus, were expected to pay a temple tax. Matthew 17:27 tells how Jesus told Peter to go out on a boat and cast a line. The first fish he caught would contain a coin large enough to pay the tax for both of them.

The solution to Peter's tax problem had likely been set in motion before Peter was even aware of it. A coin of the correct amount fell into the water at the right time and right place. A fish caught it in its mouth and made its way through the sea to be near Peter's line when it entered the water.

Peter had a need, but he discovered that God was several steps ahead of him. More than the money to pay his tax, Peter received a striking lesson in God's sovereignty that day.

 Make It Personal

*How have you seen God's sovereignty at work in your life—
where He's been several steps ahead of you?*

Speaking the Truth

"I, the Lord, have not changed."

—MALACHI 3:6

We live in a world that's constantly changing. Innovative technology, updated styles, news at a moment's notice—sometimes it seems that nothing stays the same.

Yet Hebrews 13:8 tells us that God never changes! He is "the same yesterday, today, and forever."

The Lord isn't like shifting sand. There is no shadow of truth with Him. He doesn't flip-flop on issues, depending on His audience. He is always true.

My words have not always been true. As a young woman in my twenties, wanting to make a good impression on others, I would sometimes exaggerate the truth. God showed me that my pride had resulted in a root of deception in my heart. By His grace, God granted me repentance. Over time, He removed those roots of deceit and replaced them with truthfulness.

Spiritual victories are won when we speak the truth. In real life, it often seems that people who lie succeed. But Proverbs says that in the long run, the effect of true words will be enduring and those who deceive will not last.

Make It Personal

Ask the Lord to examine your heart and show you if there are any areas where you are guilty of not speaking the truth.

The Only Difference

Remind them to submit to rulers and authorities, to obey, to be
ready for every good work, to slander no one, to avoid fighting,
and to be kind, always showing gentleness to all people.

—TITUS 3:1–2

When Paul urges Titus to teach what accords with
sound doctrine, he implies that some ways of life are
not in accordance with sound doctrine. Throughout the book
of Titus, Paul identifies ways that Christians' lives should differ radically from those of unbelievers.

The distinction between Christians and the world should
be crystal clear. Not because we're better people or come from
better upbringings. In fact, we're not inherently different from
anyone else. Our hearts would love to march to the same
self-absorbed cadence that drives the rest of the world.

The only difference is Jesus. The gospel. But what a difference that makes. What a difference *He* makes!

And the means by which the Spirit keeps loosening our
grip on old patterns of behavior, releasing us from the bonds of
cultural conformity, and awakening our hearts to the beauty of
Christ and His ways, is through the implanted truth of His Word.

 Make It Personal

*Before you spend time in God's Word today, ask Him to
awaken your heart to the beauty of Christ and His ways.*

A Servant of the Lord

My soul magnifies the Lord, and my spirit rejoices
in God my Savior, because he has looked with favor
on the humble condition of his servant.

—LUKE 1:46–48

Equipped with the promises of God, Mary's response to the angel's impossible announcement was simply, "See, I am the Lord's servant. . . . May it happen to me as you have said" (Luke 1:38). In other words, "Lord, I'm available. You are my master; I am Your servant. I'm willing to be used however You choose."

In that act of surrender, Mary offered herself to God as a living sacrifice. She was willing to be used by God for His purposes—willing to endure the loss of reputation that was certain to follow when people realized she was with child, willing to endure the ridicule and even the possible stoning permitted by the Mosaic law, willing to go through nine months of increasing discomfort and sleeplessness, willing to endure the labor pains of giving birth to the Child. Mary was willing to give up her own plans and agenda so that she might link arms with God in fulfilling His agenda.

 Make It Personal

Ask God to reveal to you the condition of your heart. Are you
surrendered to Him like Mary was? What needs to change?

The Anthem of Heaven

Blessing and glory and wisdom and thanksgiving and honor
and power and strength be to our God forever and ever.

—REVELATION 7:12

Giving thanks—it's what we'll be doing forever. Oh, I'm sure it's not *all* we'll be doing forever, and yet I'm confident that every action, thought, word, or undertaking throughout our endless life with the Lord will be an expression of gratitude.

Gratitude is the unending anthem of heaven. Revelation 11:17 says the twenty-four elders fall on their faces before Him, saying, "We give you thanks, Lord God, the Almighty, who is and who was, because you have taken your great power and have begun to reign." Even now. Right this minute.

Every time we speak and live out our thankfulness here on earth, we join our voices with the grand chorus of gratitude that wells up before the throne of God and prepare ourselves for what we'll be doing throughout all eternity, glorifying and thanking Him for all He is and has done.

So, think of today as a "dress rehearsal." And do it just the way you will when you're doing it at the actual performance.

✎ Make It Personal

*What are some ways that you can practice your thankfulness
today for the live performance that is to come?*

A Deep Friendship

LORD, you have searched me and known me.

—PSALM 139:1

As a result of extended time spent in the presence of God, Moses enjoyed an unusually deep friendship with God. Whereas others in the camp could not draw near to God or look on His glory, "the LORD would speak with Moses face to face" (Ex. 33:11).

Moses was not allowed to see God's face but God spoke with Moses directly, not through an intermediary.

"Face to face" is a picture of intimacy. It is a picture of lovers. On the other hand, when something comes between two friends it can be awkward and uncomfortable to be face-to-face.

If you have walked with God for any length of time, you know what it is to have a breach in the relationship—to find it difficult to look Him "in the eyes." The purpose of a daily devotional time is to get back into His presence, to find out what has caused the breach, and to reestablish fellowship. Then we can once again look in His face without shame or fear.

 Make It Personal

Can you look the Lord "in the eyes"?
Spend time in His presence today, seeking fellowship with Him.

Channels of Blessing

[Dorcas] was always doing good works and acts of charity.

—ACTS 9:36

I love the New Testament account of a follower of Christ named Dorcas. Here was a woman whose relationship with Christ moved her to pour out her life in practical acts of kindness toward those in need. Her life was a picture of true kindness in action. That became even more clear when tragedy struck and Dorcas died (Acts 9:37–39).

The poignant description of the widows she had blessed, grieving next to her lifeless body, suggests that Dorcas genuinely cared for the people she served. They didn't just miss what she had done for them. They missed *her*.

Her kindness stood in stark contrast to the unbelieving world, where widows were often left to fend for themselves and faced probable destitution. Dorcas's life shone a spotlight on the love of Christ. And as a result of her being raised back to life, "many" put their faith in Him (v. 42).

And that's the impact Christian kindness can have on our witness in the world.

 Make It Personal

Ask God to help your life be a picture of true kindness,
so that it may shine a spotlight on the love of Christ.

One Day

"If the Son sets you free, you really will be free."
—JOHN 8:36

To pursue holiness is to move toward joy—joy infinitely greater than any earthly delights can offer.

Why do we make holiness out to be some austere obligation when the fact is that to be holy is to be clean, to be free from the weight of sin? Why would we cling to our sin any more than a leper would refuse to part with his oozing sores, given the opportunity to be cleansed?

To resist holiness or to be half-hearted about its pursuit is to forfeit true joy and to settle for something less than that God-intoxication for which we were created. Sooner or later, sin will rob you of everything beautiful and desirable.

If you're a child of God, you were redeemed to enjoy the sweet fruit of holiness—to walk in oneness with Him, to relish His presence, to rejoice in His mercy, to know the joy of having clean hands, a pure heart, and a clear conscience. One day, we will stand before the Lord unashamed. Why settle for anything less?

 Make It Personal

*How can you make it a point to
pursue holiness on a day-to-day basis?*

Prince of Peace

May the Lord of peace himself
give you peace always in every way.
—2 THESSALONIANS 3:16

Every human heart longs for peace, but it's a gift that few experience. On the contrary, many of us are characterized by stress, fear, and anxiety. We lack peace in our relationships—we see conflict, tension, strife; we see divorce, church splits, and world wars.

It was into such a world that God sent an amazing gift. The gift everyone wants—peace—is a Person. The Prince of Peace is God's gift to people who desperately need peace.

The first and greatest need in our lives is to have peace with God, and through Jesus' death on the cross, we can. This is the starting place for all peace.

Then, having received peace *with* God, we can have the peace *of* God. We can cease striving and be calm in the storms of life. We think, *Oh, if this problem would go away, I could be peaceful.* But peace is not the absence of problems. Peace is the presence of Christ in the midst of problems.

 Make It Personal

How has Jesus brought you peace during a time of difficulty?
In what situations do you need His peace today?

Total Surrender

Jesus said to his disciples, "If anyone wants to follow after me,
let him deny himself, take up his cross, and follow me."
—MATTHEW 16:24

Having surrendered our lives to Christ as Savior and Lord, we must learn what it means to live out a surrendered life—to continually say no to self and yes to God.

Many Christians live perpetually discouraged lives because they've never realized and are not living out the implications of their initial surrender to Christ. Having once surrendered control of their lives to Christ, they have reverted to trying to manage their own lives. As a result, they're living out of alignment with the Lord who created, redeemed, and owns them.

It may be that even at this moment you are living in a chapter called "Unsurrendered."

Could it be that there are some issues on which you are reserving the right to control your own life?

For example, though you may have surrendered your life to God, do you realize that your money belongs to God too? And your children? And your time? All of these are the practical outworking of a surrendered life.

 Make It Personal

*Ask God to show you if there are any areas
of your life that you have not surrendered to Him.*

A High and Holy Calling

Her children rise up and call her blessed.

—PROVERBS 31:28

Kari was in her mid-thirties when she attended a True Woman conference. She was a devoted Christian and mother of seven who obviously valued children. Yet during that weekend, the Lord exposed anger and frustration that had been building up in her heart. Without realizing it, she had harbored a sense that her husband, children, and even God had drained away opportunities and freedoms from her.

Through the teaching of His Word, God renewed Kari's passion for motherhood. He had rekindled her zeal for what He'd given her to do. He can do the same for you.

No, the fresh winds of truth won't stop your toddler from throwing up the morning of vacation or bring a prodigal child to his senses. Parenting is demanding, complex, and short on immediate rewards, no matter how passionate you are about it.

But if you're a mother—or involved in nurturing children—remember you've got a vital calling and ministry right there in the house with you. And your efforts in raising those little ones for His glory are not—and *will* not be—in vain.

 Make It Personal

Pray that God would grow a passion in the hearts of mothers you know for the calling of motherhood.

Happy in the Will of God

Each has his own gift from God,
one person has this gift, another has that.

—1 CORINTHIANS 7:7

In the will of God, marriage is an incredible gift, to be received with joy and thanksgiving and to be used for the glory of God. Likewise, in the will of God, singleness is an incredible gift, to be received with gratitude and to be used for the glory of God.

In 1 Corinthians 7, the apostle Paul cautions against striving for a gift or a calling other than that which God has entrusted to us. He exhorts us not to seek to escape from binding circumstances or to insist on having a gift God has not chosen for us: "Let each of you remain in the situation in which he was called" (v. 20). The issue isn't our marital status or station in life but rather choosing to live in that state in union with God.

Paul sets forth the principle that what matters most isn't whether or not we're married but rather the will of God. What state has He called us to be? What gift has He given us?

 Make It Personal

Today, how can you receive the gifts God has given you with joy?
How can you use them for His glory?

Still and Always

Our God is in heaven and does whatever he pleases.

—PSALM 115:3

I can't recall a time when I didn't know and believe that Heaven rules at some level. But increasingly, this way of viewing the complexities and crises of life in this broken world has captured my heart. It has become a lens through which I see and process everything.

"Heaven rules" reminds us that our God in heaven is actively controlling and working through every single happening, event, and circumstance taking place on the earth, and He is doing it to accomplish His good, eternal, redemptive purposes.

He is doing it despite whatever you may hear concerning the state of our world while watching or scrolling through the news of the day.

He is doing it despite whatever pops up as you check your email or social media feeds after you emerge from a long meeting. He is doing it despite the nervousness that's ticking under your wristwatch while you're perched in yet another doctor's office, listening for your name to be called.

Heaven is still ruling. Heaven is *always* ruling.

 Make It Personal

How does the truth that "Heaven rules" reassure you that God is in control of your life and our world?

A Serious Sin

For though they knew God, they did not glorify him as God
or show gratitude. Instead, their thinking became worthless,
and their senseless hearts were darkened.

—ROMANS 1:21

Ingratitude is our first step away from God. In the first
chapter of Romans, Paul talks about "God's wrath" being
revealed against the "unrighteousness of people" (v. 18). He
lists "all unrighteousness, evil, greed, and wickedness" (v. 29),
and just about every awful thing you can imagine.

But what starts people (and civilizations) down this path
toward ever more serious sin? The answer is found in verse 21:
They didn't give thanks to Him.

That seemingly insignificant, innocuous matter of ingratitude turns out to be at the fountainhead of all the other evils
listed in this chapter!

Do you see how serious this sin of ingratitude is? When we
give in to whining, murmuring, and complaining—not honoring God or giving thanks to Him—we embark on a destructive slide that can take us down to depths we never could have
imagined going.

Make It Personal

*How can ingratitude lead to other sin in our lives? Take time
now to stop and thank God for all He has done for you.*

Ready for Revival?

Let's strive to know the LORD.
His appearance is as sure as the dawn.
He will come to us like the rain,
like the spring showers that water the land.

—HOSEA 6:3

Are you tired of trying to be a good Christian? Are you overloaded and worn out with church activities? Do you sometimes feel as if you're just going through the motions of the Christian life? Do you often find yourself running on empty spiritually? Do you experience heaviness or shame more than joy and freedom? If you answered yes to any of these questions, then perhaps God is calling you to something deeper. Maybe you're ready to experience personal revival!

God wants to reveal Himself to you; He wants to fill your heart with Himself. He wants to set you free from every unholy passion; He wants you to drink deeply of the joys found in His presence. He wants your service for Him to be the overflow of genuine love and an authentic life; He wants you to be a reflector of His glory in our dark world. He wants you—and His entire church—to be revived!

 Make It Personal

Imagine what "something deeper" between you and the Lord could look like. Make that your prayer today, and every day.

Clothed in Humility

In humility consider others
as more important than yourselves.

—PHILIPPIANS 2:3

Our natural bent isn't toward humility; it's toward pride. We're naturally motivated to seek attention, praise, honor, and glory for ourselves. But when we're proud, we make ourselves to be God's enemies because we're exalting ourselves rather than exalting Him.

As humans created in God's likeness, we're at our very best when we make much of Him! Jesus said in the Sermon on the Mount, "Blessed are the poor in spirit" (Matt. 5:3). Those who are spiritually bankrupt, who realize they have nothing to offer, are blessed. Those who push themselves up are the ones God pushes down.

In Philippians 2, we're pointed to the supreme example of the humility of Christ, who took the form of a servant and humbled Himself by dying on the cross. And what did God do? God lifted Him up. When we humble ourselves, God will lift us up in due time. When our hearts are humble, all we care about is that God gets the glory and that Jesus is recognized, worshiped, and applauded as Lord!

 Make It Personal

What are some ways you could humble yourself today?

Root for the Home Team!

Therefore encourage one another and build each other up.

—1 THESSALONIANS 5:11

I'm an editor by trade. That means I've spent most of my adult life trying to correct mistakes. My husband says I can spot an error on a billboard while speeding by at eighty-five miles per hour.

But while that's useful for proofreading, it's not particularly helpful in relationships, especially marriage. If I'm not careful, I'm prone to point out the one thing that's wrong (in my view) and slower to identify the ninety-nine things that are right.

On occasion, Robert has said, "I feel like you're editing me." I know in those moments he feels I'm not pulling for him. What he needs is an encourager, not an editor. So, I've made it my aim to build Robert up.

We all need honest input from those who know us best and can help us see blind spots. But our ability to give humble, helpful critique and have it be well-received is in direct proportion to the effort we make to give the gift of encouragement.

Make It Personal

Are there areas where you're "editing" someone in your life? How can you focus on encouraging and building them up instead?

An Unshakable Truth

> "With flattery he will corrupt those who act wickedly
> toward the covenant, but the people who know
> their God will be strong and take action."
> —DANIEL 11:32

On any given day, it can feel like our world is spinning out of control, that evildoers are winning, and that God is helpless (or unwilling) to do anything about it.

On a more personal level, it may seem that God is dismissive toward your situation, sluggish to act, even coldly unconcerned about matters weighing heavily on your mind and heart, difficulties that distract and distress you and sabotage your joy. But for those who "know their God" (Dan. 11:32), not even the most dreaded, drastic, or deathly occurrences can steal their hope and confidence in Him. All will be well, even though at the moment nothing seems to be well.

This truth is unshakable, despite any and all indications to the contrary. Even when storms are raging within and around us, you and I can sleep in peace each night, and each morning we can awaken to renewed comfort and courage because of this immutable, irrefutable reality. Because Heaven rules.

 Make It Personal

Has it ever seemed like God wasn't intervening in a painful situation? Looking back, how can you see Heaven's rule?

A Model of Faith

"Daniel, you are a man treasured by God."

—DANIEL 10:11

Throughout his long life, Daniel remained a stalwart pillar of faith, exerting a righteous influence in an unrighteous environment. This is because he fixed his sight on the long view—the certainty of God's everlasting kingdom.

Can you see why the account given to us in the book of Daniel is so applicable and needed today? Here where we live and serve in the "Babylon" we know, the life, words, and demeanor of this faithful, faith-filled man provide a model for believers of every generation.

That's why I don't consider it any coincidence that the Lord turned my attention to Daniel's story in Scripture as my own world was roiling in 2020. As I soaked in this book, the truth of "Heaven rules" proved to be a solid rock for my faith. The things God taught me through Daniel have caused this phrase to become my true north in an even richer, sweeter way than I had ever experienced before. And today, when life and the world so often feel upside down, this enduring truth keeps me right side up.

 Make It Personal

How does the life of Daniel encourage
you in your present-day circumstances?

Giving Grace

With all humility and gentleness, with patience,
bearing with one another in love.

—EPHESIANS 4:2

B oth you and your spouse are humans with the capacity
for love, hate, support, and betrayal. Both of you make
mistakes. Both of you need daily doses of grace.

And the more you keep that in mind, the freer you will
both be to grow in love for one another. Even the best marriage involves two sinners perpetually humbling themselves,
getting to Christ, and receiving and dispensing grace.

Growing in grace as husband and wife involves a lot of acceptance and a lot of "I'm sorry; I was wrong." It means assuming the best of each other, not insisting on perfection. It also
means extending mercy and forgiveness. But it helps to remember your spouse's strengths *and* weaknesses are what you need to
become the person God wants you to be. And vice versa.

Maintaining this awareness isn't dependent on how well
your spouse accepts and extends grace to you. It's a matter of
relying on God to give grace to both of you as you persevere in
learning more about love.

 Make It Personal

How can you show grace to your spouse today?

An Available Life

"See, I am the Lord's servant," said Mary.
"May it happen to me as you have said."
—LUKE 1:38

Mary's cry of surrender in Luke 1:38 ought to be the heart-cry of every child of God.

"I am Your servant, Lord; I'm available. Do You want me to be married? I'll be married. Single? I'll be single. Do You want me to have children? I'll raise them for Your glory. Do You want me to be childless? Then I will be a reproducer of spiritual fruit in the lives of others. Do You want me to suffer with a physical affliction? Do You want me to love and serve this spouse who is so hard to live with? Do You want me to take that young person under my wing and mentor him or her in Your ways? Do You want me to give up my free time to serve in the community? Do You want me to take meals to that cranky neighbor who is ill?

"Lord, whatever You want! I am Your servant. May it happen to me as you have said."

 Make It Personal

Ask God to make your heart willing to
follow Him in whatever He calls you to do.

Spilling Over

Let us continually offer up to God a sacrifice of praise.

—HEBREWS 13:15

My responsibilities sometimes require me to drive over a bridge that spans a river. Numerous times, I've been enthralled by the sight of the sun sparkling on the rippling water and haven't been able to restrain myself from saying aloud, "Thank You, Lord, for this scene—it's beautiful!"

Similar words of thanks often rise from my heart to my lips—after listening to a sermon that has spoken to my heart, when touched by the kindness or generosity of a friend, when I receive some unexpected blessing, or when I witness God's amazing grace at work in the life of another.

Occasions for gratitude are all around us. If we recognize them at all, our general reaction is to let the thought we hear in our minds suffice for our gratitude. But the Bible says, "Let us continually offer up to God a sacrifice of praise, that is, the fruit of lips that confess his name" (Heb. 13:15).

It's important not only to have a heart of gratitude but to let your heart spill over into words.

Make It Personal

Today, as you see things to be grateful for,
say your thanks out loud.

Light of the World

"I have come as light into the world, so that everyone
who believes in me would not remain in darkness."

—JOHN 12:46

During the Feast of Tabernacles, an annual event cele-
brated by the Jews, a ceremony took place called the
Illumination of the Temple. Every night during the feast, four
young men would climb ladders to fill four golden lamp bowls
with oil and light giant, seventy-five-foot-tall candelabras. The
light not only lit up the temple but also the whole city. It reminded the people of that great light promised by the prophet
Isaiah for those who walk in darkness.

John 8 records a dramatic scene that took place the day
after this ceremony. Jesus boldly proclaimed, "I am the light
of the world. Anyone who follows me will never walk in the
darkness but will have the light of life" (John 8:12).

He was saying that the light of the temple, though truly
magnificent, inevitably sputters out; but those who believe and
follow Him will never walk in darkness. He is our Light—not
just an occasional, annual blaze but a light we will have forever!

Make It Personal

*Ask God to shine His light into your life, your home, your church,
and your community; that He would dispel any darkness.*

How to Hallow God's Name

I . . . urge you to walk worthy of the calling you have received.

—EPHESIANS 4:1

Jesus lived His life for the glory of God. So, if we want to be like Jesus, we will strive to hallow God's name, just as Christ did.

But practically, how can we do this? First, we can hallow His name *in our hearts* by choosing thoughts, desires, priorities, and prayers that are worthy of Him.

Second, we can hallow God's name *in our talk*. So often we use His name glibly and throw out spiritual phrases flippantly and thoughtlessly.

And third, we can hallow Him *in our walk*. God takes it seriously when we fail to uphold Him as holy before others.

As Bible commentator William Barclay said, "The name of God can only be hallowed when every action of our life is a witness to our faith in Him, and when we continuously bring credit to the name we bear."[9]

Make It Personal

Take some time to reflect on how you do at hallowing God's name through your heart, your talk, and your walk.

Sharp Relief

> Woe is me for I am ruined because I am a man
> of unclean lips and live among a people of unclean lips,
> and because my eyes have seen the King.
>
> —ISAIAH 6:5

Throughout Scripture, when even the holiest men and women were confronted with the awesome holiness of God, they were moved to deep contrition and brokenness before Him.

The closer we get to God, the more clearly we will see ourselves as we really are. As long as we compare ourselves to others, we can always find someone who makes us feel good about how well we are doing. But when we step into the light of God's holiness, our lives are brought into sharp relief. What once may have seemed clean and pure suddenly looks soiled and tarnished. The pure light of His holiness exposes the nooks and crannies, the cracks and crevices of our innermost being.

To know God, to live in His presence, and to be occupied with a vision of His holiness is to know how foolish and frail we are apart from Him and to be broken from a preoccupation with ourselves.

 Make It Personal

*Ask the Lord that as you grow closer to Him,
He will help you see yourself more clearly.*

A Deliberate Choice

"Indeed, God is my salvation;
I will trust him and not be afraid."

—ISAIAH 12:2

Heaven rules" is how Robert and I, by God's daily, enabling grace, are seeking to face all of life. Mercifully, as I'm writing today, we are looking at Robert's two bouts with cancer through the rearview mirror, although the journey has entailed more surgical procedures, blood transfusions, needle sticks, chemo treatments, biopsies, scans, and hospital stays than we thought our two calendars (and one man's body!) could possibly accommodate. You just make room when Heaven rules.

But even with the sense of relief we're currently feeling on that front, we still must deliberately choose to trust and praise God each day, regardless of what He apportions to us in His all-good, all-wise design for our lives. Our confidence as we wait for Him to unfold our next season remains the same today as it was back before his diagnoses.

Heaven rules. It really is true. And no threat, no problem, whether in our own little world or in the great big world around us, can ever steal that assurance from us.

Make It Personal

How can you deliberately choose to trust God in the situations and circumstances you experience today?

Not Too High

"If anyone wants to follow after me, let him deny himself,
take up his cross daily, and follow me."

—LUKE 9:23

Betty Scott grew up in China, where her parents were missionaries. During college, Betty penned a prayer of unconditional surrender to Jesus:

> Lord, I give up my own plans and purposes, all my own desires, hopes and ambitions, and I accept Thy will for my life. I give up myself, my life, my all, utterly to Thee, to be Thine forever. I hand over to Thy keeping all of my friendships; all the people whom I love are to take second place in my heart. Fill me now and seal me with Thy Spirit. Work out Thy whole will in my life at any cost, for to me to live is Christ. Amen.[10]

Betty returned to China in 1931 to serve with China Inland Mission and later married John Stam. Just three months after their daughter was born, they were taken hostage by Communist soldiers and beheaded. Although some might consider the cost exorbitant, I'm confident that Betty, having laid down her life for Christ, wouldn't think the price too high.

 Make It Personal

Reread Betty Stam's prayer and make it your own.

Kindness Begins at Home

Her mouth speaks wisdom,
and loving instruction is on her tongue.
—PROVERBS 31:26

Nowhere am I more tempted to be selfish than in my home and closest relationships. I fear this is true for most of us. Too often, we show more concern and kindness for neighbors, colleagues, or complete strangers than for those who live under the same roof with us or who are related to us by blood or marriage.

Dealing with the responsibilities of home requires diligence and discipline every day. But it also requires kindness.

And that's where things can get challenging. It's easy to be like the woman who once lamented to me, "I'm only good enough to look good to the world." At home, it's often another story.

Yes, kindness at home takes extra effort. But if we all demonstrated true kindness toward the people who know us best and see us at our worst, our more public displays of affection would likely ring truer. And I suspect that if we showed more kindness at home, we'd also find ourselves growing genuinely kinder toward everyone else.

 Make It Personal

*What does it reveal about our hearts when we are kinder
to strangers than to those who are related to us?*

Point to Jesus

"Do whatever he tells you," his mother told the servants.

—JOHN 2:5

In the Gospel of John, we find the account of Jesus at the wedding feast in Cana. When faced with a shortage of wine, Mary pointed the servants to Jesus: "Do whatever he tells you." She used her influence to direct others to Jesus and to encourage them to obey and follow Him.

We would do well to follow Mary's example. When friends and acquaintances come to us with problems, our role is not to solve their problems but to point them to Jesus and to encourage them to "do whatever he tells you."

Mary apparently was also influential in leading her own children to follow Jesus. During His earthly ministry, Jesus' half brothers did not believe in Him (John 7:5). However, by the time the early church was birthed, they had become believers (Acts 1:14); two of them—Jude and James—penned the New Testament books that bear their names. I believe that Mary was likely one of the key influences in bringing them to faith in Jesus.

 Make It Personal

How can you be quick to point others to Jesus
when they come to you with questions or for advice?

The Biggest Picture

Look at the nations and observe—be utterly astounded!
—HABAKKUK 1:5

The big picture." This phrase gets thrown around in the business world to describe a company's overall mission. An employee is encouraged to look at the big picture when details threaten to overwhelm him.

But an executive's "big picture" can never compare to God's. The most meaningful mission comes from setting aside our own plans and getting perspective from the One who sees eternal time and infinite space. God told the prophet Habakkuk, "Look at the nations and observe—be utterly astounded!" (Hab. 1:5).

One of the reasons Habakkuk's prayers seemed to be unheard was that he was looking in the wrong place for the answer. He was focusing on his own nation and his own people while God was orchestrating world events.

We always ought to pray with the awareness that God may be doing something far bigger than we can imagine. Even though we can't see the big picture, we can trust the One who does. We can pray like our Savior, "Not my will, but Yours be done."

 Make It Personal

Ask God to help you see His big picture
and pray for His will to be done in your life.

Whatever He Says

Open my eyes so that I may contemplate
wondrous things from your instruction.
—PSALM 119:18

A practice that's made an enormous difference in my devotional life is that of beginning my time in the Word each day by praying words of Scripture back to the Lord. Scriptures like Psalm 119:18. Or Psalm 25:4–5:

Make your ways known to me, LORD;
teach me your paths.
Guide me in your truth and teach me,
for you are the God of my salvation;
I wait for you all day long.

As I pray this prayer, I'm committing to God that whatever He says to me through His Word I will obey. "Help me understand your instruction, and I will obey it and follow it with all my heart" (119:34). I'm saying to God, "Whatever You say, whether I like it or not, whether it's easy or not, by Your enabling grace and power, *I will obey.*"

 Make It Personal

Choose one of the above verses to pray before you read the Word today, and commit that whatever God says to you, you will obey.

Looking Back

A person's heart plans his way,
but the LORD determines his steps.

—PROVERBS 16:9

God's providence is often better seen in retrospect. Looking back often gives us a more accurate picture of where we've been and what it means. That's not to say that every look back will show us all there is to see. But if we continue to ponder where we've been and look with the eyes of faith, the view in the rearview mirror will often snap into focus and we'll get a clearer vision of how God has been working in our lives.

The view out the front windshield is a different story. We may think we know where we're headed, only to discover we had no earthly idea. What actually takes place may not at all be what we had envisioned or anticipated. What we see looking ahead is our story—our circumstances seen from our finite, limited perspective. What appears when we look back is God's Story—what He sees and knows and has in mind, how He is always at work for our good and His glory.

Make It Personal

Take time to reflect on ways you've seen God at work in your life. What were moments when you can clearly see His hand working?

The Fruit of Deception

There is a way that seems right to a person,

but its end is the way to death.

—PROVERBS 14:12

As Puritan pastor Thomas Brooks put it, "Satan promises the best, but pays with the worst; he promises honor, and pays with disgrace; he promises pleasure, and pays with pain; he promises profit, and pays with loss; he promises life, and pays with death."[11]

Satan uses deception to win our affections, influence our choices, and destroy our lives. In one way or another, every problem we have is the fruit of deception—the result of believing something that isn't true.

Satan holds out the glittering promise of "real life"; he knows, however, that those who respond to his offer will certainly die.

Anytime we receive input that's not consistent with God's Word, we can be sure Satan is trying to deceive and destroy us. It may sound or feel right, but if it's contrary to the Bible, it *isn't* right. If we could only see that the forbidden fruit, which looks so ripe and tastes so sweet in the first moment, always leads ultimately to death and destruction.

 Make It Personal

As you go throughout your day, how can you make sure
that what you hear and see lines up with God's Word?

The Good Shepherd

The Lamb who is at the center of the throne will shepherd them; he will guide them to springs of the waters of life.

—REVELATION 7:17

Sheep can't fend for themselves, which is why they need a shepherd. In truth, we're not much different than sheep— shepherding is necessary for our survival. So, what a joy when we realize God has always been the Shepherd of His people, collectively and individually. We find His shepherding all through the Old Testament, and there's also the promise of a Shepherd to come.

That Shepherd did come! His name is Jesus. The sheep belong to Him, and He knows them. Our Good Shepherd has a personal relationship with His sheep. We can be in a crowd and feel unknown, but in Jesus' fold, we don't get lost. He knows each of us by name. He knows our background, tendencies, and vulnerabilities. He knows where we're tempted and tested, and He knows our needs.

This Good Shepherd leads His sheep. He goes before them. He knows the terrain, and He can lead them through the most difficult places. Will you let Him lead you?

 Make It Personal

How does knowing that Jesus is your Shepherd encourage you today? How has He led you through difficult places in the past?

Through the Fog

For now we see only a reflection as in a mirror,
but then face to face.

—1 CORINTHIANS 13:12

Once while on vacation near the Grand Teton mountains in Wyoming, I decided to take a hike. In spite of the fact that the view was shrouded in fog, I chose to press on.

I knew there was a stunning view, but I couldn't see it. The apostle Paul describes the Christian life that way in 1 Corinthians 13. We know there is a purpose out there, but it's obscured by the fog of time and space. Yet Paul goes on to give us reason for great hope: "Then I will know fully, as I am fully known" (1 Cor. 13:12).

Yes, the pathway of faith may be steep. But for those who press on to know Him, we have God's promise that one day we will step out of the fog into brilliant, clear, dazzling sunlight. The view at the top will be spectacular, for that is where at long last we shall behold Jesus. That's one view that will be well worth the wait!

 Make It Personal

How does knowing there's a spectacular "view at the top"
give you hope to keep pressing on in your Christian life?

A Guarded Mouth

LORD, set up a guard for my mouth;
keep watch at the door of my lips.

—PSALM 141:3

The presence of a guard indicates the possibility of danger. We don't guard something that doesn't need to be protected.

Notice where the guard is posted in Psalm 141:3. Not at the ear to protect us from being hurt by words we might hear. Nor at the heart to shield us from the wounds that are sometimes caused by what others do. Rather the psalmist asked God to post a sentinel at his own mouth, knowing that the greatest danger he faced was not what others might do to him but rather what he might say that would harm others.

Our tongues can be dangerous weapons. Careless, harsh, or untimely words inflict pain on those who hear. Too often we let our words run unrestrained. Even though we may later regret our words, we can never take them back. Better to set a guard at our mouth, preventing the danger from getting loose, than trying furiously to "take back" words we never should have spoken in the first place.

 Make It Personal

*What are some practical steps you can take today
in order to guard your words and control your tongue?*

It's for Us All

As the one who called you is holy,
you also are to be holy in all your conduct.

—1 PETER 1:15

Everyone who names the name of the Lord is called to live a holy life!

Holiness is for moms who battle a sense of discouragement and who are tempted to escape into self-pity or the arms of an attentive man. It's for students constantly bombarded with pressure to conform and to indulge in ungodly forms of entertainment.

It's for lonely widows, divorcees, and singles who struggle to stay sexually abstinent. It's for husbands and wives who wrestle with bitterness toward mates who have abused or abandoned them. It's for men who are tempted to cheat on their wives or to abdicate their spiritual leadership in the home.

God knows we cannot possibly be holy apart from Him. That's why He has made provision for us to overcome sin through Christ. That's why He has sent His Spirit to live in our hearts. And that's why He has given every believer a supernatural resource called grace that gives us the desire and the power to be holy.

 Make It Personal

Ask God to pour out His grace on your life, so that you can be holy in whatever challenging situation you face.

Immanuel

"Therefore, the Lord himself will give you a sign:
See, the virgin will conceive, have a son,
and name him Immanuel."

—ISAIAH 7:14

The prophet Isaiah encouraged Ahaz to ask for a sign of God's promise, but Ahaz didn't want a sign. He was unwilling to put his trust in the Lord. But God was going to give Ahaz a sign, whether or not he wanted one—not just for Ahaz's sake but also for God's covenant people.

This was a promise that the nation of Judah wouldn't be snuffed out, no matter how many threatening kings and nations surrounded them. A child named Immanuel would come to deliver, and they would have a glorious future.

Bible scholars differ as to the extent to which this prophecy was fulfilled in Ahaz's day. But we know the prophecy found its ultimate fulfillment some seven hundred years later in the birth of Jesus.

Immanuel means that we have a God who is not far away, but One who is with us—a God who came to share the experiences of our lives and our humanity.

 Make It Personal

How does knowing that you have a God who is right here
with you encourage you with whatever you're facing today?

Hidden in Her Heart

I have treasured your word in my heart.

—PSALM 119:11

The book *Evidence Not Seen* is the moving story about Darlene Deibler Rose, an American missionary who spent four years in a Japanese prison camp during World War II. She recalls the way God used Scripture she had memorized as a child to sustain her through her ordeal:

> In the cell I was grateful now for those days . . . when I had memorized many single verses, complete chapters, and Psalms, as well as whole books of the Bible. In the years that followed, I reviewed the Scriptures often. The Lord fed me with the Living Bread that had been stored against the day when fresh supply was cut off by the loss of my Bible. He brought daily comfort and encouragement—yes, and joy—to my heart through the knowledge of the Word.[12]

We may never be held in a prison camp, but when we memorize Scripture, it will bring us comfort, encouragement, and joy throughout our own dark days.

 Make It Personal

How could memorizing Scripture help you during times of trial?
What verses could you start memorizing today?

Don't Worry; Just Worship

I have trusted in your faithful love;
my heart will rejoice in your deliverance.

—PSALM 13:5

Several decades ago, a popular song encouraged listeners to "Don't worry, be happy." Perhaps this call to a carefree life caused some to relax, but it's unlikely that the song had a lasting impact.

The prophet Habakkuk worried about his people and their lack of holiness. He worried about evil nations that terrorized their neighbors. He worried that God didn't seem to care.

While a catchy tune isn't the answer, singing can combat worry. The psalmist also often expressed worry, only to watch it disappear in the light of God's glory. Psalm 13 begins, "How long, LORD? Will you forget me forever?" (v. 1). But by the end of the chapter the psalmist has been transformed by worship: "I will sing to the LORD because he has treated me generously" (v. 6).

Even as you face the struggles of the day, will you respond in faith by worshiping and singing to the Lord?

 Make It Personal

What worries are on your heart today?
Worship and sing to the Lord—and watch what happens!

It's All Been Erased

He has rescued us from the domain of darkness
and transferred us into the kingdom of the Son he loves.

—COLOSSIANS 1:13

At one time, the "record" of our sin was out in the open—accusing us, exposing us, and vindicating God's righteous anger against us. But with one press of the delete key, our holy, merciful God erased the whole thing. Nothing was saved on the cloud. Nothing printed out in hard copy. Nothing stored in a separate folder or filing cabinet in case it proved useful to whip it out again someday.

All of it, deleted. Forever. All because of Christ's death on the cross—in our place. Our debt was canceled.

Colossians 2:13–14 puts it this way: As believers, we are told that God has forgiven "all our trespasses. He erased the certificate of debt, with its obligations, that was against us and opposed to us, and has taken it away by nailing it to the cross." We're then treated as if the sin never occurred in the first place. This is the incredible way God has forgiven us.

 Make It Personal

*Thank the Lord for His forgiveness of your sins and
ask Him to help you truly forgive others in the same way.*

More Costly Than Surrender

"For whoever wants to save his life will lose it, but whoever loses his life because of me and the gospel will save it."

—MARK 8:35

Do you fear what a lifestyle of full surrender to Christ might cost you? Then consider the cost of holding out on God. I think of professing believers I know who have tragically wasted what could have been the most productive, fruitful years of their lives. They have settled for wartime conditions when they could have been enjoying the blessings of peace.

The truth is that resistance is far more costly than surrender. To reject God's gracious provision of salvation and to refuse His command to repent means eternal punishment for sin. For those who are followers of Christ, any resistance to the will of God will keep us from enjoying an abundant life and will create barriers in our fellowship with God.

But our God abounds in mercy and grace: He is willing to offer a full and complete pardon to those who lay down their weapons.

 Make It Personal

What price have you paid for resisting God in an area of your life? What blessing have you experienced by relinquishing control to Him?

The Resurrection and the Life

"Don't be afraid. I am the First and the Last, and the Living
One. I was dead, but look—I am alive forever and ever,
and I hold the keys of death and Hades."

—REVELATION 1:17-18

Ever since the Fall, death has been an inevitable and painful part of life. Sooner or later, we all taste the grief it brings and face it ourselves.

But Jesus gives abundant, eternal life to those who place their trust in Him. He brings hope where there would otherwise be only despair. In Jesus, death is not final.

At the funeral of my youngest brother, David, the minister said, "We think of David as having gone from the land of the living to the land of the dead, but the fact is David has gone from the land of the dying to the land of the living." That is the truth—for those who believe in Jesus.

He came to redeem not just our souls but our bodies as well. Every part and particle of our beings will one day share in His resurrection life.

Make It Personal

*How does knowing Jesus as the Resurrection and the Life
give you hope in the present? How does it give you hope
for your future?*

Tremble at His Word

How I love your instruction!
It is my meditation all day long.
—PSALM 119:97

The Scripture says that God has exalted His Word above even His own name (Ps. 138:2 KJV). If God esteems His Word that highly, what should be our attitude toward the Word?

In Psalm 119, David speaks of loving the Word, reverencing it, delighting in it, longing for it, trusting it, and fearing it. God says through the prophet Isaiah, "I will look favorably on this kind of person: one who is humble, submissive in spirit, and trembles at my word" (Isa. 66:2).

What does it mean to tremble at the Word of the Lord? It means to have an attitude of reverential awe and fear. It's the opposite of a cavalier attitude.

My father had a great reverence and love for the Word of God. As a way of demonstrating that respect, it was his habit never to place anything on top of the Bible—a practice I've adopted, not because the paper and leather have any mystical properties or inherent value but to visibly demonstrate honor for what's contained in those pages.

 Make It Personal

What is your attitude toward the Word of God?
How can you increase your love and reverence for it?

Telling the Truth

Pray for us, for we are sure that we have a clear conscience,
desiring to act honorably in all things.

—HEBREWS 13:18 ESV

This particular church service was years ago, but I still remember how miserable I was under the Spirit's conviction. A few years earlier, as a college student, I had lied on a number of weekly reports we had to turn in to our department. I knew I had to make it right.

Because of my desire to be truthful in my communication, the Lord led me to commit to speak the truth to every person, in every situation, regardless of the cost. I've also committed that anytime I fail to speak the truth, I will go back and make it right. I've had to confess being untruthful, both privately and publicly; as a result, I've experienced the great freedom and joy of having a clear conscience before God and others.

As we get the truth of God's Word into our hearts, it protects us from deception and from sinning with our tongues. Sometimes it's hard to speak the truth. But the consequences of lying are much more costly.

Make It Personal

Are there any areas in your life where you haven't been completely truthful? What do you need to do to make it right?

King Over All

"It is necessary for me to proclaim the good news
about the kingdom of God."

—LUKE 4:43

God's kingdom is a thread that runs throughout Scripture. Luke 4 tells us Jesus came to preach the kingdom of God (v. 43). Matthew has approximately forty references to the kingdom of God or the kingdom of heaven.

The kingdom of God isn't a geographical territory; it speaks of God's sovereign control. To pray for His kingdom to come is to acknowledge and submit to His rule in every matter, large or small.

God is King over all the earth. All other powers and rulers are subject to Him. They may seem powerful today, but they only have that power insofar as God allows them to.

God's kingdom also has a personal aspect. For those who have received Christ, He reigns and rules in our hearts. As that happens, our lives should reflect His kingdom values.

Whether you're at work, at home, or in church—at all times and in all situations, our lives should reflect what it means to love the King and His kingdom.

 Make It Personal

*How would things in your life be different if your heart
were completely surrendered to God's reign?*

Going Over His Head

Wait for the LORD and keep his way.

—PSALM 37:34

I had a boss once who kindly told me, "It's fine to put your cards on the table, but once you do, take your hands off."

My natural temperament is to sink my teeth into something and not let go until the other person says, "Fine, you win." Unfortunately, such tendencies are seldom effective in marriage—or in any relationship. When I approach Robert about a concern with a gentle spirit, then leave the matter with him, things go much better. When he knows I'm trusting God to work through his leadership, he's *more* inclined to listen to me.

What a relief it is to know we're not responsible for wringing obedience out of our husbands. Only God can do that. What we need to do is *pray* for the men we married—and our issues of disagreement.

If there's wisdom in what we're asking them to consider and they don't seem inclined to listen, then the best way to get through to him is go "over his head" to the One who can move his heart to do what is right.

Make It Personal

Do you have an issue of disagreement with an authority figure? Ask God to help you trust Him to direct that person to what's right.

The Best Response

"There is nothing covered that won't be uncovered,
nothing hidden that won't be made known."

—LUKE 12:2

Why do you think God asked Adam, "Where are you?" when Adam hid from Him in the garden rather than simply telling him that He had seen everything Adam had done?

This teaches us in part about how God deals with us when we sin. God faithfully gives His straying children the opportunity to repent. He wants us to break the silence and admit our wrongdoing.

He may do this by sending one of His servants to confront us, by causing us to suffer the consequences of our sin, or by allowing us to experience a deeper sense of His love and mercy. However God chooses to get our attention, the best response to Him is an honest one.

The Scripture reminds us that we're accountable to an all-seeing, all-knowing God. We can be sure that every attempt to hide our sins will fail.

Make It Personal

Is there anything you're trying to hide from God? Confess it to Him and experience His forgiveness and cleansing today.

A Different Focus

Everyone should look not to his own interests,
but rather to the interests of others.

—PHILIPPIANS 2:4

Grateful people are loving people who seek to bless others, while ungrateful people are bent on gratifying themselves. They tend to focus on "my needs," "my hurts," "my feelings," "my desires." An unthankful person is full of himself, seldom pausing to consider the needs and feelings of others.

I believe this is why a common end result of ingratitude is the sin of moral impurity. A person who is wrapped up in himself, whose whole world revolves around getting his own needs met, is prime bait for a tempter who thrives on accusing God of being unfair and ungenerous.

An ungrateful heart is quick to notice when self is feeling unsatisfied and is vulnerable to resort to sinful acts and behaviors in an attempt to eliminate pain and experience personal pleasure.

As we mature in Christ and focus more on pleasing Him, our natural inclination will shift toward serving God and meeting others' needs out of sheer gratitude for what we know God has done for us.

 Make It Personal

*Ask God to help you focus more on serving Him
and meeting the needs of other people.*

Taking God at His Word

"Blessed is she who has believed that the Lord
would fulfill what he has spoken to her!"

—LUKE 1:45

When the angel appeared to Mary with a message from God, she took God at His word. She exercised faith in His ability to fulfill His promise—His seemingly impossible promise. It was that faith in God and His Word that activated the power and blessing of God in her life. As a result, God fulfilled His promise and a Savior was born.

Years ago Dr. Adrian Rogers said, "We have no right to be believed so long as we can be explained."[13] Most of our lives are so very explainable because we rely on natural, human efforts and energy, abilities and plans, programs and methods. What would happen if God's people believed His promises and laid hold on Him in prayer, believing Him for the impossible—for reconciliation of broken marriages, for the salvation of unbelieving friends and relatives, for spiritual transformation of wayward children, for a fresh outpouring of His Spirit in genuine revival? We might see God release from heaven the greatest awakening our world has ever known.

 Make It Personal

What "impossible" thing do you need to believe God for today?
Choose to take Him at His word and trust Him to work.

If Only

Godliness with contentment is great gain.

—1 TIMOTHY 6:6

Over the years, I have come to realize that contentment is a choice. True joy is not the result of having everything I want but of gratefully receiving exactly what God has given me. The enemy has robbed many of us of joy by getting us to live in that foolish realm of "if only . . ." We feel that we would be happy, "if only . . ."

"If only I had a husband . . ." or "If only I *didn't* have a husband . . ." or "If only I had a *different* husband."

"If only we had children . . ." "If only we didn't have so many children . . ." "If only I had a different job . . ." "If only I lived in a different place . . ." "If only I could own my own home . . ." "If only I made more money . . ."

The fact is that if we're not content with what we have, we will never be content with what we think we want.

 Make It Personal

*How can you put aside the "if onlys" and
live in the joy of the gifts God has given you?*

A Single Lens

"What I'm doing you don't realize now,
but afterward you will understand."

—JOHN 13:7

I don't know a lot about photography, but I know that most serious photographers use what's called a single-lens reflex camera (SLR). This was a significant breakthrough in camera technology when it first came on the market. Other cameras at the time required the photographer to look through a view-finder rather than through the lens itself. The best you could do was guess at what the picture would ultimately look like. Because the real picture wasn't what you saw in the viewfinder—it was only on the other side of that lens.

You and I, in looking at what's going on in our world, in our home, in our relationships, or in our bodies, have a variety of viewfinder options we can choose from, different ways of trying to perceive and interpret what we're seeing. But though we inevitably "see through a glass darkly" (1 Cor. 13:12 KJV), we will see a lot more clearly if our eyes are on what's actually taking place, not on the many earthly, temporal viewpoints masquerading as what matters most.

 Make It Personal

How does looking through the lens of "Heaven rules"
change your viewpoint of current events?

Our Advocate

I am writing you these things so that you may not sin.
But if anyone does sin, we have an advocate
with the Father—Jesus Christ.

—1 JOHN 2:1

In the American justice system, anyone accused of a crime has the right to legal representation. If someone can't afford an attorney, the court will appoint an advocate for him—someone who will stand alongside him and plead his case.

Our defense attorney is Jesus. He advocates for us before the Father, applying to us the sufficiency of His sacrificial death. He reconciles us to God and restores our fellowship with Him.

An attorney's job is to defend his client, to do everything possible to show the defendant isn't guilty, or if proven guilty, to be sure his client isn't treated unjustly.

Jesus advocates for us in a different way. He knows we're guilty of breaking God's law, and He doesn't pretend we're innocent. He always tells the truth, and the truth is we're rebels. The reason He advocates for us is that justice has already been served. Those who have been justified in Christ can stand before God as if they had never sinned.

Make It Personal

Take time to express gratitude to Jesus for interceding for you at the cross and for offering grace and forgiveness to cover your sins.

The Privilege of Giving Life

The man named his wife Eve because
she was the mother of all the living.

—GENESIS 3:20

The name *Eve* holds enormous significance, both in God's plan for women and in redemption. For when Adam named his wife, the two of them had just made a fatal choice. In violating God's command not to eat from the one tree, they called down upon themselves and future generations the justified curse of death.

Yet it was that moment when Adam named his wife Eve, which sounds like the Hebrew for "life-giver." The woman whose actions had brought death would now become the one whose body would produce physical *life*. This legacy can be seen in the hearts and physical capabilities given by God to generations of women who've carried on the giving of life.

The tremendous value and responsibility invested in us as women by God means we all share in His purpose whether we bear physical children or not. We all participate in Eve's life-giving legacy. And when we love children as He has instructed us to do, the gospel grows and brings forth the fruit of eternal life.

 Make It Personal

What are ways that God has used you to be a life-giver in the past? How might He be calling you to do that today?

Wasted Years

"Separate yourself from your sins by doing what is right. . . .
Perhaps there will be an extension of your prosperity."

—DANIEL 4:27

God gave Nebuchadnezzar ample opportunity to bow before Heaven's rule. But when he persisted in his delusion of autonomy and self-grandeur, God deposed him from his throne and left him to rummage for food on his hands and knees like a soulless animal.

Seven years later, the once-arrogant king of Babylon had finally come to see life through a completely different lens. "At the end of those days," he said, "I . . . looked up to heaven, and my sanity returned to me" (Dan. 4:34). He'd wasted all those years pushing back against what the angel and Daniel had said about the Most High being ruler. And yet the truth was still the same.

How much better if we just go ahead and live now inside the comfort and courage of God's forever rule. It's where the future meets the present. Where His omnipotence meets our frailty. Where comfort meets courage. And where nobody ever has to go crazy in the process.

Make It Personal

What can you do today to acknowledge
Heaven's rule in your life?

Follow to the Cross

Standing by the cross of Jesus were his mother, his mother's
sister, Mary the wife of Clopas, and Mary Magdalene.

—JOHN 19:25

Although the life of Jesus' mother didn't unfold the way she
thought it would, it far exceeded her expectations. Why?
Because Mary knew Jesus was her Savior and she chose to follow Him, even when others rejected Him or turned away. She
was one of the few who followed Him all the way to the cross.
When others fled for their lives, she remained loyal, regardless
of the personal danger or risk.

Many so-called disciples today will follow Jesus as long
as it doesn't cost them too much, as long as their family and
friends are followers, or as long as they are getting their needs
met and following Him is rewarding and exhilarating. They're
willing to obey the Word when God's ways seem to work. But
few are willing to follow Him when the apparent outcome
isn't as they had hoped, when they have to live with those who
resist Him, or when there is no end in sight to the sacrifice and
suffering they must endure.

 Make It Personal

Will you follow Christ even when the outcome
of your circumstances is not as you had hoped?

Make Me a Servant

Having been set free from sin,
you became enslaved to righteousness.
—ROMANS 6:18

Being a servant is not a politically correct concept. However, as Paul explains in Romans 6, we're all servants—either to sin and disobedience or to Christ and His righteousness. And there is no higher, holier calling (nor one with greater rewards) than to be a servant of Jesus Christ!

God has chosen us as believers to be His servants, to join Him in serving others. As we do, we follow in the example of Christ, the humble Servant of the Lord. In Mark 10:45, Jesus says about Himself, "For even the Son of Man did not come to be served, but to serve, and to give his life as a ransom for many."

No matter how menial the task or unfulfilling the responsibility, we can joyously accept it and count it as an honor, for we're following the example of our Lord Jesus of what it means to be the servant of all.

 Make It Personal

*What would it look like if you thought of yourself
as a servant of Christ? How would it affect
your words, attitudes, and priorities?*

Our Redeemer

In him we have redemption, the forgiveness of sins.

—COLOSSIANS 1:14

From Genesis to Revelation, the Bible is a drama of redemption. Redemption is about deliverance. It speaks of rescue, release, and recovery. It's a word of hope in the midst of seemingly hopeless circumstances.

When your situation is dark and there appears to be no light at the end of the tunnel, redemption promises a brighter future ahead. When you can't dig yourself out of the hole of guilt and shame, redemption promises that your failure and the losses caused by your sin can be overruled and you can be restored to usefulness.

On our own, we're trapped and cannot free ourselves from sin's vise. We need someone to reach out and help us.

That's exactly what Jesus Christ did for us on the cross. He is our Redeemer. He provides deliverance for us from the penalty and the power of sin—and one day from the very presence of sin. Our blessed Redeemer has paid the price for us and saved us from destruction.

 Make It Personal

What has Christ redeemed you from?
What does it mean to you in the present to have a Redeemer?
In eternity?

The Giving Tree

"Every man shall give as he is able."
—DEUTERONOMY 16:17 ESV

Shel Silverstein's *The Giving Tree* is a wonderful story illustrating the blessings of being a giver. The apple tree in this parable gives gifts to a boy—apples to eat when he's hungry, shade when he's hot and tired, and branches on which he can climb and play.

As the years pass, the tree gives up all its branches to meet the boy's needs. Finally, all that's left is a stump, which the tree offers as a seat to the grown man who has returned to his childhood home. The man, who's spent his life taking from others, is now disconsolate and empty, while the tree that's always been so generous is content and happy.

Unfortunately, our natural instinct is to be takers rather than givers. Perhaps no society in history has been more materially prosperous than ours. Yet studies reveal that our giving is on the decline rather than the rise. Our prosperity has bred increased selfishness, stinginess, and insecurity. How contrary this is to the heart of God and to the nature of the gospel itself!

 Make It Personal

Ask God to help you look for opportunities to share with others the blessings and resources He has entrusted to you.

A Greater Story

> The Lord handed King Jehoiakim of Judah
> over to [King Nebuchadnezzar], along with
> some of the vessels from the house of God.
>
> —DANIEL 1:2

The story of Daniel takes place in the context of the Babylonian captivity—when the Jewish people endured seventy years of exile in Babylon under the iron fist of a tyrannical despot. The experience was brutal. Seemingly endless. And pointless.

That's what it felt like from the vantage point of God's chosen people. And that's what our story and our world sometimes feel like to us. Proud people and senseless policies. Devaluing and disrespecting what we hold dear. Wearing us out with assaults on truth and those who treasure it. And don't forget that tireless enemy of God and His people, the devil, inserting himself into this world and attempting to wreak havoc in every direction.

It's all vexing and wearying, to say the least. But above and beyond all that we see and experience here on earth is a far different, far greater story unfolding. And that story would become clear to us if only we could see life's happenings and hardships from heaven's perspective.

Make It Personal

*Ask God to help you see everything happening in your life
and our world right now through heaven's perspective.*

A Painful Privilege

"A sword will pierce your own soul."
—LUKE 2:35

Inherent within the privilege of motherhood is also the potential for pain, because anyone who accepts this call risks having her heart broken as a result.

Mary experienced this more deeply than any mother who has ever lived. Yes, she was uniquely blessed to be the mother of the Son of God. And yes, this calling would bring exquisite joys. But with the privilege came excruciating pain. Not pain caused by her Child's sin but the painful price her Child would pay for the sin of the world.

You're not Mary, of course. But no mother escapes the pain of motherhood entirely. Your children will disappoint you at times, just as you will disappoint yourself as a parent. Even on the best days, a mother's job can be fraught with worry, fear, and guilt—which means moms must recognize their utter dependence on the grace of God.

When mistakes rear their ugly heads, moms can experience afresh the truth of the gospel that invites them to turn to Christ, receiving His mercy and forgiveness, and walking in renewed hope.

 Make It Personal

*What does it look like for a mother
to be utterly dependent upon God?*

Open Before Him

> We all, with unveiled faces . . . are being transformed
> into the same image from glory to glory.
>
> —2 CORINTHIANS 3:18

Exodus 34:29 tells us that when Moses came down from receiving God's Law on Mount Sinai, "he did not realize that the skin of his face shone as a result of his speaking with the LORD."

Paul referred to this account and explained its significance for our lives in 2 Corinthians. He compared the glory of the old covenant, which faded away and ministered condemnation and death, to the far superior glory of the new covenant, which gives life and never fades away. Then he explained that as Moses gazed upon the glory of God with an unveiled face and was transformed, so we will also be transformed as we behold God's glory "with unveiled faces."

To me, this is one of the most wondrous verses in all of God's Word. As we come into God's presence, without pretense but with our lives open before Him and as we steadfastly gaze on Him, we will gradually take on His likeness—we will be transformed.

Make It Personal

Pray for your life to be open and exposed before the Lord— and that He would transform you to look more like Him!

Without a Roof

The sacrifice pleasing to God is a broken spirit.
You will not despise a broken and humbled heart, God.

—PSALM 51:17

I f we want to live a lifestyle of humility and brokenness, we must learn to live with the roof off of our "house" and the walls down. One practical way to do that is to make a habit of acknowledging and verbalizing our spiritual need to God and to others.

Living with the "roof off" toward God is having a heart attitude that says, "It's not my father, not my brother, not my mate, not my kids, not my roommate, not my boss, not the pastor—it's *me*, oh Lord, standin' in the need of prayer!" To live with the roof off toward God means that I no longer blame others, but I take personal responsibility for my sin. There is no brokenness where the finger of blame is still pointed at another; brokenness means no excuses, no defending, no rationalizing my sin.

When I acknowledge my need to God, I say:

Nothing in my hand I bring,
Simply to Thy cross I cling.[14]

Make It Personal

Ask God to help you live with the "roof off."

A Slippery Slope

Guard me and rescue me; do not let me be disgraced,
for I take refuge in you.

—PSALM 25:20

Generally speaking, people don't fall into bondage overnight. They don't just wake up one morning and discover they're addicted to food or have a temper they can't control. There's a progression that leads to bondage, and it always begins when we listen to a lie.

That's how it all began in the garden of Eden. Eve *listened* to the lies told her by Satan. I'm confident she had no idea where those lies would ultimately lead her and her family. Perhaps it didn't seem particularly dangerous just to listen to the Serpent, to see what he had to say. Listening in itself wasn't disobedience. But—and here's the key—listening to a viewpoint that was contrary to God's Word put Eve on a slippery slope that led to disobedience, which led to physical and spiritual death.

Listening to things that aren't true is the first step toward ultimate bondage and death. That's why I believe it's so important to carefully monitor the input we allow into our minds and hearts.

Make It Personal

Is there anything you're listening to that's not true? How can you shut out that voice and listen to God's truth instead?

Our Friend, Jesus

[Jesus] was delivered up for our trespasses
and raised for our justification.

—ROMANS 4:25

D o you ever feel lonely, even in a crowd? I do sometimes. But we have a constant friend in Jesus. Perhaps you identify with those sinners He spent time with on earth, and you worry that if others really knew you, they'd shun you. Well, if you're that sinner (and who of us isn't?), you have a friend in Jesus.

At the same time, we must remember Jesus isn't a friend of sin. He never condoned sin but came to deliver sinners from their sin. Sin has to be paid for, and Jesus paid for it with His life. He's a friend to all who acknowledge their sin and will receive His friendship. Once you receive His friendship, you can't keep going on in your sin. It will take away your desire for sin.

As sinners who have been befriended by Jesus, we should be known for welcoming and befriending other repentant sinners and for taking friendship and the gospel to them, even those we're not comfortable with. Let's be faithful to introduce them to Jesus.

 Make It Personal

What kind of people make you most uncomfortable?
Are you willing to befriend them in Jesus' name
and point them to His redeeming love?

What's at Stake

That God's word will not be slandered.

—TITUS 2:5

Throughout his short letter to Titus, Paul gives instructions to believers in various seasons and stations in life. He shows what it looks like when all believers live in a way that's "consistent with sound teaching" (2:1).

But Paul didn't just toss around these concepts as being good ideas, nor did he intend that they were solely for our personal spiritual growth or even for the benefit of other believers. In Titus 2, he lays out the purpose that gives us an even grander, greater motivation for taking this message seriously: "that God's word will not be slandered" (v. 5).

Paul's point is simple and sobering. When we call ourselves Christians and claim to believe God's Word but don't live according to it, the Scriptures will be dishonored in the eyes of those watching us. Any disconnect between what His Word says and the way we live will give them ammunition to speak evil of God and His ways.

Instead, the example of our lives should earn the respect of onlookers, making God's Word more attractive and compelling.

Make It Personal

As you've observed others who identify as followers of Christ, how have their lives made the gospel more attractive to you?

God Is Working

We were predestined according to the plan of the one who
works out everything in agreement with the purpose of his will.

—EPHESIANS 1:11

It's not enough just to say that things happen for a reason; the point is that things happen for God's reasons. God
Himself is actively at work in our world and in our lives to
carry out His own objectives.

Will we always understand what God is doing? Of course
not. But here's what we can be sure of. God's sovereignty and
His providence are able to shield us and our often-quaking
hearts inside an impenetrable fortress.

This tells us that even in those hard, scary places of life,
there's more to what's going on than just what can be seen
from earth's perspective. There's another way of looking at it, a
heavenly perspective.

And though earth's happenings often seem random, meaningless, hopeless, and even cruel, what is happening in the
heavenly realm is infused with such wisdom and goodness,
with such a plan and a purpose, that if we knew what God was
doing, we would worship and praise Him.

 Make It Personal

*What are some ways we can remind each other that God
is in control and is working when we can't see how?*

Purity Restored

Mary asked the angel, "How can this be,
since I have not had sexual relations with a man?"

—LUKE 1:34

When God was ready to send His Son into the world to bring about His eternal plan of redemption, He placed the seed of His Son into the womb of a pure vessel. He selected a woman who had kept herself for the Master's use.

In a world that flaunts perversion and scoffs at purity, women of God must be willing to walk in purity and to teach their daughters the value of a commitment to moral virtue.

You may be reaping the blessings of a lifelong commitment to personal purity. Or you may be living with a deep sense of regret from having made wrong choices. Perhaps you feel that God will never be able to use you because you have not kept yourself pure.

The wonder of God's grace is that He can and will restore purity to those who come to Him in true repentance. He cannot restore the virginity you sacrificed, but by His grace He can restore true virtue.

 Make It Personal

What are ways you can walk in purity today?
How can you model purity to those around you?

Growing Pains

Christ also suffered for sins once for all, the righteous
for the unrighteous, that he might bring you to God.

—1 PETER 3:18

As you better understand how God desires for you to live, there may be times you feel woefully inadequate. But the point of exposing our insufficiency isn't to burden us down with our failure. It's to get us to Christ, whose mercy and grace are our only hope and to make us realize our utter dependence on Him.

If you're a believer in Christ, He has already imputed to you His righteousness. You couldn't be any more pleasing to Him, even if you tried—because His love is based on *His* performance, not yours. And it's His love and faithfulness that enable you to walk in a way that honors Him.

The conviction you feel, therefore, isn't meant to induce you to try harder, as if you could work yourself into better favor with God. It's intended to let true repentance lead you back to the true Source of all this love, kindness, and self-control—the only One who's able to make you into what He wants you to be.

Make It Personal

Spend time thanking God for Christ's righteousness on your behalf, and ask Him to form you into who He wants you to be.

The Heart of Revival

Will you not revive us again
so that your people may rejoice in you?
—PSALM 85:6

Depending on your background, the word *revival* may sound old-fashioned. Revival is a label that's been applied to a variety of happenings, including a series of religious meetings, evangelistic campaigns, seasons of increased religious fervor, and moral and social reformation.

While all these elements may be present, they don't adequately get to the heart of true revival. Revival isn't an event we can schedule on the calendar. Nor is it synonymous with evangelism, though when revival comes, unbelievers will be born into God's family. Further, though our emotions will be involved, revival shouldn't be confused with mere emotionalism. So, what is revival, really?

The word *revive* literally means "to bring back to life." Revival is what happens when God's people, whether individually or corporately, are restored to a right relationship with Him. Revival is a supernatural work of God—it's not something we can manufacture or package.

 Make It Personal

What comes to mind when you hear the word "revival"?
Ask God to do a work of revival in your heart and life.

Setting the Captives Free

"I will bring you out from the forced labor of the
Egyptians and rescue you from slavery to them."

—EXODUS 6:6

As Yahweh delivered His people from slavery in Egypt, Jesus delivers and sets captives free. He has rescued us from slavery to Satan and sin. He continues to rescue us from ourselves, the power of sin, and the entanglements of this world.

As Yahweh led His people into the promised land in the Old Testament, so Jesus came to lead many sons and daughters to glory. He leads us today by His Spirit, who lives in us. As God promised to be with Moses, Jesus is with us today. He will enable you to do whatever He calls you to do.

Jesus gives us Himself to fill up whatever we need or lack. Do you have a thirsty soul? He is living water. Do you have a hungry heart? He is the bread of life. Do you feel the weight of sin? He is the resurrection and the life. Do you feel lost? He is the way. Jesus says, "I am all that you need. I am the great I AM."

 Make It Personal

What needs are you looking to Jesus to meet in your life today?
How are you trusting Him to care for you?

Spread It Out

We do not know what to do, but we look to you.

—2 CHRONICLES 20:12

Second Chronicles 20 tells the story of a vast army of Moabites and Ammonites that came together to make war against Judah. We read that King Jehoshaphat was alarmed and "resolved to seek the LORD" (v. 3).

Before calling a meeting of the National Defense Council, he called a solemn assembly for the people to fast and seek the Lord. Jehoshaphat laid out the facts before the Lord and closed his prayer by emphasizing their reliance on the Lord (v. 12). In answer to that prayer, God dramatically and decisively defeated the enemy, using one of the most unusual battle plans in history.

Years later, King Hezekiah learned Jehoshaphat's prayer defense. When he received an intimidating message from an enemy, "Hezekiah took the letter from the messengers' hands, read it, then went up to the LORD's temple, and spread it out before the LORD. Then Hezekiah prayed before the LORD" (2 Kings 19:14–15).

What is the crisis, the difficulty, the decision you are facing? Spread it out before the Lord and pray.

🌿 Make It Personal

Take time today to lay your decisions before the Lord, thanking Him for His wisdom and expressing your desire to rely on His direction.

The Joy of Relationships

Two are better than one because they have a good reward for
their efforts. For if either falls, his companion can lift him up.
—ECCLESIASTES 4:9-10

E ven with life a complicated maze of obligations, disappointments, longings, and uncertainties, God settles and
stabilizes our hearts.

He places us in close-knit, Christ-centered relationships,
through which we can experience and express more of His
love. He makes us at home in others' homes—and others at
home in ours—to unite us across generations and protect us
against our tendencies toward insecurity and isolation.

To give us friendship. To give us growth. To give us hope.
To give us joy.

Yes, we will feel overwhelmed at times. Choosing to invest
in others or to receive another's counsel and care involves cost
and sacrifice. But none of that can compare with the refresh-
ment, connectedness, and joy we receive from these relationships, not to mention the greater joy of glorifying God through
fruitful lives.

 Make It Personal

*When have relationships with other believers strengthened
your faith, refreshed your soul, brought you joy?
Thank God and pray for these individuals.*

Pure in Heart

For the LORD is righteous; he loves righteous deeds.
The upright will see his face.

—PSALM 11:7

Ever since I was saved as a young girl, I've longed to experience a more intimate relationship with God. The psalmist expressed the same desire when he asked, "Who may ascend the mountain of the LORD? Who may stand in his holy place?" (Ps. 24:3). His answer ("The one who has clean hands and a pure heart") reminds us that only those who have holy hearts and lives can draw near to God.

"Blessed are the pure in heart," Jesus said, "for they will see God" (Matt. 5:8). Unholy people cannot fellowship with a holy God. I cannot cling to my impatience, gluttony, slothfulness, and moodiness and have fellowship with God at the same time.

A teenager who willfully violates his parents' instructions is going to have a hard time looking them in the eye when he gets home late. A wife who lies to her husband isn't likely to enjoy marital intimacy when the lights are turned out at night.

So sin destroys our fellowship with God.

 Make It Personal

Ask God to search your heart and show you any sin that's putting up a barrier in your relationship with Him.

The One to Call

How long, LORD, must I call for help?
—HABAKKUK 1:2

One of the most challenging aspects of parenting toddlers is the constant calling out to their parents. When a child has a question or is afraid, his first response is "Mommy!" As adults, we don't normally call for our mothers, but we still have a reflex to call out to someone when we feel helpless.

In the book of Habakkuk, the prophet's first words are significant. He could have considered the power structures of his day and tried to figure out who was most likely to meet his needs. But like a trusting child calling for his parent, Habakkuk knew the source of all love, power, and protection. He called, "O LORD."

How often do we cry out to the experts, looking for help, when we would be much better off calling, "O Lord"? Ultimately, the peace, perspective, and answers we need won't be found by going to a counselor or a therapist, by reading a book, or by pouring out our hearts to a trusted friend. Ultimately, what we need is found by going to the Wonderful Counselor.

 Make It Personal

When crisis hits, where do you first go for help?
How does the Lord help you in ways that no one else can?

The Power of Kindness in Marriage

She rewards him with good, not evil,
all the days of her life.

—PROVERBS 31:12

In the short time I've been a wife, I've witnessed at moments the distance-creating, intimacy-killing impact of a lack of kindness on my part toward my husband. Unkind words spoken thoughtlessly, kind words left unspoken, inconsiderate actions.

But I've also experienced the incredible importance and power of kindness in a marriage. And Robert's tender heart and consistent kindness have inspired me to be more tuned in to how I can do good to him.

Often it's the little things that express love to my husband and set the tone in our relationship. Leaving encouraging sticky notes in his Bible. Honoring his preferences over mine. Choosing to overlook some perceived (or real) slight rather than grinding his nose in it.

A kind heart expressed in kind words and deeds oils our relationship and softens and draws our hearts toward each other.

 Make It Personal

What can you do to show kindness in the little things today to your spouse or someone else close to you?

A New Nature

I have been crucified with Christ,
and I no longer live, but Christ lives in me.
—GALATIANS 2:20

I don't think I've met anybody who was "born submissive." I surely wasn't. I came into this world with a strong will that wanted to be in control of everything around me. So did you. The idea of submitting to another is contrary to our old nature.

When we became children of God, we received a new nature, one that recognizes God's right to rule over us and wants to submit to His will. However, although our spirit wants to obey God, our flesh wants to have its own way.

As a result, there are times when we resent, resist, or run from the circumstances God has brought into our lives. When difficulties arise, we tend to view the person or circumstance as our problem and to resist the pressure it places upon us. In so doing, we end up pushing against God and resisting His will. Only in our new nature and only with God's help are we able to say, "Your will be done."

Make It Personal

What circumstances are you resisting today that God has brought into your life? How can you say, "Your will be done"?

All the Difference in the World

Do you not rule over all the kingdoms of the nations? Power and might are in your hand, and no one can stand against you.

—2 CHRONICLES 20:6

If "Heaven rules" were nothing more than a comforting way of processing the news, this quality alone would make it invaluable. Think back to all that's happened since 2020: COVID, a contentious election, racial strife, runaway inflation, the war in Ukraine—just to name a few.

This relentless deluge of disasters has exacted an emotional toll that most weren't prepared for and left us with questions we don't know how to answer. How are we to handle more upsetting news? And how are we to deal with the pandemic of depression, loneliness, and fear that's gripped so many?

This is where it makes all the difference to affirm by faith what we cannot always see: that Heaven rules over everything, even over those things that threaten the world's peace and well-being. God is sovereign over leaders, nations, the weather, and all the affairs of our world. Heaven rules over everything, everywhere.

Make It Personal

How should believing that Heaven rules change your reaction to upheaval both in your own life and in the world around you?

Where True Worship Begins

"Love the Lord your God with all your heart, with all your soul, with all your mind, and with all your strength."

—MARK 12:30

There's a lot being said today about freedom, love, and worship, and a fervent attempt is being made in many circles to cultivate love in the body of Christ and create worshipful experiences. However, true freedom, love, and worship cannot be manufactured. Part of the problem is that we're short-circuiting the process God has established that leads to these things.

True worship begins with *brokenness and humility* over whatever God reveals to us in His Word. Poverty of spirit and mourning over our sin lead to genuine *repentance*, which in turn leads to *forgiveness*. Forgiveness will produce *freedom*—freedom from guilt and bondage. When we have freedom that has been birthed out of brokenness, repentance, and forgiveness, we will have a greater capacity for *love* and for *worship*. And of course, true love and worship will lead us back to a new level of brokenness, which leads to greater and deeper repentance, increased forgiveness, newfound freedom, and an even greater capacity for love and for worship.

 Make It Personal

Ask the Lord to help you start the cycle of true worship in your life.

The Lion and the Lamb

I saw one like a slaughtered lamb
standing in the midst of the throne.

−REVELATION 5:6

In Revelation 5, John had a vision where Jesus was called a Lion, but John also saw Him as a slain Lamb. So, which is He? Lions and lambs are radically different.

The truth is that Jesus is *both*. He has supreme dominion over heaven and earth, yet He submitted to the cross. And He is worthy to open the scroll because He conquered sin through His atoning death.

The Lion's triumph was accomplished by His death as a Lamb. He conquered by His suffering. And as the Lion of the tribe of Judah, Jesus is both the protector of His people and the prosecutor of His enemies. If you belong to Him, He will be as a Lion to defend and protect you.

If we have put our faith in Jesus, we share in His victory. He triumphed by laying down His life, and we, too, will triumph as we take our place with Him. We conquer with Him by being willing to take up our cross and follow the slain Lamb.

 Make It Personal

How has Jesus been like a lion in your life? How does knowing that He is the conquering Lion of Judah encourage you today?

A Matter of Time

"Seek first the kingdom of God."
—MATTHEW 6:33

Although God is King over all the earth, most people don't acknowledge His reign. Currently, this world is under the reign of Satan. But that's temporary.

One day all kingdoms of this world will be brought into complete submission to Christ. As we pray, "Your kingdom come" (Matt. 6:10), we long for the day when every knee will bow and every tongue confess that Jesus is Lord.

But what does this prayer mean for us right here, right now?

First, we need to ask ourselves whose kingdom we're building and seeking. Second, history shows that rulers, philosophers, and people in all walks of life have tried to build their own kingdoms and destroy the kingdom of God, but that will never happen because His kingdom will endure forever.

When it seems like the kingdoms of this world are prevailing against God, we need to realize we're not seeing the final picture. The rulers of the world won't live forever. That person who makes your life difficult won't reign forever. Neither will we. Ultimately, God is the One who will overcome.

 Make It Personal

How can you seek God's kingdom throughout your everyday life?

Rest in His Providence

[Job] was a man of complete integrity,
who feared God and turned away from evil.

—JOB 1:1

The book of Job is a stunning story of God's control over the happenings in our lives. It opens with a ringing endorsement of Job's character. Yet this God-loving, sin-hating man wasn't insulated from suffering.

At the outset, Job held fast to his confidence that God is worthy to be blessed, even when God's good gifts are removed. As time wore on, however, that confidence sometimes wavered.

Finally, God reminded Job of His greatness, power, and care of the universe. Job responded in awe-filled wonder: "Surely I spoke about things I did not understand, things too wondrous for me to know" (42:3). In other words, "God, You are good. You are faithful. I trust You to write my story."

Chances are, your story isn't as dramatic as Job's, yet your problems and pain are no less real. You may not be able to see God's plan, but by His grace, you can rest in His providence, confident that He is good; He is faithful. And you can trust Him to write your story.

 Make It Personal

What are some ways that you've seen God's
hand of providence at work in your own life?

No Small Matter

Make sure that no one falls short of the grace
of God and that no root of bitterness springs up,
causing trouble and defiling many.

—HEBREWS 12:15

A "root of bitterness"—it may not seem like a big deal if you've been hurt. In fact, given the circumstances, it may seem perfectly understandable and justifiable. But unacknowledged and unaddressed, its poison will affect and infect you and others beyond anything you ever imagined possible.

When you're unjustly maligned or injured by others, bitterness may feel like a birthright. But it is a fallback position doomed to failure. Not only is it sin, it's senseless.

The root of bitterness will infest every inch of ground in your life if you let it. But God invites you to reach out and receive His grace. In so doing, your heart will be set free from the vise of unforgiveness; you will be released to love and serve Him and others. No longer will that root of bitterness trouble you and "defile" others.

Instead, His grace will flow through you to others, blessing everything you touch.

Make It Personal

What's one area of your life where you need to receive God's grace so a root of bitterness doesn't spring up in your heart?

Give It Up

> "The one who loves his life will lose it, and the one who
> hates his life in this world will keep it for eternal life."
>
> —JOHN 12:25

What was Jesus saying to His disciples? The only way to gain your life is to give it up. The only way to win it is to lose it. We think we're giving up so much by dying. But in reality, it's those who refuse to die who are giving up everything. When we choose the pathway of brokenness and humility, we're choosing to receive new life—His supernatural, abundant life—flowing in us and through us.

Of course, the ultimate picture of that kind of brokenness is Jesus Himself. He's the One who said, "This is my body, which is [broken] for you" (1 Cor. 11:24).

The prophet Isaiah spoke of Jesus when he said, "He was pierced because of our rebellion, crushed because of our iniquities. . . . Yet the LORD was pleased to crush him severely" (Isa. 53:5, 10). Jesus was willing to be crushed, to die, so that through His death, eternal life could be released for us.

 Make It Personal

Are you holding on to your life or giving it up to Christ?

Putting God's Heart on Display

Just as the Lord has forgiven you, so you are also to forgive.
—COLOSSIANS 3:13

Forgiveness is more than a way to find personal freedom, more than a way to ease the pain we feel in our hearts. It's even more than a way to hold out the hope of reconciliation to those who have wronged us.

All those benefits are secondary to an even higher outcome. The ultimate goal of forgiveness is to bring glory and honor to God.

Forgiveness in the life of a believer showcases the astounding, redemptive heart of God. It puts on display the riches of His abundant mercy and amazing grace for all to see. Every opportunity you encounter to practice forgiveness is an opportunity to draw attention to the God who so delights to show mercy and to pardon sinners that He gave His only Son to make it possible. When those around you see you forgiving, they may be seeing Christ in a way they've never known Him before. And they may be drawn to love, worship, and trust God.

 Make It Personal

How have you seen God's mercy and grace
displayed through the forgiveness of others?

It Started with a Lie

[The serpent] said to the woman, "Did God really say,
'You can't eat from any tree in the garden'?"
—GENESIS 3:1

Take a walk with me back to where all our problems began: the garden of Eden, the first home of Adam and Eve—a perfect, ideal environment. What took place in that setting has an inescapable bearing on each of our lives today.

A lie was the starting place for all the trouble in the history of the universe. Eve had listened to that lie, believed that lie, and acted on that lie. Every problem, every war, every wound, every broken relationship, every heartache—it all goes back to *one simple lie.*

As lies have a way of doing, that first lie grew and spun off more lies. Eve believed the lie, and we, the sons and daughters of Eve, have followed in her steps—listening to, believing, and acting on one lie after another. We've believed some lies so long that it may be difficult to recognize them as lies. The "best" lies are those that look the most like the truth. The "newest" lies are the oldest ones.

Make It Personal

What lies do we often believe that look a lot like the truth?
How can you train your mind to recognize them?

Be a Student

"Where your treasure is, there your heart will be also."
—MATTHEW 6:21

My husband, Robert, is a lifelong Chicago Cubs fan. Becoming a Cubs fan myself has proven to be one practical way for me to love my husband. Showing interest in Robert's home-construction projects is another way I express my love. When he built a deck on our home, I took periodic time-outs from working to cheer him on and replenish cold drinks. This said to him, *I care about the things you enjoy.*

If you invest time, effort, and attention in your job or a hobby, your heart will be drawn in that direction. And when you invest "treasure" in your husband, your heart will be drawn to him. But if you choose to invest in someone else, you may soon begin to feel things toward them you've not felt for your husband in a long time.

This is how an affair can begin or you and your husband can simply "drift apart." But if you make the choice to focus your time, attention, and interest in your husband, you'll find your love for him growing.

Make It Personal

What are some ways you can be a student of your husband and choose to invest in him and the things he enjoys?

Nothing to Fear

"I do not seek my own will, but the will of him who sent me."
—JOHN 5:30

Y our will be done." This may be the hardest four-word prayer to say—and mean it. We are born wanting our own way. But if we claim to be God's children, we must submit to Him in all areas of life.

To pray this prayer means we relinquish our own sense of how things should be done. It means asking, "Lord, what would please You in this situation?"

It means we don't dictate to God what we want to see happen or ask Him to fulfill our will. It's seeking to know what He wants on a matter and then praying and asking for it to be done.

When we pray, "Your will be done," we might be fearful of what might happen if we pray this and really mean it. Will God make us do something we don't want to do? But according to Romans 12:2, the will of God is *good*; it's *acceptable*; and it's *perfect*. If we truly believe that about His will, why would we ever reject it?

 Make It Personal

*How can you be intentional about seeking
to know what would please God?*

He's Watching Over Us

Esther was taken to the palace,
into the supervision of Hegai, keeper of the women.

—ESTHER 2:8

By the time Esther entered into the king's "beauty pageant," her young life had already been marked by the tragedies of being orphaned and living in exile from the Jewish homeland.

Though she may have felt alone, separated from all that was familiar, Esther was being watched by someone who deeply cared for her. Each day her only living relative, her cousin and guardian Mordecai, paced back and forth in front of the harem's courtyard. He had to know how Esther was doing and "what was happening to her" (2:11).

Mordecai's watchful care over Esther is a picture of God who is the Keeper of those who belong to Him. He faithfully watches over us, never sleeping (Ps. 121:3–4). Though often unseen by us, God's care is certain. He watches what is happening to us and "learns" how we are doing. He is working behind the scenes, putting everything in place. And in time, He will be the means of upending our enemy's objectives and fulfilling God's holy purpose for our lives.

 Make It Personal

*How does knowing that God is working behind the scenes
in your life provide hope for your current circumstances?*

Journey to Freedom

"You will know the truth, and the truth will set you free."

—JOHN 8:32

If you are a follower of Jesus Christ, then you are more than likely dealing with an issue that includes the need to forgive or be forgiven.

I realize this journey into forgiveness may require you to delve into areas of your life that are sensitive and still hot to the touch. But I'm also aware that our natural way of handling these hurts only results in keeping them sore and inflamed.

It is God's way—and His way alone—that holds out any hope of healing and rescue from the inevitable troubles of life that we face.

It was no idle promise or wishful thinking for Jesus to say, "The truth will set you free." To choose forgiveness and to walk in His truth is God's prescribed pathway—your journey to freedom. Only those who walk it will find out.

Can you think of a situation where you retaliated or became resentful rather than forgiving someone? How was your relationship with that person affected? How did your response change you? How did it affect your relationship with God?

Make It Personal

How has choosing forgiveness
in the past helped you to find freedom?

Burning Words

So too, though the tongue is a small part of the body, it boasts great things. Consider how a small fire sets ablaze a large forest.

—JAMES 3:5

On August 24, 2000, a forty-six-year-old woman tossed a burning match onto the ground when she stopped by the road to light a cigarette. Rather than putting out the burning match, she just glanced at it and left the area.[15] Many days later, the fire she had recklessly begun was finally contained. Timber worth more than $40 million was destroyed, and over 80,000 acres were burned.

It's easy to think, *How dare she leave a burning match in a dry forest!* Yet how often do we throw out burning words without thinking about the consequences? You may even walk away after saying words that deeply wound others—not wanting to look back at the enormous damage you caused.

If you're like me, you may sometimes talk without thinking. It's easy to blurt out words when you're under pressure. Although we may have no intention of hurting others, our words can inflict great damage which can take years to restore.

 Make It Personal

Ask the Lord to help you more carefully consider your words, so that no one will be burned by them.

Molded and Shaped

Search me, God, and know my heart;
test me and know my concerns.

—PSALM 139:23

D o you ever wonder why God is allowing certain difficult circumstances in our lives? Perhaps He wants to expose our need and bring us to the end of ourselves. The circumstance He uses may be a stressful job, a difficult marriage, a chronic illness, a financial crisis, or some other issue that brings pressure to bear on our lives. In the face of such pressure, we can choose to respond in pride, by resisting and resenting the circumstance, or by giving in to despair. Or we can choose to respond in humility, to submit to the hand of God and allow Him to mold and shape us through the pressure.

He also gives us the body of Christ. As we walk in the light with our fellow believers, they can help us see areas where we need to be broken. "The wounds of a friend are trustworthy" (Prov. 27:6)—whether that friend is a pastor, a parent, a partner, or another believer—who loves us enough to point out our spiritual blind spots.

Make It Personal

What methods is God using in your life right now to mold and shape you into the person He wants you to be?

A Grateful Spirit

Give thanks to the LORD, for he is good;
his faithful love endures forever.

—PSALM 118:1

D o we live with a sense that we are the recipients of lavish, underserved grace? The problem is that we don't stop and think about that often enough.

Too often we are like the ungrateful workers in the vineyard in Matthew 20. We let ourselves be pulled down by comparison to others and unfulfilled expectations. But God calls us to give thanks in everything—to acknowledge and express the benefits and blessings we have received from Him and others.

When we live as grateful people, it will affect the atmosphere of our homes, our workplaces, and our churches. Whether we are grateful or ungrateful will determine whether our presence is toxic to those around us or a gracious fragrance.

When our hearts are tuned to sense and appreciate the blessings and mercies of God, He can use us as an instrument to turn the hearts of those around us to desire Christ.

Make It Personal

*What keeps you from continually
being a profoundly grateful person?*

Servant of the Lord

"This is my servant; I strengthen him,
this is my chosen one; I delight in him."

—ISAIAH 42:1

God's people, Israel, were called to serve the Lord, but they failed. As a result, they became servants of their enemies. But in God's mercy and grace, He would send a righteous, ideal Servant to rescue them.

God's perfect Servant would be tender with bruised lives (Isa. 42:3). Some people seemed unfixable, but the Servant of the Lord would repair and strengthen them.

Of course, Jesus, God's own Son, was this promised Servant. While on this earth, Jesus cared for those who were blind, deaf, lame, lepers, marginalized, demonized, and sexually promiscuous.

Isaiah foretold that this Servant wouldn't become weak, despondent, or disheartened (v. 4). Instead, He would help despondent, broken people. He wouldn't give up until God's purposes were accomplished through Him.

Jesus willingly embraced this calling. He came to do what Israel had failed to do.

Make It Personal

*What is an appropriate response to the fact that
the Creator of the universe stooped down and
became a humble servant of His creatures?*

Speaking Words That Heal

The tongue that heals is a tree of life,
but a devious tongue breaks the spirit.

—PROVERBS 15:4

Our words can do enormous damage. Even one thought-less word has consequences. It's hard to believe that the same tongue that speaks life-giving words can also speak words that bring destruction.

Perhaps you heard such destructive words as a child—words you've never been able to forget. Even though you know today that those words weren't true, they still hurt deeply. We can't control the words that are spoken to us, but we can focus on the words that we say to others. Sometimes it's easy to say careless or destructive words without thinking when you're with those you know the best. But don't let your guard down and say discouraging, impatient words that wound rather than heal.

Oftentimes we are blinded concerning how our words offend. Ask the Lord to open your eyes to ways that your words are hurtful or damaging. Then ask Him for wisdom in the moment to speak words of blessing and hope to those around you.

Make It Personal

*Today, choose to say words of healing
and hope to those around you.*

An Everlasting Love

The God of old is your dwelling place,
and underneath are the everlasting arms.

—DEUTERONOMY 33:27

During my fifty-seven years as a single woman, I had times of loneliness and longing for deeper companionship. But I also experienced sweet contentment, joy, and fruitfulness as I learned to trust God to direct my life, meet my needs, and walk with me through challenges. Now that I'm married, I know that Christ—not my husband—is my highest good, my unfailing hope, and that I can trust Him with whatever this chapter of my life may hold.

You may have unfulfilled longings for a mate—or find yourself in a troubled marriage where you feel alone. I can't promise God will change your situation. But I can assure you that you are deeply loved, with a love that never fails. The everlasting arms of God are supporting and surrounding you, carrying and caring for you.

Do you long for a friend who knows and desires you? In Christ, you have the dearest Friend a soul could have, one who walks with you today and will be yours for all of eternity.

Make It Personal

Think about the ways God has provided for you and how He's worked in your life, then thank Him for His unfailing love.

A Cosmic Conflict

Let all kings bow in homage to him,
all nations serve him.

—PSALM 72:11

As followers of Christ, we often call what's happening in our world today a culture war, but it's really a cosmic war between kingdoms. Man doesn't want to acknowledge the reign of God, something that can be traced back to Genesis 3. We're born wanting to be our own god.

It can be overwhelming to look at everything going on in our society. But it's encouraging to remember that the kingdoms of this world will not prevail against the kingdom of God. They're fighting a losing battle, one already won by Jesus!

The concept of the kingdom of God means we're not at the mercy of earthly rulers, political systems, cultural programs, and immorality. It means we realize history isn't an endless, meaningless cycle of the triumph of evil. We understand that life has meaning and that God has a purpose and a plan.

We serve King Jesus, and we pray "Your kingdom come" with confidence that He is coming, that He is the King, that He will rule and reign. We can count on it.

Make It Personal

Take time right now to pray for the Lord's interests to reign supreme in your heart and in the world around you.

Anointed One

The LORD has anointed me to bring good news to the poor.
He has sent me to heal the brokenhearted, to proclaim liberty
to the captives and freedom to the prisoners.

—ISAIAH 61:1

All through the Old Testament we find God's promise of a Messiah. In fact, there are hundreds of prophecies that give us glimpses and clues about Him. The word *messiah*, which means "anointed one," is the Old Testament counterpart to the New Testament term *Christ*.

This promised anointed one was to be supernaturally born in Bethlehem, a direct descendant of David. He would perform miracles, heal the brokenhearted, and set captives free. He would put an end to sin and bring in everlasting righteousness. There's only one person who fulfilled these prophecies—Jesus. In so doing, He proved beyond the shadow of a doubt that He was the promised Messiah.

Jesus is the One who came to deliver His people from enemies of sin and death and ultimately from all the consequences of the Fall. He is God's anointed King who will reign forever and ever.

Make It Personal

Spend time praising God that He keeps the promises He's made in His Word . . . and He'll keep the promises He's made to you.

Theology 101

It is God who is working in you both to will
and to work according to his good purpose.
—PHILIPPIANS 2:13

During my sophomore year in high school, I took a world
cultures class. As we studied the rise and fall of nations,
my heart became grounded in the conviction that God reigns
over both the big events of history and the minute details of
His creation.

This wasn't a new concept. But now I was seeing God's sovereignty being worked out in the panorama of world history,
and the sight was stunning to my young heart.

During that same year, through a series of difficult circumstances for my family, I also experienced the comfort, calm, and
confidence that come from knowing a wise, good, sovereign
God is intimately involved in every chapter of our lives.

My parents' example, along with that class, gave me a year-long course in Theology 101. What I gained was a living, pulsating, vibrant faith in the God who reigns over every part and
particle of His creation, tenderly cares for His own, and is always
accomplishing His eternal redemptive purposes in this world.

 Make It Personal

Pray that God would grow your confidence and trust that
He is intimately involved in every chapter of your life.

Glad Surrender

In the beginning God created the heavens and the earth.
—GENESIS 1:1

In the first recorded act in time and space in Genesis 1, God exercised control over His universe. He spoke with authority and power, bringing light, life, and order to the darkness and chaos of the universe.

When He said, "Let there be light," there was light. When He said, "Let the . . . fruit trees" bear fruit, the trees bore fruit (v. 11). All creation, including—initially—the first man and woman, lived in glad, wholehearted surrender to the sovereign control and will of the Creator.

This surrender didn't strip the creation of dignity or freedom; to the contrary, surrender was—and still is—the source and means of true freedom and fullness. The sovereign Creator ruled over His creation with tender love, inviting His creatures to engage with Him in a divine dance-of-sorts, in which He led and they followed. They responded to His initiative with trust, love, and surrender. In turn, their needs were abundantly met, they fulfilled their created purpose, and they existed in harmony with God and with each other.

 Make It Personal

What evidence do you see of nature being surrendered to
God's control? How can you experience that same freedom?

Living by Faith

The righteous one will live by his faith.

—HABAKKUK 2:4

A re you living by faith, or are you struggling to live for God through your own power? Relying on yourself leads to discouragement and condemnation. But living by faith brings confidence and peace. The God who has power to save you is also living in you, ready to help every moment.

The apostle Paul said those who have been justified by faith should continue to live by faith. He quoted a verse from Habakkuk: "The righteous will live by faith" (Gal. 3:11).

Not only is this a crucial part of Paul's letter to the Galatians, but it's also the turning point in the book of Habakkuk. In just a few words we see how the prophet could handle the issues that had perplexed him earlier. By faith he could patiently wait for justice. By faith he could undergo the coming Babylonian persecution.

Like Habakkuk, we can live by faith amid uncertainty and difficult circumstances. That means we stop relying on ourselves to change things and rely on the God in us, who will help us face whatever comes our way.

 Make It Personal

What does living by faith look like in your life right now?

A Light in the Dark

"I am the light of the world. Anyone who follows me will
never walk in the darkness but will have the light of life."

—JOHN 8:12

Light is more powerful than darkness. When you turn on
the light, darkness flees. For centuries people have tried
to extinguish the light of God's Word and of Jesus. Our world
remains in moral and spiritual darkness. We're confronted
with injustice, hopelessness, despair, cruelty, hatred, and broken lives. There's darkness in our own hearts as well.

But Light has come into the world. Jesus is the "star . . . from
Jacob" (Num. 24:17), the "sun of righteousness" (Mal. 4:2), the
"bright morning star" (Rev. 22:16), and the "Sunrise from on
high" (Luke 1:78 NASB). One day He will return, and there will
be a final great sunrise—the new Jerusalem that doesn't need
the sun or the moon, "because the glory of God illuminates it,
and its lamp is the Lamb" (Rev. 21:23).

No more darkness. No more night. Only eternal, brilliant,
glorious Light. His name is Jesus. In the meantime, He shines
through us into our dark world.

Make It Personal

*Are there any dark places in your heart that you need to bring
into Christ's light? Ask Him to shine brightly in your life today!*

Not a Coincidence

[Ruth] happened to be in the portion of the field
belonging to Boaz, who was from Elimelech's family.
—RUTH 2:3

After the loss of her husband and sons, Naomi returned to Bethlehem, along with her daughter-in-law. Ruth attempted to sustain their family by becoming a gleaner—gathering up bits of grain left after the harvesters had finished.

Ruth 2:3 says she "happened to be" in Boaz's field. "Happened to be" . . . That's what it looked like from an earthly perspective. The job search of this needy woman "happened" to lead her to the employment of a wealthy landowner, who "happened" to be a relative of her deceased father-in-law . . . and who through an ancient legal provision would "happen" to become her husband and lifelong provider.

A happy coincidence? Hardly. A stroke of luck? Not at all.

This is a story of a wakeful, watchful God who knows the number of hairs on our head and the number of stars in the universe. A God who ordains and superintends all the details of our lives from the tiniest to the greatest. It's a story of divine providence.

 Make It Personal

*Think of moments in the past when God provided for your needs.
How does that help you trust Him in your current struggles?*

Hold Your Tongue

The mind of the righteous person thinks before answering,
but the mouth of the wicked blurts out evil things.

—PROVERBS 15:28

A New Jersey teen, Brett Banfe, decided he was spending too much time talking and too little time listening to others. So, he took a vow of silence for a year.[16] This inspired me to take a vow of silence—for forty hours. I didn't think it would be too hard since I was by myself the entire time!

That reminds me of an old story of a monk who joined a monastery where he was permitted to say only two words every ten years. After ten years, the monk said, "Bed hard!" Ten years later, the monk said, "Food bad!" After ten more years, the monk spoke for the third time: "I quit!" His superior said, "I'm not surprised. All he did for the past thirty years was complain!"

Holding our tongues is a challenge! Proverbs 29:11 says, "A fool gives full vent to his anger, but a wise person holds it in check." What would an impartial observer say about your tongue? Do you carefully choose your words?

 Make It Personal

Ask the Lord to help you carefully choose
and measure the words you speak today.

Alpha and Omega

"I am the Alpha and the Omega," says the Lord God,
"the one who is, who was, and who is to come."

—REVELATION 1:8

John was an old man when he was given a vision while in exile on the isle of Patmos. More than sixty years had passed since he had last seen Jesus, but he was given a glimpse of things to come. He heard Jesus say, "I am the Alpha and the Omega, the first and the last, the beginning and the end" (Rev. 22:13).

Alpha and *omega* are the first and last letters of the Greek alphabet; they represent the entirety of the alphabet. Jesus is the sum total of all of life. He is the God of beginnings and endings, of time and transitions.

He was there at the beginning of time, and He will be there at the end. He is also the author and finisher of our faith.

Jesus wants to be "first and last" in your life—the first One you think about in the morning and the last One you think about as you sleep at night. Is He?

 Make It Personal

*What would it look like for Jesus to truly be
the Alpha and Omega of your life—at home,
at work, at church, in your neighborhood?*

As It Is in Heaven

"Your will be done on earth as it is in heaven."

—MATTHEW 6:10

It's important we pray for God's will to be done in our own lives, but He also wants us to have His heart for the world.

When we pray Matthew 6:10, we're asking that every person in the entire world be brought into obedience to the will of God. We're praying that unbelievers, either next door or thousands of miles away, be brought to repentance and faith in Christ. We're actively seeking God's will for our families, our workplaces, in every person we know, and in every nation.

God doesn't intend for us to sit back and wait for the rapture. He's left us here to be His ambassadors and part of advancing His kingdom on this earth.

While it's easy to feel helpless in the face of huge global crises or to feel paralyzed in the face of encroaching evil, we forget something when we do. Whether the problems are in our homes or next door or around the world, we need to remember how powerful God is and that our strength lies in prayer.

Make It Personal

Make it a priority to pray for God's will—not just in your own life and community—but throughout the whole earth.

Ashes into Beauty

"The woman you gave to be with me—
she gave me some fruit from the tree, and I ate."

—GENESIS 3:12

Adam and Eve weren't just the first humans. They were also the first humans to betray one another. Once their relationship with God was shattered, it wasn't long before their relationship with each another devolved into blame and accusations. Being sinned against (and sinning against others) has been part of the human story from those earliest days through today.

The ways people sin against others are the poisonous, heartrending fruits of humankind's treachery against God. Sometimes these sins hit our lives with the force of a wrecking ball. It may take years to regain our equilibrium. In some cases, the perpetrator may never (in this life) be brought to justice or repentance. All of which may lead us to feel that someone other than God is writing our story and to wonder whether He can be trusted.

Yet our faithful, loving God has the power to redeem the unredeemable and to turn ashes to beauty, not just *in spite of* the injuries we've suffered but actually *through* those very wounds.

Make It Personal

Have you ever seen God redeem the unredeemable or turn ashes into beauty? How did that affect your trust in Him?

Too Much to Say

When there are many words, sin is unavoidable,
but the one who controls his lips is prudent.

—PROVERBS 10:19

After participating in a multi-hour meeting some time ago, I sensed that perhaps I had said more than I should have. I asked one of the men who was in the meeting if I had talked too much. He said, "Well, perhaps you could have condensed that long story you told!"

I am so thankful to have real friends who will help me know when I'm not walking wisely, in accordance with the Word of God. God wants our lips to be controlled by the Holy Spirit. We need His wisdom and grace to measure our words and to speak to others only after listening to Him.

People who are measured in their words are thought to be wise. Many women express frustration that their husbands don't listen to them. I don't mean to be unkind, but sometimes I wonder if men might listen more attentively if we women didn't have so much to say!

Make It Personal

Ask the Lord to bring to your mind those moments when you spoke too many words. What would have been a better response?

The Flag of Surrender

When arrogance comes, disgrace follows,
but with humility comes wisdom.
—PROVERBS 11:2

If you want to experience the blessings of brokenness and have a revived heart, you must choose to run head-on into whatever it is your pride is telling you not to do.

As I speak across the country about brokenness, I generally ask at the close, "How many of you know there is some step of brokenness God wants you to take, but there's a battle going on inside, and your pride is keeping you from taking that step?" Invariably, many hands go up. I tell them the same thing I want to tell you: The battle inside will stop the moment you wave the white flag of surrender and say, "Yes, Lord."

The longer you delay, the harder you resist, the more difficult it will be to obey God. Don't hesitate a moment longer. You can't begin to imagine the joy that awaits you on the other side of the cross, the power of His resurrection life that will be released through your death of self, and the wholeness that will emerge out of your brokenness.

 Make It Personal

What step of brokenness do you need to take today?

Healed by His Wounds

He himself bore our sins in his body on the tree.

—1 PETER 2:24

Trusting God to write our stories in a world where we have been sinned against might seem unattainable and perhaps even ludicrous—if we didn't have a Savior who knows what it is to be sinned against through no fault of His own. Though He was the object of unimaginable abuse, He trusted God to write His story.

And what was the outcome? "By his wounds you have been healed" (1 Peter 2:24).

In Christ's willingness to bear the wounds we inflicted on Him, we have been healed of the wounds inflicted on us by our sin and that of others. Through His trust in the Father, our hearts have been brought back to God.

Even so, as we entrust ourselves to God when we've been sinned against, He may not only bring us healing but may also use us to be instruments of healing and repentance to our offenders. Regardless of whether we ever live to see that fruit in this life, we know the One who judges justly will one day right every wrong.

 Make It Personal

Praise God that one day, He will right every wrong—
the ones done to you and all those throughout history!

Living in Bondage

"A thief comes only to steal and kill and destroy. I have come
so that they may have life and have it in abundance."

—JOHN 10:10

Most people I meet today aren't free, often by their own admission. Many live under a cloud of personal guilt and condemnation. They're not free to enjoy the grace and love of God.

Many are in bondage to their past. Whether the result of their own failures or that of others, their past hangs like huge weights around their necks. Others are in bondage to the "fear of man"—gripped by fear of rejection, fear of what people think of them, and a longing for approval. Still others are emotional prisoners, enslaved by worry, fear, anger, depression, and self-pity.

I don't want to suggest that everybody is a basket case. But overall, many Christians are in trouble—the kind that requires more than superficial solutions and remedies.

When we turn to Scripture, we're reminded that God didn't intend for it to be this way. We read the words of Jesus in John 10 and know God has something better for us—abundant life.

 Make It Personal

Are you living in bondage to anything?
How can you experience the abundant life God has for you?

What Makes the Difference

The LORD was with Joseph.

—GENESIS 39:2

As the favored son of eleven brothers, Joseph had been singled out by his father, Jacob, and lavished with affection and gifts. However, that favor incurred the jealousy of his brothers, who threw him in a pit and then sold him to passing merchants.

How could Joseph have seen that these tragic events were not random acts but carefully scripted scenes in a great, eternal drama of redemption? Of course, he could not. From his finite point of view, all Joseph could have known was what he faced in the moment.

From our vantage point, we can see God's purposes carefully being brought to pass in and through Joseph's life. But for him, there must have been little more than unanswered questions, unjust circumstances over which he had no control, continuing year after year.

Yet we know something important about Joseph's situation—something he could only have grasped by faith. We know "the LORD was with Joseph" (Gen. 39:2). That reality made all the difference in the world and in the outcome of Joseph's story.

 Make It Personal

As you look back on difficult seasons of your life,
what evidence do you see that the Lord was with you?

Ready for the Bridegroom

The marriage of the Lamb has come,
and his bride has prepared herself.

—REVELATION 19:7

It had been a short night of sleep. But that didn't matter. I knew this day—November 14, 2015—was one I'd never forget. Today I would say "I do" before God and several hundred witnesses and become Mrs. Robert Wolgemuth.

I spent more hours than usual on my makeup and hair, getting my nails done, and putting on a beautiful new dress and sparkly shoes. I got more dressed-up than I had ever been. So, why did I go to so much trouble?

I'll tell you why; I wanted to be *adorned*—beautiful, ready for my bridegroom. I wanted to bring Robert joy, just as his love brought me joy and made me feel beautiful.

Just as I wanted to look beautiful for my earthly bridegroom, we as believers are called to prepare ourselves for our heavenly Bridegroom—to be ready when Jesus returns.

What if His return was today? Would He find His bride ready to meet Him, without spot or wrinkle, holy and blameless? Or will she be dirty, disheveled, and stained?

 Make It Personal

*Are you ready for Christ to return? What steps
can you take today so that you will be prepared?*

Flirting with Disaster

Then after desire has conceived, it gives birth to sin,
and when sin is fully grown, it gives birth to death.

—JAMES 1:15

For more than a dozen summers, Timothy Treadwell, an avid outdoorsman and "bear specialist," lived peacefully and without weapons among Alaskan grizzlies, living alone with and videotaping the bears.

In an appearance on *The David Letterman Show*, Treadwell described the bears as mostly harmless "party animals." Two years later, on October 6, 2003, the bodies of Treadwell and his girlfriend were discovered after they were fatally mauled in a bear attack.

The lesson was all too obvious—wild animals can't be "reformed." Regardless of how comfortable or trusting you may become around them, sooner or later they will act according to their nature. To assume otherwise is to flirt with disaster.

A healthy fear and respect keeps most people from getting cozy with wild beasts. So, what makes us think we can get close to a far more deadly beast called *sin*—and survive?

 Make It Personal

Have you ever underestimated the danger of sin? What was the result? How can you guard against this in the future?

A Thousand Different Things

We know that all things work together
for the good of those who love God.

—ROMANS 8:28

More times than I can count, I've shared with others something unforgettable I heard Pastor John Piper say years ago: "In every situation you face, God is always doing a thousand different things that you cannot see and you do not know."

Oh, if we think hard, we may be able to discern a few things He's doing amid the mess around us. Looking back, we might be able to see a few more. But unseen and unknown to us, He is in fact doing a *thousand* or more things. Things that one day become clear to us, either in this world or the next.

Perhaps from where you sit today, you can see only miscellaneous, frayed, disconnected strands that make no sense, no matter how hard you try to figure it out. But on the flip side of the tapestry God is weaving in and through our lives—the tangle of threads that we can see—He is creating a picture of great beauty and worth for those who will trust Him.

 Make It Personal

*Thank God that He is always at work in and through you—
even when you cannot see what He's doing.*

Guard Your Mind

I will not set before my eyes anything that is worthless.

—PSALM 101:3 ESV

I'm the oldest of seven children, and I thank the Lord for the conviction God gave my parents about controlling the kinds of influence that were allowed in our home as we were growing up.

As an adult, I still find it is crucial to guard my mind—to carefully choose the input I allow into my life and to reject that which promotes ungodly thinking. The world's deceptive way of thinking comes to us through so many avenues—television, movies, music, friends, and social media, to name a few. A steady diet of these worldly influences will shape our view of what is valuable, what is beautiful, and what is important.

There are no harmless lies. We cannot expose ourselves to the world's false, deceptive way of thinking and come out unscathed. Eve's first mistake wasn't eating the fruit; it was listening to the Serpent.

Listening to counsel or ways of thinking that aren't according to the truth is the first step in developing wrong beliefs that will ultimately place us in bondage.

 Make It Personal

How can you guard your mind today
against the influences of the world?

A Reflection of the Heart

Let your speech always be gracious, seasoned with salt,
so that you may know how you should answer each person.

—COLOSSIANS 4:6

Perhaps you, like me, want to speak encouraging, life-giving words. The key to a transformed tongue is a transformed heart. A person who is righteous loves what God loves and hates what He hates.

Jesus said, "A good person produces good out of the good stored up in his heart. An evil person produces evil out of the evil stored up in his heart, for his mouth speaks from the overflow of the heart" (Luke 6:45). The words we speak actually reflect our hearts.

If I am a foolish person, then I will speak foolish words. If I am a wicked person, I will speak wicked words. But if I am a godly woman whose heart is connected to Jesus Christ, then I will speak wise words that are full of grace, mercy, and truth. Wise, kind words flow out of wise, kind hearts. When we fill our hearts with the Word of God, what flows from our heart to others will reflect Him.

 Make It Personal

*Ask the Lord to help the words of
your mouth be a reflection of Him.*

God's Timetable

He had sent a man ahead of them—
Joseph, who was sold as a slave.

—PSALM 105:17

Given the opportunity, no doubt Joseph would have written a different plot for his life. But with each twist and turn of his story, this young man was being shaped and transformed by God.

Joseph was "sent ahead" by God to a foreign land where God intended to use him to provide for His people. Once there, he was sold and shackled as a slave. And in those horrendous circumstances, the "word of the LORD tested him" (Ps. 105:19)—shaped him, honed him—until the time came for God's predictions through him to be fulfilled.

Taking this message to heart can make a huge difference as you navigate your own challenges. The hardest parts of the story God is writing in your life aren't random or meaningless. They're full of purpose. And in due time, all that He has intended for you and for this world will come true. In the meantime, He will always be with you. That's a truth you can always trust.

 Make It Personal

How can knowing that God is working out
His purposes for your life according to His timetable
assist you in navigating challenges?

Choosing to Worship

Rejoice in the Lord always. I will say it again: Rejoice!

—PHILIPPIANS 4:4

The book of Habakkuk suggests that worship is more than singing songs. For the prophet, worship was the act that gave him balance. It was the antidote to the worry that threatened his earlier perspective.

Habakkuk had learned some important things since his first moments of worry in chapter 1. He learned that utter devastation was in his near future. Yet he also learned that the righteous shall live by faith.

It was in faith that he chose not to obsess on the material things he currently had nor on the scarcity he was about to experience. Instead, he took joy in the one thing he would never lose—God Himself. This led him to sing, "Though the fig tree does not bud and there is no fruit on the vines, though the olive crop fails and the fields produce no food, though the flocks disappear from the pen and there are no herds in the stalls, yet I will celebrate in the LORD; I will rejoice in the God of my salvation!" (Hab. 3:17–18).

Make It Personal

Choose to worship the Lord today, whether you are in a season of scarcity or one of abundance.

Why Ask?

"Ask, and it will be given to you. Seek, and you will find.
Knock, and the door will be opened to you."
—MATTHEW 7:7

Do you actually ask God to meet your needs? This sounds so basic, but it's such a simple concept that we sometimes miss it. Throughout the Gospels, Jesus urges us to ask our heavenly Father for what we need—not just to hope He will provide but to take the step of *asking* Him to provide for our daily needs. Then we're to *expect* Him to meet those needs.

But Jesus says God already knows what we need before we ask (Matt. 6:8). That raises the question: Why ask if He already knows?

We don't tell God our needs in order to inform Him but because He wants a relationship with us. He wants us to keep communicating with Him, needing Him, and desiring Him.

God knows what we really need. Those are the things for which we should pray and which we can rightly expect Him to provide. When we come before Him, we don't have to beg or be frantic. We just need to ask.

 Make It Personal

*What needs do you have today? Ask God—humbly and not
in a demanding way—and then expect Him to provide.*

The Answer to Death

"I am the resurrection and the life.
The one who believes in me, even if he dies, will live."

—JOHN 11:25

In John 11, we find death confronting a family in the village of Bethany. Lazarus had died, and four days later Jesus arrived. He said to Martha, Lazarus' grieving sister, "Your brother will rise again" (v. 23).

Martha knew Jesus could raise her brother from the dead someday, but she needed faith for her present situation. Life is wrapped up in Jesus. There's no physical life apart from God, and there's no spiritual life apart from Jesus. The resurrection isn't just an event—it's a Person.

"Do you believe this?" Jesus said to Martha. Martha replied, "I believe you are the Messiah, the Son of God, who comes into the world" (v. 27). At that moment, faith overcame her confusion and despair.

Jesus went to Lazarus' grave, where He demonstrated His power. He declared His authority over life and death, saying, "Lazarus, come out" (v. 43). And Lazarus came walking out of that tomb!

Make It Personal

Do you believe those who die believing in Jesus have eternal life?
How does that belief affect your perspective on death?

God Sent Him

"Don't be grieved or angry with yourselves for selling me here,
because God sent me ahead of you to preserve life."
—GENESIS 45:5

After Joseph revealed himself to his brothers, they were terrified he would retaliate against them. But Joseph reassured them that wasn't his intent, as God had sent him to Egypt for a purpose.

You *sold* me. But God *sent* me.

Eventually, long after Joseph's death, it became clear that the story God had written in the life of this patriarch foreshadowed another, far greater Story. The beloved, favored Son of the Father of life was also envied and mistreated by His brothers. Though He had done no evil and had steadfastly refused the tempter's lure, He was sold for a pittance, cruelly abused, and violently murdered.

We sold Him. But God sent Him.

We meant evil against Him—but God meant it for good, to bring about life for many who were destined to die, that they might become His sons as well. What a wonder this Story is!

 Make It Personal

*Ask God to help you refrain from taking control of
your story and trust Him to be the Author of it instead.*

A Longing for Intimacy

I have loved you with an everlasting love;
therefore, I have continued to extend faithful love to you.
—JEREMIAH 31:3

Everyone loves a love story. That's because we were made to give and receive love. We were made for intimacy.

Yet most of us know more about the absence of intimacy than the reality. That sense of aloneness we've all experienced is a God-created hole that cries out to be filled; it's a longing for intimacy with God.

From earliest childhood, we've sought to fill that vacuum. We crave closeness, warmth, and affection; we long to know that someone cares, that someone who really knows us still loves us.

However, even in the best of human relationships, the most we're able to do is somewhat dull the sense of longing. Other humans can never completely fill the hole.

That's because the God who created that hole is also the only One who can fill it. In the Scriptures we encounter a God who moves toward us, who seeks to draw us to Himself, who knows us intimately and passionately, and who invites us to know Him in the same way.

 Make It Personal

What have you used in the past to try
and fill that vacuum in your heart?

Words Like Honey

Your lips drip sweetness like the honeycomb, my bride.
Honey and milk are under your tongue.

—SONG OF SONGS 4:11

At one point in the Song of Songs, the groom takes time to praise his bride for how she blesses him and others with her words.

This woman doesn't babble on and on. Her words, like honey, are measured. They are thoughtful and sweet.

Her tongue has a filter. It has a governor—much like the safety mechanism that limits the speed on a car or boat. And her words strengthen and encourage the hearts of those who hear them instead of causing harm and contention.

I want to be like that woman, don't you? I want my words to minister grace to others, starting with my heavenly Bridegroom.

With God's help, let's use our tongues to build up those around us rather than tearing them down. Above all, let's speak words that make much of Christ. Words that adorn His gospel and put His loveliness on display. Words worthy of people whose hearts have been won by His amazing grace.

 Make It Personal

Meditate on God's Word and ask Him to help
you speak words that make much of Christ.

Give It Away

A woman came with an alabaster jar of very expensive perfume
of pure nard. She broke the jar and poured it on his head.

—MARK 14:3

Mary of Bethany loved Jesus deeply. The greatest expression of her love was when she anointed the feet of Jesus with a pound of costly ointment. Those who observed were indignant. *How fanatical! Such a waste*, they thought. But what could be more wasteful than to lavish such costly gifts on ourselves? Unfortunately, the more we have, the more we think we need, the more we want, and the more those things begin to control our lives.

Years ago I decided that I didn't want to own anything I didn't need, unless it enabled me to invest more effectively in the kingdom of Christ. This is easier said than done! But I don't want things to have a grip on my life. I continually look for ways to counter my natural bent toward covetousness by giving away items I don't need. These are wonderful opportunities to prove my heart is surrendered to Jesus by faith and to consciously depend on Him to meet my needs.

Make It Personal

Today, how can you look for opportunities to share with others the blessings and resources God has entrusted to you?

Small Yet Powerful

The one who guards his mouth and
tongue keeps himself out of trouble.

—PROVERBS 21:23

On September 11, 1995, a squirrel climbed onto the Metro-North Railroad power lines near New York City. This set off on an electrical surge, which weakened an overhead bracket, which let a wire dangle toward the tracks, which tangled in a train, which tore down all the lines. As a result, 47,000 commuters were stuck in Manhattan for hours that evening.[17]

This story reminds me of what we do with our tongues. Something very small can cause a lot of damage!

We might think, *It's just a tiny lie, a little argument, a few contentious words.* . . . Yet we're reminded time and time again in Scripture that if we guard our mouths and tongues from saying words we'll later regret, we will save ourselves from disaster.

Innocent loved ones can be harmed because of our ill-spoken words. The life of a loving child, loyal spouse, or committed friend may be harmed because of a "little" word.

 Make It Personal

*What are some practical steps you can take now
to avoid saying words you'll later regret?*

A Humble Heart

"I live in a high and holy place, and with the oppressed
and lowly of spirit, to revive the spirit of the lowly and
revive the heart of the oppressed."

—ISAIAH 57:15

According to Isaiah 57:15, God has two "addresses." The first comes as no surprise. The high and exalted God of the universe lives forever "in a high and holy place." Yet God has another "address" I find astounding. He lives with those who have a humble and contrite spirit. Generally, we think of kings as being comfortable with the high and mighty, with the wealthy and the successful. But this King chooses to dwell with those who are contrite and humble.

To what kind of person does God draw near? Who does He rescue and deliver? Those who have a broken, contrite spirit.

Psalm 51 is the prayer written by King David after he committed his sin with Bathsheba. He realized there was nothing he could do to earn his way back into God's favor. David understood that God wasn't looking for religious acts or devout behavior. The only offering God really wanted was a humble, contrite heart.

 Make It Personal

*Ask God to help you have a humble
and contrite spirit before Him.*

Pressing On . . . Together

A man will leave his father and mother and be joined to his wife,
and the two will become one flesh. This mystery is profound.

—EPHESIANS 5:31–32

Robert and I love each other even more than when we said "I do," and we've experienced many happy times in our marriage. But we've also had our share of misunderstandings and stressful moments—figuring out how to blend our different lifestyles into our new life as one.

Some tears have been shed. At times we fight the temptation to become isolated from one another and independent in spirit—to forget we need each other.

Yet even in our more difficult moments we press on—together—because we believe we are called to this. We remember we can't do this alone. We realize that the dailyness and even the struggles we face are forging for us a deeper oneness and joy than would otherwise be possible.

We believe it's worth the price for our marriage to be able to point others to the loveliness of Christ. And we know that unfettered, unsullied joy will ultimately be ours at the end of the journey.

 Make It Personal

What benefits come from pressing on together through difficulties in your relationship with your spouse or with other believers?

The Ultimate Goal

The law of the Spirit of life in Christ Jesus
has set you free from the law of sin and death.

—ROMANS 8:2

We know from God's Word that our fight against sin won't be completely won until we're at home with Him. What He wants us to learn is that this gospel that saved us can also *keep on saving us.* The battle here on earth can keep us continually turning to Christ.

It's actually His love for us, then, that causes God to lead us down this long, hard road, putting to death all our unwholesome substitutes one obedient choice at a time.

As we persevere, we begin to experience a richer, more satisfying, more enduring victory over our habits and addictions than any divine snap of the fingers could provide.

That's because our goal isn't merely to get better. The goal is to draw near to our God, who is more desirable, attractive, and fulfilling than any pleasurable, exciting, yet enslaving enticement.

Than anything.

 Make It Personal

*How does knowing the ultimate goal—to draw near
to God—help you in your current struggle with
unhealthy habits, temptation, or sin?*

An Incredible Opportunity

"If anyone is thirsty, let him come to me and drink."

—JOHN 7:37

Few subjects evoke more feelings of guilt among believers than the matter of "daily devotions." But I've come to see that "having devotions" isn't so much an obligation as it is an incredible opportunity to know God.

He has issued an invitation for us to draw near to Him, to walk right into the "Holy of Holies," to enter into an intimate love relationship with Him.

Wherever God finds you, if you're His child, I believe there is within you something that will never be satisfied with anything less than intimate fellowship with your heavenly Father. Until you see Him face to face, you'll never cease to hunger and thirst to know Him more.

Jesus' words in John 7:37 are an invitation to come to Him, not to another program, thing on your to-do list, or requirement but to Jesus, the Source of all Life. Come to Him and drink.

Drink deeply; keep on drinking; let Him quench your thirst. And then watch as rivers of living water flow out through you to quench the thirst of those around you.

 Make It Personal

Today, come to Jesus, the Source of all Life. Take the time to drink deeply, asking Him to quench your thirst.

Channeled Water

God had granted Daniel kindness and
compassion from the chief eunuch.

—DANIEL 1:9

Who gave Daniel favor with the supervisor of the young men in Daniel 1? God did. Even here in this quote-unquote "advancement program," which was intended to instill progressive Babylonian thought in these Hebrews, God intervened on Daniel's behalf and moved the hearts of his pagan handlers. So, when Daniel appealed to the "guard" (1:11) and suggested a ten-day dietary experiment of vegetables and water for him and his three friends, the man agreed to it. Why? Because God had gone before them. Protecting them. Providing for them.

"A king's heart is like channeled water in the LORD's hand," the Bible says (Prov. 21:1), as are the hearts of all those in authority, even if they don't acknowledge God. Even if they hate and resist God. Even if they worship other gods, our God still "directs" their hearts "wherever he chooses."

There's not a king or leader or president, not even your boss at work, whose heart God cannot touch and turn; not a person God cannot cause to carry out His will. Because Heaven rules.

 Make It Personal

Pray for your leaders, both on a local and national level,
that God would direct their hearts to do His will.

Zero-Tolerance Policy

Let all bitterness, anger and wrath,
shouting and slander be removed from you.
—EPHESIANS 4:31

In Ephesians 4, Paul instructs us to impose a zero-tolerance policy concerning the sharing of unkind, untrue, unhelpful information about others.

I understand you may be dealing with situations where people have sinned against you. But before you air your grievances, take a minute to check your motivation.

Is it to see the offenders exposed? To punish them? To gain an outside ally? Are you as concerned about the people you're criticizing as you are about how their actions are affecting you?

And then consider: Have you prayed for the people who have hurt you? And have you gone to them directly in a genuine appeal for their personal welfare and restoration?

When it becomes necessary to expose the sin of another, be sure the exposure comes from a heart that wants to see them restored to a right relationship with God. And be sure to pick your confidants carefully.

 Make It Personal

*How can you impose a zero-tolerance policy
on your words when it comes to sharing things
that are unkind, untrue, and unhelpful?*

Crying Out to God

"If my people who are called by my name humble themselves,
and pray . . . then I will hear from heaven."

—2 CHRONICLES 7:14 ESV

One of the greatest roles in which God has used women as instruments of revival is in the matter of prayer. In 1949–1951 God used two sisters, Peggy and Christine Smith, in the Lewis Revival in Scotland.

Both women were in their eighties. Peggy was blind, and Christine was crippled with arthritis. They couldn't leave their cottage. But they knew how to pray. God used their prayers to plant seeds of longing in the hearts of men who then began to pray for revival. God sent a great spiritual awakening in response to the earnest prayers of these two obscure women.

As I read reports of violence and perversion, as I receive letters from women whose family members are far from God, as I look at the backslidden condition of so many churches and homes, I wonder, *Where are the praying women who are carrying these burdens on their knees and crying out to God for mercy and divine intervention?*

 Make It Personal

*Take time today, and every day, to cry out to God
for mercy and divine intervention in your family,
your community, and your world.*

True Brokenness

Holy, holy, holy is the Lord of Armies;
his glory fills the whole earth.

—ISAIAH 6:3

In Isaiah 6, Isaiah encountered God in a way he never had before. The prophet was struck with a vision of God's holiness—holiness so intense that even the temple pillars had the good sense to tremble.

Isaiah no longer saw himself in contrast to all the depraved people around him. Now he saw himself in the light of the holy, high, supreme God of the universe. The words out of his mouth were no longer, "Woe to *them*." Now they were, "Woe is *me*!"

Prior to this Isaiah had been a good man; he was gifted and committed to God. But in chapter 6 Isaiah came to true brokenness. From then on he operated not out of natural strength but out of an intense sense of his own neediness.

To know God, to live in His presence, and to be occupied with a vision of His holiness is to know how foolish and frail we are apart from Him and to be broken from a preoccupation with ourselves.

 Make It Personal

*How would seeing yourself in the light of the Lord's
holiness change how you go about your day today?*

A Powerful Witness

Daniel determined that he would not defile himself
with the king's food or with the wine he drank.

—DANIEL 1:8

Daniel and his friends hadn't forsaken their God or pursued idolatrous lifestyles. And yet they were dealing with the same sense of loss and displacement as the people whom God was disciplining for their disobedience.

The four teenagers could have thought they had every reason to misunderstand God's actions or resent where He had placed them. You may feel that way, too, at times. Your life may have been made more difficult by the choices and sins of others.

Rain falls on both "the righteous and the unrighteous" (Matt. 5:45). Yet in every trial, God will do whatever is necessary to protect and provide for His children. He won't forget you in the swirl of what's happening around you.

These kinds of settings, the ones in which the "why me?" questions are easy to ask, are purposeful. In and through the unknowns, God is carrying out His good, eternal plan. And He often uses these injustices to create a platform from which your life can give powerful witness to His greatness.

 Make It Personal

*How has God worked through difficulties in your past
to help your life be a witness for the gospel?*

The Lamb of God

"Look, the Lamb of God,
who takes away the sin of the world!"
—JOHN 1:29

Before Christ came, sacrificing lambs was a part of every-day life for the Israelites, which is why the above words of John the Baptist were so significant. That was a stunning declaration to the Jews, and it should be stunning to us because it contains the heart of the gospel message.

The lamb symbolizes innocence, submission, vulnerability, quiet suffering, and sacrifice. The King of the universe came to earth as a gentle, sacrificial Lamb. He suffered quietly for sins not His own. And He figures prominently in God's eternal plans for His people.

His sacrifice results in salvation for God's people, but un-repentant sinners will be conquered by His wrath. This Lamb, who strikes terror in the hearts of unbelievers, strikes praise and worship in the hearts of those who have believed in Him.

One day you will face the Lamb, either as your Judge or as your Savior. Which will it be for you? Either He will conquer you, or you will be one of those who conquers *with* Him.

Make It Personal

If you haven't already, place your trust in the Lamb of God
who takes away our sin. Take time to worship Him today.

Just the Necessities

Give me neither poverty nor wealth.... Otherwise, I might
have too much and deny you ... or I might have nothing
and steal, profaning the name of my God.

—PROVERBS 30:8–9

The writer of this proverb recognized that we can dishonor God's name as a result of having wealth or poverty. He doesn't want too much, and he doesn't want too little.

This writer is describing a life of moderation; a life not given to excess, and one that is content with God's provision of basic necessities. Choosing that kind of self-controlled, moderate lifestyle is a means of guarding our hearts.

This ties in with the Lord's Prayer. When we pray, "Give us today our daily bread," we're asking God for the basic, simple necessities of life. God may be pleased to bless us with far more than we need, but we're told to ask for only what's essential. Jesus is teaching us to say, "Lord, I want as much as is sufficient for each day."

Whether we're wealthy or poor, if we have nothing else but God as our portion and allotment for this day, we're still rich.

 Make It Personal

When you pray, do you ask God to provide
for what you need or what you want?

Fighting Together

Therefore encourage one another with these words.

—1 THESSALONIANS 4:18

Part of the beauty—and the power—of a Christian lifestyle is that we're not in this battle alone. We tend to think of our struggles as a personal issue. But the directives God has given us in His Word aren't just about us as individuals but also about how we live out the beauty of the gospel—*together*.

We do this in community with others, and we do it for the sake of others. What a joy—and responsibility—it is to fight together for grace and freedom in Christ and to take others with us into a place of victory where together we can worship at the feet of Christ.

The mandate we see in Scripture is about sharing and receiving from one another the gifts of transparency, accountability, mercy, and encouragement, reminding one another who our Master really is. And it's about teaching one another as well.

Just think what life could be like with all of us running together, fighting together—rather than shadowboxing all alone with such stubborn opponents.

 Make It Personal

Why do we often think we have to face struggles alone?
Why is it important to enlist others to fight with and for us?

By Life and By Death

Though [Jesus Christ] was rich, for your sake he became poor,
so that by his poverty you might become rich.

—2 CORINTHIANS 8:9

As the son of a wealthy businessman, William Borden could have settled for a life of ease. Instead, he chose to lay down his life for Christ. When William graduated from high school in 1904, his father sent him on a worldwide cruise. Brokenhearted by the spiritual needs of the people he met, William committed his life to be a missionary.

He dedicated his college years to mastering God's Word and reaching those around him with the gospel. When it was time to leave for the mission field, he headed for China, sailing first to Egypt, where he contracted spinal meningitis and died less than a month later.

He left his entire fortune of over one million dollars to be invested in the cause of Christ. After his death, the following phrases were found in his Bible: No reserves. No retreats. No regrets.[18]

It's when we choose to follow in Jesus' steps that we'll be able to look back on our lives with no regrets.

 Make It Personal

As you go throughout your day, think about how you can live for Christ in a way so that you'll have no regrets.

Satan's Strategy

"When he tells a lie, he speaks from his own nature,
because he is a liar and the father of lies."

—JOHN 8:44

Deception was—and still is—crucial to Satan's strategy. Sometimes, as was the case with Eve, Satan deceives us directly. Sometimes, however, he uses other people as instruments of deception. Paul warns in Ephesians 5:6, "Let no one deceive you with empty arguments." Repeatedly he challenges God's people to speak truth to one another.

According to the Scripture, we can even be deceived by spiritual leaders—those who have been entrusted with the responsibility of shepherding God's flock and communicating the truth to His people.

Regardless of the immediate source, anytime we receive input that is not consistent with the Word of God, we can be sure Satan is trying to deceive and destroy us. What we read or hear may sound right, may feel right, may seem right—but if it is contrary to the Word of God, it isn't right.

 Make It Personal

*Ask God to help you evaluate what you hear
today in light of the truth of His Word.*

Your First Love

Cursed is the person who trusts in mankind. He makes human flesh his strength, and his heart turns from the LORD.

—JEREMIAH 17:5

A major city in western Asia Minor, Ephesus was a center of early Christianity. But over the years, the Christians there had somehow lost sight of the Savior. They had transferred their affection elsewhere, and this deviation threatened to cost them dearly.

God wants us to love Him first and foremost. When we find ourselves trusting in people instead, this indicates that our heart's focus has shifted from Him. Love for people—friends, family members, or even ourselves—can compete with our love for Christ (Matt. 10:37). Other substitutes for a God-centered love relationship may include money, pleasure, friends, work, the teachings of respected leaders, or Bible knowledge without a relationship with Christ.

Revival doesn't begin when struggling, wayward people decide to return to the Lord but rather when the loving heavenly Father, wanting His people to enjoy the safety and security of His love, calls them back to Himself. God is the initiator; the call to revival is a plea of love from His heart.

 Make It Personal

What are some things that may be competing with your love for God?

Wonderful Counselor

The Spirit of the LORD will rest on him—a Spirit of wisdom
and understanding, a Spirit of counsel and strength.

—ISAIAH 11:2

In the midst of dark days, Isaiah prophesied about the coming Messiah who would bring hope out of despair and light out of darkness: "For a child will be born for us, a son will be given to us, and the government will be on his shoulders. He will be named Wonderful Counselor" (Isa. 9:6). Maybe you find yourself today in a dark place, wondering if God really cares.

He does. He's the Wonderful Counselor. In Scripture the word *wonderful* is only used of God, never of man. Is He wonderful to you or have you lost the wonder of who He is and what He has done? There are many good counselors in this world, but Jesus surpasses them all.

Do you want to know God's will for your life? Do you want to know how to respond to your husband, raise your children, or deal with that difficult coworker? Are you facing a circumstance of which there seems to be no solution? Turn to the Wonderful Counselor, ask Him for wisdom, and then trust His counsel. He will never mislead you.

 Make It Personal

Where do you turn for counsel when you're desperate?
How has Jesus been a Wonderful Counselor in your life?

When Your Freezer Is Full

"Give us today our daily bread."
—MATTHEW 6:11

When we already have most of our needs met, it's hard to have a sense of dependence on God. But when we ask Him for daily bread, we're recognizing He is our provider.

Whether we're barely scraping by or can easily make our mortgage payment, as God's children we're supposed to ask for daily bread. As we do, we recognize we need Him for everything, including necessities that may be plenteous in our lives. Something as simple as food—and every other provision—should be received with a grateful heart. We need to realize that even if our freezer is full, we're dependent on Him.

The child of God who doesn't ask God to meet her basic needs is unlikely to recognize that He's the source of every good gift. As a result, we may become ungrateful and tend to take things for granted. Then when the provision is removed or delayed, our hearts can become bitter.

There's nothing wrong with having plenty if we recognize where it came from and keep a heart that's grateful, humble, and dependent on our heavenly Father.

Make It Personal

Ask God to provide for your basic needs today; then when He does send provision—whether big or small—thank Him for it.

Speak Well of Others

No foul language should come from your mouth,
but only what is good for building up someone in need.

−EPHESIANS 4:29

Perhaps the best way to curb our bent for picking at others' faults is to go out of our way to say *good things* about them—not by being insincere but simply by making the effort to voice what we notice.

You might be surprised how many opportunities present themselves to pay a compliment.

As the wife of a busy pastor and the mother of eleven children, Sarah Edwards (1710–1758) certainly faced temptation to speak ill of others. But she was known for the opposite:

> Sarah made it her rule to speak well of all so far as she could. . . . She was not [prone] to dwell with delight on the imperfections and failings of any; and when she heard persons speaking ill of others, she would say what she thought she could with truth and justice in their excuse.[19]

What a commitment—to speak well of all. And what a calling—to reflect the heart of Christ to those around us.

 Make It Personal

How can you speak well of others today? Write a note of encouragement, pay a compliment—be creative in building them up!

He's Writing Your Story

"For I know the plans I have for you, declares the LORD, plans
for welfare and not for evil, to give you a future and a hope."

—JEREMIAH 29:11 ESV

God sovereignly and purposefully orchestrates the circumstances of our lives. There is no such thing as happen-
stance or accident. Nothing catches Him off guard. We need
to remember that what we see now is not the whole story. If we
could see what God sees and know what He knows, our hearts
would be at peace.

The challenges we face may also be a part of God writing
someone else's story. God wants to use our story to be a means
of His grace in the lives of others—even those who may have
"wrecked" our story.

Those who trust in Him will never be disappointed (Isa.
49:23). Not every chapter in this life has a happy ending. But
every true child of God will live "happily ever after." We can
be sure of that.

You can trust God to write your story—and you can be
sure that in the end, He will right your story!

 Make It Personal

Spend time thanking God that He not only writes
your story but will one day make all things right!

Sorrow into Joy

Jesus wept.
—JOHN 11:35

As a boy, Jesus was misunderstood by His parents. During His earthly ministry, His brothers didn't believe in Him. He experienced hunger, exhaustion, and temptation. As the Man of Sorrows, He witnessed the ravages of sin in a broken world—sickness, death, grief, pride, prejudice, and hatred.

He wept at the grave of His friend Lazarus. He wept over Jerusalem for her rejection of her Savior. He wept in the garden as He prepared to go to the cross and endure the ultimate suffering. This Man of Sorrows was betrayed, mocked, beaten, and crucified.

Much of the sorrow that abounds in the world is readily visible, but there is also much private pain that most never see. Yet Jesus has always seen, and He cared enough to do something about it. He drank the full cup of sorrow and pain that every person in the world through all of history has experienced.

At the cross, judgment and salvation met so we could receive forgiveness, comfort, and healing. One day, every sorrow of those who have placed their faith in Him will be turned to joy.

 Make It Personal

Take time to express your gratitude to Jesus for carrying your sin, sorrow, and pain—and for giving you joy in exchange.

A Tree of Life

Pleasant words are a honeycomb:
sweet to the taste and health to the body.

—PROVERBS 16:24

I f you look up the word *healing* in a thesaurus, you will likely find these words: therapeutic, medicinal, curing. What a blessing it is to experience physical healing from sickness. An even greater blessing is when God uses us as an instrument of spiritual healing in the lives of others.

Proverbs 15:4 says, "The tongue that heals is a tree of life." Picture a lush redbud or dogwood in the peak of spring. Its branches are filled with dense blossoms announcing that spring has arrived. Its roots dig deeply into the soil, soaking up valuable nutrients, and its leaves are green and healthy—full of new life.

God says that the tongue can be like a tree of life. It can give refreshing words and encouragement to the weary. It can provide support for the anxious. It can freely give kindness to young and old alike.

May God keep watch over our lips. May our tongues minister grace, help, and healing through words of encouragement and blessing.

 Make It Personal

*Ask the Lord to let the words you speak today be
like healing medicine to those who receive them.*

Bookends

> The fruit of the Spirit is love, joy, peace, patience, kindness, goodness, faithfulness, gentleness, and self-control.
>
> —GALATIANS 5:22–23

Did you notice the two bookends of Paul's list? *Love* and *self-control*. Between these two lie all those other qualities that characterize a fruitful life. I'm convinced the order is no accident.

Wherever we lack love and self-control, we invite all manner of breakdown and discord to take up residence in our midst. Bitterness and anger in our hearts, expressed in evil speaking, vengeful words, malicious gossip, and talebearing—these are the signs that love and self-control are in short supply.

I imagine Satan cheers as we bite and devour one another rather than being like our reconciling, life-giving Father. So, let's join together in shutting down the slander machine.

Instead, "let us pursue what promotes peace and what builds up one another" (Rom. 14:19). And let's pray earnestly with the psalmist: "Lord, set up a guard for my mouth; keep watch at the door of my lips" (Ps. 141:3).

 Make It Personal

How does practicing the qualities of love and self-control make a difference in how you speak to and about others?

Ordinary and Unqualified

God has chosen what is foolish in the world to shame the wise.

—1 CORINTHIANS 1:27

Regardless of how ordinary and unqualified we may be, all of us as children of God can walk with Him and be used by Him—not because we're inherently significant but because of our relationship with Christ. Our true identity isn't found in a job, mate, child, position, or possession. It's our connection to Jesus that gives our lives value and significance and makes us usable in His kingdom.

The significance of the life of Mary, the mother of Jesus, wasn't based on any of the things our world values so highly—physical beauty, intelligence, education, natural gifts and abilities. It was her relationship to Christ that gave her life significance. "The Lord is with you," the angel said (Luke 1:28). This is what made all the difference in this young woman's life. And it's what makes all the difference in our lives.

Don't assume you have to be extraordinary to be used by God. God specializes in using ordinary people whose limitations and weaknesses make them ideal showcases for His greatness and glory.

 Make It Personal

How have you seen God use ordinary people to bring Him glory?
How can He use your life to showcase His greatness?

Real Gratitude

Thanks be to God, who gives us the victory
through our Lord Jesus Christ!

—1 CORINTHIANS 15:57

To send up a "thank you" in heaven's general direction at the sudden appearance of a good parking spot, the dismissal of a speeding ticket, or a phone call from the doctor's office that tells you all your tests came back negative is not distinctively Christian gratitude.

This kind of me-first thankfulness is the sort that only kicks in when things are going well and when positive blessings are flowing our direction. It's little more than an automatic reflex, like saying, "Excuse me," after accidentally bumping into someone or, "You too," after being encouraged by a sales clerk to have a nice day.

Christian gratitude, on the other hand, involves *recognizing* the many benefits we've received from God and others, *acknowledging* God as the ultimate Giver of every good gift, and *expressing* appreciation to Him (and others) for those gifts.

 Make It Personal

How would choosing to practice true Christian
gratitude make a difference in your day today?

Ten Times

In every matter of wisdom and understanding that the king
consulted them about, he found them ten times better than
all the magicians and mediums in his entire kingdom.

—DANIEL 1:20

From earth's perspective, Daniel and his friends were nobodies. No sooner had they walked into the palace than
they'd been assigned new Babylonian names. Everything involved in this forced reeducation program was designed to
show the Hebrews that their old ways were outdated and their
old God outmatched by Babylon and its gods, including Nebuchadnezzar who thought he was a god.

Nobody names their sons Nebuchadnezzar anymore. But
they sure do call a lot of them Daniel. They do it because
there's something different about people who are so convinced
God is ruling over the macro world that they can genuinely
trust Him to supply and care for them in their micro world.
There's something "ten times" more notable about nobodies
who only have one answer for what makes them stand out in
ways that even the somebodies can't help but notice, desire,
and wonder about.

 Make It Personal

What differences do you see in the lives
of those who truly trust in the Lord?

Passing It On

Older women . . . are to teach what is good,
so that they may encourage the young women.

—TITUS 2:3–4

Many years ago, my friend Susan gave birth to a son with multiple, life-threatening defects, including having no esophagus. She hardly slept his first four years because she had to watch to make sure he didn't choke.

But during that season, Susan was driven to the Word. She developed a sound mind, grounded in the Word, the character, and the ways of God. That is where she found perspective, comfort, and strength.

Years later, when another one of her children faced a prolonged health crisis with her own child, Susan was able to walk her daughter through that difficult season with wisdom and grace. Susan has also been used to minister to and mentor hundreds of other young moms, passing on to them what God taught her.

This is the dynamic Paul had in mind when he wrote Titus 2. The younger women in your life need your example, your encouragement, and your prayers. And they need you to help them get into the Word and get the Word into them.

 Make It Personal

How could you use what you've learned about developing a sound mind and lifestyle to help the younger women in your life?

All I Have Needed

"Therefore don't worry about tomorrow,
because tomorrow will worry about itself."
—MATTHEW 6:34

When we ask God to "give us today our daily bread," what are we really saying? There are several attitudes implied with this petition.

First, there's *the attitude of gratitude*. This petition for daily bread is a grateful acknowledgment of God's faithfulness.

Then this request implies *an attitude of contentment*. It's the realization that God has already provided for me today all I need for my present peace and happiness.

And lastly, there's *an attitude of faith*. If we're grateful and content, if we believe and trust God, then there's no room for worry, anxiety, or fear.

If we have God as our King, how can we be anxious? There's something wrong with the picture of fearful, anxious, worrying children of God. When people see how we operate in our relationships and responsibilities, we want them to be challenged to trust our heavenly Father for their every need, without anxiety or care.

Make It Personal

Confess any areas of life where you have anxiety or fear, and ask God to help you trust Him to provide for your every need.

All the Answer We Need

This wondrous knowledge is beyond me.
It is lofty; I am unable to reach it.
—PSALM 139:6

An old hymn expresses the thoughts many of us have about eternity. We sing, "We'll understand it better by and by." When we get to heaven, the questions that perplex us on this earth will be answered.

There's some truth in that perspective. But while some of our questions may be answered in heaven, we will not suddenly know everything. It's not like God is going to take out a computer screen and put all the answers up for us. I'm not sure we will care so much, because when we look at Him as He is, He will be answer enough.

The same is true in our life on this earth.

God isn't going to answer all your questions. If you knew all the answers, you would be God and you wouldn't need Him. God won't answer all your questions, but I'll tell you what He will do: as you ask honest questions and then listen, He will reveal Himself to you.

 Make It Personal

What questions do you have for God?
Do you think they'll matter when you see Christ?

The Lion of the Tribe of Judah

The LORD will roar from Zion and make his voice heard
from Jerusalem; heaven and earth will shake. But the LORD
will be a refuge for his people, a stronghold for the Israelites.

—JOEL 3:16

In Revelation, John had a vision about the end of history. In this vision, he was shown a scroll with seven seals. What John saw caused him great distress—there was no one able to break those seven seals.

But then John was told, "Do not weep. Look, the Lion from the tribe of Judah, the Root of David, has conquered so that he is able to open the scroll and its seven seals" (Rev. 5:5). There's someone worthy after all. It is Jesus, the risen Savior.

Jesus alone has the authority to open the scroll that contains God's eternal purposes. He is able to prevail where others have failed. He is omnipotent where others are impotent. He is essential to the unfolding of God's eternal purposes. Lions are thought of as the king of beasts that rule the jungle. Jesus is the Lion who rules the universe and all that happens in it.

Make It Personal

*How does the thought of Jesus as the Lion who rules the
universe comfort you in your struggles and circumstances?*

The Importance of Self-Control

Be transformed by the renewing of your mind.

—ROMANS 12:2

Too often, I believe, we focus on trying to change our behavior without understanding the real trigger behind our actions. That's because those actions originate not in our wills or stressful circumstances but in our minds.

The reason you lashed out at that person again isn't that he or she did something to hurt you. It's because in that moment when the frustration erupted in impatient, fiery words, you weren't operating from a sound mind.

Or you look up one day, sick from the bitter consequences of a reckless, shortsighted decision and wonder, *Why didn't I stop before it came to this?*

Here's why. It's because you weren't self-controlled.

If we don't master this, we will struggle with every other virtue and spiritual discipline. To be self-controlled is basic to every believer in every season of life.

 Make It Personal

Do you agree that if we don't master self-control we will struggle with every other virtue and spiritual discipline? Why or why not?

Responding to God's Initiative

Moses hid his face because he was afraid to look at God.

—EXODUS 3:6

Moses and God came to experience an extraordinary relationship. But it didn't start out that way. In fact, Moses' first encounter with God could hardly be called intimate. As he stood next to that burning brush on the side of a mountain and heard the voice of God, Moses was terrified.

But once God had Moses' attention, He shared with Moses things no other man of his time had ever known. He revealed His deep concern about the children of Israel in Egypt. He revealed His plan to use Moses as their deliverer. And He revealed that He had all the power and resources to make it happen.

As Moses thought back over his checkered past and his very average aptitudes, he must have wondered how this could be. He felt insecure and inadequate.

Nonetheless, he responded to God's initiative, and from that day his life was never the same—just as your life will never be the same once you embark on the adventure of a growing, vital relationship with God.

 Make It Personal

What was your first encounter with God like?

Grave Danger

For the wages of sin is death, but the gift of
God is eternal life in Christ Jesus our Lord.

—ROMANS 6:23

If I noticed my neighbors' house was on fire, I would do whatever I had to do to get them out of danger. If necessary, I would scream and pound on their door. I wouldn't worry about whether they felt annoyed or about hurting their feelings. Their lives are at risk.

That's the picture of someone who's engaged in sin and won't stop. They're in grave danger. Because this is a desperate situation, I'll do whatever I can to warn them and help them get out of that burning house before it's too late.

If you know you're engaged in thinking or behavior that God says is sin, then I implore you to take immediate, drastic steps to extricate yourself from the dangerous situation you've allowed yourself to get into. The grace of God will enable you to take one difficult step after another past emotions, old habits, and deeply ingrained (but false) ways of thinking. He will lead you in a whole new way of life.

 Make It Personal

*Ask the Lord to show you anyone around you
who needs to be rescued—and then go help them!*

A Hammer

The voice of the LORD in power. . . . The voice of the LORD
breaks the cedars; the LORD shatters the cedars of Lebanon.

—PSALM 29:4–5

When you recognize your need for a broken and a contrite heart, when you want to choose the pathway of brokenness, begin by opening the Word of God.

God's Word has the power to soften the hardened soil of our hearts and shatter our stubborn self-life. God says, "Is not my word . . . like a hammer that pulverizes rock?" (Jer. 23:29). The psalmist stood in awe of the power of His Word: "The voice of the LORD in power. . . . The voice of the LORD breaks the cedars" (Ps. 29:4–5).

Each time we open His Word, whether in private or public settings, it should be with the intent of allowing the Word to break us. The same Word that serves as a hammer to break us will then become a balm to heal our hearts and a light to guide our footsteps in the pathway of humility.

 Make It Personal

How has God's Word both broken you and healed you?

The Gift of Peace

"I have told you these things so that in me you may have peace.
You will have suffering in this world. Be courageous!
I have conquered the world."

—JOHN 16:33

B ecause we live in a fallen, broken world, there will always be trials and disappointments. But in the midst of all of that, we can be at peace if we are rightly related to the Prince of Peace. It's a gift He gives as we trust Him.

You can't buy the peace you long for; you won't find it in a bottle, a pill, a trusted friend, or different circumstances. We experience peace when we rest in Jesus. If we focus on ourselves and our trials, we won't have peace. Peace was purchased by the Prince of Peace, and it's given to us as a gift. "Punishment for our peace was on him, and we are healed by his wounds" (Isa. 53:5).

Do you have that peace, even though your circumstances today might be painful? The Prince of Peace will go with you where no one else can go. If you'll look to Him, He'll give you His peace.

Make It Personal

Spend time thanking God for the peace that only He can bring and ask Him to help you experience that gift in your present difficulties.

A Beautiful Thing

He gave himself for us to redeem us from all lawlessness
and to cleanse for himself a people for his own possession,
eager to do good works.

—TITUS 2:14

Decadence, perversion, substance abuse, and immorality—
this was the prevailing culture of the Roman Empire
in the first century. In the midst of that darkness, followers of
Christ were called to be sober-minded and self-controlled.

They stood out. They made a difference. They reflected the
beauty, balance, and stability the gospel brings to a mind, a life,
a culture.

Few things should be of higher priority to us than the development of a clear-thinking, gospel-saturated, sound mind.

The change isn't always a dramatic one. It often occurs in
the simple, everyday spaces and places of our lives.

It's a beautiful thing when our minds are renewed by the
truth, freed from the shackles of our peevish, demanding selves,
living under the control of God's Spirit—and joy filling the
space invaded by His grace.

Make It Personal

Ask God to help your life reflect the beauty
of the gospel to the world around you.

An Eternal Perspective

[Daniel] declared: May the name of God be praised forever
and ever, for wisdom and power belong to him.

—DANIEL 2:20

Through no fault of his own, Daniel faced an almost unbroken succession of difficulties throughout his life, from his teen years until his eighties. His story inspires us to believe that it's possible for us, too, to remain calm and courageous in the face of crises—both in the way we respond to the macro headlines in the world and the way we deal with the micro headaches in our personal lives. How?

By lifting our eyes from earth's perspective to see what's going on from God's perspective. By remembering, as Daniel did, that our confidence isn't in the powers that be but in the all-powerful God of heaven whose we are and whom we serve. By viewing everything that's happening around and to us through the lens of "Heaven rules." And by trusting that, though His ways may not always be easy to discern, our sovereign and providential God is always at work, always carrying out His grand and gracious purposes in all that transpires in this world.

 Make It Personal

Ask God to help you see both the good and hard
things of today through an eternal perspective.

The Blessing of the Thorn

I take pleasure in weaknesses, insults, hardships,
persecutions, and in difficulties, for the sake of Christ.
For when I am weak, then I am strong.

—2 CORINTHIANS 12:10

The hymn writer Fanny Crosby had a choice to make. I'm sure when she learned a doctor's mistake caused her blindness, she was forced to deal with wondering "what might have been."

Few of us know what it's like not to see. We forget to be thankful for the blessing of sight. Yet Fanny Crosby, writer of more than eight thousand hymns, saw things another way. She was *thankful* for the blessing of blindness.

She said, "I could not have written thousands of hymns if I had been hindered by the distractions of seeing all the interesting and beautiful objects that would have been presented to my notice." As she wrote in her autobiography, "It seemed intended by the blessed providence of God that I should be blind all my life, and I *thank Him* for the dispensation."[20]

"I thank Him." For blindness. Wow.

Make It Personal

Is there a difficult situation in your life that God has used to help you grow? How could you thank Him for this "thorn"?

At the Core

When you were dead in trespasses and
in the uncircumcision of your flesh, he made you
alive with him and forgave us all our trespasses.

—COLOSSIANS 2:13

This truth seems to capture forgiveness well: forgiveness is a promise never to bring up that sin against that person again—not to God, not to the person who committed it, and not to anyone else. It's a deliberate decision to deal with another's sin by doing away with it.

Forgiveness is truly at the core of the gospel. Even our excuses for *not* forgiving keep bringing us back to the cross where forgiveness was perfectly applied, not to a group of people who'd gone through all the right steps to become forgivable but to us—to people who didn't deserve it, didn't know we needed it, perhaps didn't even want it!

We of all people should appreciate the joy of forgiveness . . . by knowing what a treasure it is to be perfectly forgiven.

But beyond that, when we extend to others the forgiveness that Christ extended to us on the cross, we reflect God's mercy and grace to a world that desperately needs to be forgiven.

 Make It Personal

How does your choice to forgive testify to your
understanding of your own salvation?

Carry the Light

"You will conceive and give birth to a son,
and you will name him Jesus."

−LUKE 1:31

There is a sense in which God has chosen all of us for a similar task as Mary of Nazareth—to bring forth spiritual life. Whether or not He grants us physical children, He wants to use us to carry the life and light of Jesus into the world—to be spiritual reproducers, bringing forth His life in the lives of others.

We may look at certain prominent or unusually gifted people and think they've been uniquely chosen by God. The fact is that if you're a child of God, you've been chosen by God for a task of supreme significance—to be a bearer and nurturer of spiritual life by carrying the life of Jesus to others.

Look at your life that way and you'll never have a self-image problem. Many people today carry scars of rejection. What a joy to discover that though we deserve to be rejected by God, we have been chosen to belong to Him and to be a part of His redemptive plan in the universe.

 Make It Personal

Ask God to give you opportunities to be a
nurturer of spiritual life in those around you.

Getting Rid of Debt

"Lord, how many times must I forgive my brother or
sister who sins against me? As many as seven times?"

—MATTHEW 18:21

Most of us are more conscious of how other people have sinned against us than we are of how we've sinned against our heavenly Father. That's why we pray, "Forgive us our debts" (Matt. 6:12) so that we may be as conscious of our own sins in broken relationships as we are that of the other person.

There are two essential ways of dealing with others' sins. We can keep the debtor on the hook and hold out for payment. Or we can write those debts off and forgive them.

We can't hold back pardon from anyone and expect God to forgive us. Our pardon must extend to everyone who has sinned against us and to all of their sins.

As long as we're on earth, we're not going to stop sinning entirely. There will always be sins for which we need to be forgiven, and there will always be sins we need to forgive on the part of others.

Make It Personal

Ask God to search your heart for any unforgiveness you may be holding on to. Then choose to release those debts and find freedom.

A Seed of Unforgiveness

"If [your brother] sins against you seven times in a day, and comes
back to you seven times, saying, 'I repent,' you must forgive him."

—LUKE 17:4

I've come to believe that unforgiveness is a very real issue
for *most* people. Almost everyone has someone they haven't
forgiven. I've seen it over and over again.

Whenever I have spoken on this subject, after defining forgiveness from a biblical perspective, I've asked the audience,
"How many of you would be honest enough to admit that there's
a root of bitterness in your heart—that there are one or more
people in your life, past or present, that you've never forgiven?"

I've asked for a response from tens of thousands of people,
including long-time believers, Bible study leaders, and voca-
tional Christian workers. In virtually every case, somewhere
between 80 and 95 percent of the people in the room have
raised their hands.

It still affects me profoundly to think that the vast majority
of people sitting in church (and many who are sitting at home,
having left the church, disillusioned) have at least a seed—if
not a forest—of unforgiveness in their heart.

 Make It Personal

Is there someone in your life that you've never forgiven?
What steps can you take today to forgive?

He's the King

Your throne, God, is forever and ever.

—HEBREWS 1:8

When Jesus was on trial for His life, Pilate asked him, "Are you the king of the Jews?" To which Jesus responded, "You say so."

As the trial unfolded, Jesus was rejected for His claim. Soldiers twisted together a crown of thorns and dressed Him in a purple robe. Crowns and robes belong to kings, but the people were not sincere in crowning Jesus. To the contrary, they mocked Him.

When Pilate said to the Jews, "Here is your king!" they cried out, "Crucify him!" The people wanted a king, but Jesus wasn't who they wanted.

Pilate attached an inscription to Jesus' cross, which said, "Jesus of Nazareth, the King of the Jews." The leaders objected, but Pilate answered, "What I have written I have written."

Pilate got it right. Jesus is King, and there on the cross, the King of Kings laid down His life for His subjects. One day that King will return. He came first as a suffering king, but when He comes back, He will rule forever.

 Make It Personal

Today, spend time thanking and praising God
that He is the King of Kings who will rule forever.

Guarding Our Tongues

May the words of my mouth and the meditation of my heart
be acceptable to you, LORD, my rock and my Redeemer.

—PSALM 19:14

Words have power. They have the power to cut, wound, and even kill and destroy. But words also have power to give life, heal, nourish, restore, bless, strengthen, and encourage.

Our speech is a barometer because it reveals our hearts—our true spiritual condition. And the more words that come out of our mouths, the greater the potential for us to sin with our tongues.

It's so easy to say words that wound without even intending or realizing it, which is why we need the filling of Jesus' Spirit in our lives. We need to purpose to honor God with our speech and to fill our hearts with His holy Word.

We need to echo the psalmist's prayer: "LORD, set up a guard for my mouth; keep watch at the door of my lips" (Ps. 141:3)! When we ask God for help, He will answer, as we seek to say words that both honor Christ and build others up.

 Make It Personal

*Ask God to help the words that come out of your mouth
to be ones that honor Him and build up others around you.*

Strength on Request

I call to God Most High,
to God who fulfills his purpose for me.
—PSALM 57:2

I f we are to fulfill the purpose for which God has chosen us, we must be filled with His Spirit. When the angel said to Mary, "You're going to have a child," Mary responded, "How can this be? I've never been intimate with a man!" God had chosen her for a task that was humanly impossible.

In response to Mary's expression of weakness and inadequacy, the angel promised her God's strength and adequacy: "The Holy Spirit will come upon you, and the power of the Most High will overshadow you" (Luke 1:35).

The task for which God has chosen you and me is no less impossible. We can share the gospel of Christ with our lost friends, but we cannot give them repentance and faith. You can provide a climate that is conducive to the spiritual growth of your children, but you can't make them have a heart for God. We are totally dependent on Him to produce any fruit of eternal value.

 Make It Personal

Spend time thanking God for His promise of that same strength and power to live the Christian life today—available upon request!

He Allows It

[God] changes the times and seasons;
he removes kings and establishes kings.

—DANIEL 2:21

No matter how glorious or inglorious an earthly ruler's season in the spotlight, no matter how long or how brief their tenure, the sun eventually sets on their rule. Whether people love them, fear them, suffer under them, or all of the above, every person who assumes the power of office will at some point reach the end of their time in that office, either by their resignation or retirement, by a loss at the polls, by a successful coup, or, if nothing else, by their death.

But this rhythm of rising and falling is not just a function of age or political opposition or the fickle cry for change from the voting public. Above it all, across all ages of human history, both past and present, stands a God in heaven who "brings down one and exalts another" (Ps. 75:7).

Earthly rulers only rule because God allows them to rule. And they rule only for as long as He allows them.

Make It Personal

As you hear news reports, ask God to help you remember that no matter what earthly rulers are in charge, He is King over all.

Receiving Forgiveness

What, then, are we to say about these things?
If God is for us, who is against us?

—ROMANS 8:31

Who can forgive sins but God alone? No one.

This is so important to remember when all the regret, all the shame, all the guilt leads you to say, "I just can't forgive myself"—especially when your issue isn't an unresolved conflict with someone but something you've done yourself.

Perhaps you're having a hard time getting past a "grass-is-greener" decision you made that cost you a good job and a lot of your long-term security. Or a moment of negligence where you failed to keep one of your children safe from danger. Or an abortion you had ten years ago. It could be any of a million things.

A well-meaning friend or counselor may tell you that forgiving yourself is your first step toward healing and recovery. The problem is that we don't find God instructing us to deal with our heartaches this way anywhere in the Scripture. Rather He urges us to receive *His* forgiveness.

In fact, Paul writes, "If God is for us, who is against us?"

 Make It Personal

*Is there some sin for which you still struggle to "feel forgiven"?
How can you truly experience the reality of God's forgiveness?*

Get Out of the Way

God's foolishness is wiser than human wisdom,
and God's weakness is stronger than human strength.
—1 CORINTHIANS 1:25

Don't ever forget that in your own strength you cannot do what God has called you to do. You cannot parent that child, love that husband, care for that elderly parent, submit to that boss, or lead that Bible study.

I can't begin to count how many times the Lord has given me a task and I've responded, "Lord, I can't do this. Others are more qualified. I'm not prepared. I'm so tired. I don't know what I'm doing." Then I sense His response: "That's why I've given you the Holy Spirit. The Holy Spirit will enable you, and My power will overshadow you and your weakness."

God specializes in the impossible, so that when the victory is won and the task is complete, we cannot take any credit.

We can only live the Christian life and serve God through the power of His Holy Spirit. As soon as we think we can handle it on our own, we become useless to Him. Let God take over and let Him overshadow you.

 Make It Personal

Does God want to use you in some kind of "impossible" task?
How can you let Him work through you?

Choose to be Broken

Humble yourselves, therefore, under the mighty hand of God,
so that he may exalt you at the proper time.

—1 PETER 5:6

Jesus identified Himself as the rejected Stone spoken of in the Old Testament: "The stone that the builders rejected has become the cornerstone. This came from the LORD; it is wondrous in our sight" (Ps. 118:22–23). He stressed the importance of how we choose to respond to His lordship: "Everyone who falls on that stone will be broken to pieces, but on whomever it falls, it will shatter him" (Luke 20:18).

Some people who may seem "broken" have not been broken at all. Rather they have been crushed by their circumstances because of their unwillingness to voluntarily fall on the Rock and be broken. Don't wait for God to break you. Humble yourself under the mighty hand of God. Fall on the Rock—Christ Jesus, who was broken for you—and cultivate the habit of crying out with the tax collector, "God, be merciful to me, a sinner" (Luke 18:13) and with David, "Have mercy on me, O God" (Ps. 51:1 ESV).

 Make It Personal

Humble yourself before Him today,
so that you can be broken rather than crushed.

The Gift of a Rebuke

A wise correction to a receptive ear
is like a gold ring or an ornament of gold.
—PROVERBS 25:12

Someone has said, "The last person to know he has a rip in his jacket is the guy who's got it on!" We all need friends who will love us enough to tell us when they see "blind spots" in our lives. And we need to be willing to be that kind of friend to others.

It's so important to learn how to receive *and* give godly counsel and reproof. Most of us don't like the idea of being rebuked. Nor do we find it easy to rebuke others. Yet a wise person's reproof has great value and is to be desired.

According to the Scripture, a rebuke from a wise person is a *gift*. Imagine how grateful you would be if someone gave you an expensive, beautiful piece of gold jewelry—custom-designed for you! God does just that when we humbly receive wise reproof. And He does this for others when we offer wise reproof.

 Make It Personal

*Ask a good friend if you have any blind spots
and be ready to receive their correction.*

A Great Need

"Forgive us our debts."

—MATTHEW 6:12

In Matthew 6:12, sin is defined as a debt. We're asking God to forgive us of our indebtedness to Him. We tend to think of the effect our sin has on us, but at its heart, we need to remember that our sin is against God. He is the One to whom we are indebted.

If we don't often find ourselves praying this part of the Lord's Prayer, could it be that we don't often see ourselves as sinners in need of God's forgiveness? Implicit in this prayer is asking God to make us more sensitive to our sin and to help us see it as He does. We need Him to give us a penitent heart, to help us realize how great our need is to ask for His forgiveness.

Whether we tend to minimize sin or we tend to minimize the grace of God, the cure is to get a fresh view of Christ, go to the cross, and see the cost of our salvation.

 Make It Personal

Ask God to help you see your sin as He sees it and
to understand how great your need is for forgiveness.

God with Us

The virgin will become pregnant and give birth to a son, and they
will name him Immanuel, which is translated "God is with us."

—MATTHEW 1:23

I will be with you" is a promise found throughout God's
Word. God with us—that is our greatest need in every circumstance, and God is with those who know and trust Jesus.

Immanuel, God with us, transforms ordinary moments
and mundane tasks. If Jesus is your Immanuel, then in that
profane work environment, God is with you. When your bills
are greater than your income, God is with you. At the grave-
side of a loved one, God is with you. When you're lonely, God
is with you. When your heart is breaking, God is with you.

His presence can give you joy in the midst of every valley.
When you don't know which direction to go, He is the guide
for your journey.

If Jesus lives in you, then God is with you, and you can be
free from fear. You can step out in faith, obey God, and fulfill
His calling for your life. Immanuel is God with us for all of
eternity.

Make It Personal

*What difference does God's presence make in your life? Take time
to praise Him that at all times, wherever you are, He is with you!*

The True King

*In the third year of the reign of King Jehoiakim of Judah,
King Nebuchadnezzar of Babylon came to Jerusalem
and laid siege to it.*

—DANIEL 1:1

The "kings" that are exerting their power over you and me today don't exactly resemble King Nebuchadnezzar in Daniel's day. But no doubt there are people and circumstances attempting to control our lives. That's why we must learn to counsel our hearts and minds according to the truth of God's Word: that He is the true, eternal King.

That means cancer is not king. No pandemic is king. No demented dictator is king. Financial concerns and crises are not king. Injustices committed against us or against those we love are not king.

Other people may have the ability to wound us deeply or even cause our hearts to break. But none of these people is king either.

Only God is King. All others are held in check by Him, rising and falling at His command. And this truth (because it is truth) infuses us with spiritual vigor and imparts a sense of equilibrium which we'd have no hope of enjoying otherwise.

 Make It Personal

*Take time to praise and thank God that He is King
over everything in your life—and in our world.*

Dealing in Truth

The one seated on the throne said,
"Look, I am making everything new."

—REVELATION 21:5

Our hearts ache at the thought of injustice. When people tell us tragic stories of how they've been ravaged by the sin of another, our natural inclination is to wish upon those offenders at least a measure of what they deserve.

But if we're going to be true instruments of mercy, we must deal in truth—*God's* truth. Not blissful, artificial denial, trying to act as though the hurt never happened. Not rigid, mechanical words and formulas, as if following some step-by-step recipe were all that was required.

I'm talking about the sweet, rich, pure Word and ways of God, not laid perfunctorily or unnaturally atop our real-life experiences but pulsing with vitality, healing, and grace, as God wrests reconciliation from the jaws of brokenness.

His truth is even strong enough to face situations where an apology never comes—strong enough to leave us free and whole, heart and soul, by the gift of forgiveness.

That's God's way of doing things.

 Make It Personal

Are you facing any situations today that seem unjust? How can you make the choice to believe that God will make all things new?

Whine or Worship?

The humble will eat and be satisfied;
those who seek the LORD will praise him.

—PSALM 22:26

When God puts challenging circumstances in our lives, we either worship or whine. I'm ashamed to say I've done more than my share of whining—even about ministry. "Oh, Lord, I'm tired of traveling. This is hard! Why do I have to deal with that person?"

I am reminded of the Israelites in the wilderness who murmured incessantly. "If only God had just let us die in the wilderness," they whined. One day God finally said, in essence, "You want to die in the wilderness? Okay, you'll die in the wilderness!" (See Num. 14:2, 28–30.) Be careful what you murmur—God may take you up on it.

But when Mary faced a change in plans, she responded in worship: "My soul magnifies the Lord, and my spirit rejoices in God my Savior" (Luke 1:46–47). So begins her Magnificat—one of the greatest hymns of praise ever lifted to heaven. She worshiped God for His wonderful acts, for His mercy, and for choosing her to be a part of His great redemptive plan.

 Make It Personal

Make a choice to worship God in honest praise no matter what circumstances you're currently going through.

Glimpses of His Glory

You who seek God, let your hearts revive.

—PSALM 69:32 ESV

The turn of the twentieth century was marked by an unusual concern for spiritual matters. In November 1904, God began to stir in the hearts of believers throughout Wales.

Evan Roberts was one person that God used. Everywhere he went, Roberts delivered a simple, straightforward, and timeless message. Did God's people desire an outpouring of His Spirit? Then four conditions must be observed:

- Confess all known sin.
- Put away all doubtful things and forgive everyone.
- Obey the promptings of the Holy Spirit.
- Publicly confess Christ as your Savior.

The impact of the revival was felt in every nook and cranny of society and spread to other countries around the world.

One person, one family, one church—no matter how "insignificant"—that's committed to seeking the Lord can become a part of the "awakened giant" He will use to spread His glory.

Make It Personal

Follow the four conditions above, and then ask God to use you to impact those around you for His glory.

Common Mercies

Every good and perfect gift is from above,
coming down from the Father of lights.

—JAMES 1:17

Charles Spurgeon once said, "Let us daily praise God for *common mercies*—common as we frequently call them, and yet so priceless that when deprived of them we are ready to perish."[21]

Bath soap. Toothpaste. Hot water. Houseplants. Sunsets. Family photos. Warm clothes. Books. Beautiful music.

People who draw a blank when asked what they're grateful for—after running through the fairly automatic litany of faith and family and food and health—can never be those who draw nearest to God, not when He has given us so many ways to answer this simple question.

These *common mercies* are included in the biblical appeal for "giving thanks always for everything to God the Father in the name of our Lord Jesus Christ" (Eph. 5:20).

People who remember to thank God for everything from pliers and pruners to paper plates are people who know what "everything" is all about. And why shouldn't that person be you?

Make It Personal

What's on your list of common mercies? How can you make it a habit to give thanks to God "always for everything"?

Get God's Word on the Subject

Be diligent to present yourself to God as one approved,
a worker who doesn't need to be ashamed,
correctly teaching the word of truth.

—2 TIMOTHY 2:15

One of our greatest needs as followers of Christ is to become people of the Word so that our prayers and our responses are saturated with God's way of thinking.

The world doesn't need to hear our opinions. When friends approach us for advice, they don't need to hear what we think. We should take them to the Word and say, "I don't have the answers you need, but I know Someone who does. Here's what God's Word has to say about this situation."

God didn't intend for pastors to be the only ones who point people to the Word. Each of us should be able to use the Word effectively, not only in our worship and our own walk but also in ministering to others. If we're going to be people of the Word, we must make a priority of spending time daily in the Scripture.

Make It Personal

How can you further fill your life and your prayers with Scripture?
Ask God to help your words be saturated by His Word.

Once for All

[Christ] doesn't need to offer sacrifices every day....
He did this once for all time when he offered himself.

—HEBREWS 7:27

The Old Testament priests had to offer sacrifices daily, but Jesus' sacrifice was sufficient once for all. The animals sacrificed under the old covenant merely foreshadowed the one sacrifice that would fully atone for sin. Jesus offered Himself—the perfect sacrifice for every sin.

The priests entered the presence of God in the temple once a year, but when Jesus offered His perfect sacrifice, the veil that separated the Most Holy Place from the rest of the temple was torn from top to bottom, thereby opening the way of access to God. The barrier is gone; we can come with confidence into God's presence.

Jesus' priestly work on our behalf isn't over! He intercedes for us in heaven. As we cry out to Jesus, He sympathizes and understands and makes intercession for us to the Father. We don't have to worry that God might reject us for something we did. We can go with confidence in the name of Jesus, because the price for our sin has been paid.

Make It Personal

How does knowing that Christ is interceding for you in heaven help you to endure your present circumstances and press on?

Essential for Your Soul

How joyful is the one whose transgression is forgiven,
whose sin is covered!

—PSALM 32:1

Right after Jesus taught His disciples to ask for their daily bread, He followed it with a petition for forgiveness. Why would He put a request for something so simple as daily bread in the same sentence as something so profound as forgiveness?

In the same way we can't live without food for a prolonged amount of time, we can't live without forgiveness. Just as food, water, and air are essential for our bodies to survive, it's essential for our souls to have forgiveness.

In fact, we need forgiveness more than we need food. Food just feeds our physical bodies, which are temporal. But forgiveness sustains our souls, which will live forever.

Both these requests in the Lord's Prayer show we are utterly dependent on something other than ourselves. Only God can ultimately provide the things we need to sustain our bodies and souls.

So, when we say the Lord's Prayer, we're acknowledging our desperate need for our heavenly Father. We're saying, "Lord, I can't live without these things that only You can supply."

Make It Personal

How is forgiveness essential for your everyday life? Ask God to help you experience the joy that comes through His forgiveness.

Get Rid of the Roots

People are enslaved to whatever defeats them.

—2 PETER 2:19

Most of us have areas of our lives where we are in bondage because we have listened to, believed, and acted on lies. How can we move toward freedom in those practical issues of our lives?

Begin by identifying your personal area of sinful behavior. Chances are, you already know what some of those bondages are. But there may be others that are not as obvious. Are there areas where you are in physical bondage (overeating, an eating disorder, substance abuse)? Are you in emotional bondage (anxiety, fear, depression, chronic emotional disorders), sexual bondage (masturbation, pornography, lust, fornication, homosexuality), or financial bondage (overspending, greed, stinginess)? Are there sinful habits that plague you (anger, lying)?

Once you identify those areas, don't just try to eliminate them. If you want to get rid of poisonous berries, it's not enough to go out and pick all the berries off the bush. More will just grow back in their place. The only way to permanently get rid of the poisonous fruit is to pull the bush out from the roots.

 Make It Personal

Ask God to show you specific areas where you are living in bondage and for help to pull out the roots.

Peace in the Flood

The Lord gives his people strength;
the Lord blesses his people with peace.

—PSALM 29:11

Whatever the storm or flood, whether we're feeling ourselves being dragged under by life's problems and pressures or just fearing how much worse they could get, we can still live with strength and peace.

Amazing. How can such seemingly contradictory experiences coexist?

Storms and strength? Floods and peace? How can the many varieties of troubles we may face, whether in society at large or in the lives we lead at home or at work, result in something other than debilitating distress and panic?

The answer? Heaven rules. The storms and floods of life happen beneath Him, not above Him. Though their waters swell, He is in charge of how far they can reach. And just as surely as He's stirred up those waves, He can also cause them to be still. (See Ps. 107:25, 29.)

This doesn't mean the floods are not dangerous. But it does mean the floods are not final.

 Make It Personal

What floods are you experiencing in life? Ask God to give
you the peace and assurance that He is in control.

A Thankful Heart

In everything, through prayer and petition with thanksgiving,
present your requests to God. And the peace of God . . .
will guard your hearts and minds in Christ Jesus.

—PHILIPPIANS 4:6–7

If you find discouragement, depression, fear, or anxiety among your frequent companions, you may attribute them to difficult or painful circumstances surrounding you. But as challenging as your situation or season of life may be, your frame of mind likely has less to do with your distressing circumstances than with your need to develop a thankful heart.

How else can you explain those believers around the world who scrape by with less than most of us can fathom and whose days are perpetually beset with trials and tragedy, but who nonetheless manifest irrepressible peace and joy?

I'm convinced that we must cultivate the grace and spiritual discipline of gratitude if we are to avoid losing our footing in these turbulent days. An important key to not becoming overwhelmed by what is going on around us is looking for evidence of God's hand at work in the midst of turmoil and being simply overwhelmed with thankfulness to Him.

Make It Personal

How can gratitude help you with discouragement, depression, fear, or anxiety? What can you do today to develop this discipline?

Fully Pardoned

Therefore, there is now no condemnation
for those in Christ Jesus.

—ROMANS 8:1

Satan is a tireless prosecutor and accuser against God's children. He appears, at times, in the high court of heaven and before the throne of God, the righteous Judge. Satan brings charges against us, setting out our sins and failures and faults. When that happens, Jesus approaches the divine Judge and says, "This one has been fully pardoned. Justice has already been carried out, so let the prisoner go."

Because our sin has been reckoned to Jesus' account and His righteousness imputed to us, we're guaranteed an acquittal.

Is Jesus your Advocate? Have you trusted that your sins were placed on Him so His righteousness could be credited to your account? If so, then you can rejoice that there's now no condemnation. And you can have great peace knowing you don't have to fear the wrath of God and nothing can make God love you less.

Yes, we sin, but thanks be to God, we have an Advocate—Christ Jesus!

Make It Personal

How does knowing that Jesus is your Advocate affect how you approach Him? What impact will it have on your life today?

A Living Sacrifice

I urge you to present your bodies as a living sacrifice,
holy and pleasing to God; this is your true worship.

—ROMANS 12:1

Romans 12:1 is the manifesto for the Christian's surrender to God. Our "bodies" represent the sum total of all we are, all we have, and all we do. As those Old Testament believers signified their consecration by offering up sacrifices to be consumed on the altar, so we are to offer ourselves in totality to be consumed by God.

Unlike the Old Testament sacrifices, however, we're to offer ourselves as *living sacrifices*—we are to go on living in these bodies, recognizing that they're not our own, that they belong to God, whose temple we are. The surrender should be made once and for all, as well as a daily, recurring sacrifice of our lives to God.

It's a complete presentation of ourselves to God, devoting to Jesus not just our spare evenings but our whole lives. Being a *living sacrifice* pictures living out that devotion, one day at a time, as we respond to God on the basis of that initial consecration.

 Make It Personal

As you go throughout your day today, consider every act of obedience as an offering to the Lord.

God's Love Draws Us

I took them up by their arms, but they did not know that I healed them. I led them with cords of kindness, with the bands of love.

—HOSEA 11:3–4 ESV

Why does God want to revive our hearts and restore us to a closer relationship with Him? One major reason is He loves us.

We need to beware of misunderstanding the heart and ways of God when we study His dealings with His people, especially in the Old Testament. Due to the numerous accounts of God's judgment recorded there, we might get the impression He was eager to punish or He is harsh, demanding, and impatient. But the opposite is true. Times of judgment usually came after *years* of pleading with His people to come back to Him.

Hosea 11 and 14 provide "before," "during," and "after" snapshots of how and why God revives and renews His people. The constant in all three stages is His love. God loved the Israelites when they were newborns; He loved them after they returned to Him from a season of rebellion; and He loved them throughout the whole process of correcting them.

 Make It Personal

Write a prayer thanking God for His faithful love
and for His desire to restore His people when they
have wandered away from Him.

Hard to Wait

"While the son was still a long way off,
his father saw him and was filled with compassion."

—LUKE 15:20

In Luke 15, Jesus tells three stories about lost things. There's one about a coin misplaced in a house and a woman who vigorously swept the floor until it was found. Then there's one about a sheep that wandered off, and the shepherd was compelled to go searching. But the lost thing in the third story was far more precious than copper currency or a curious lamb could ever be. Unlike the coin or the sheep, the son in the story made a conscious decision to break his father's heart.

The father of the lost boy didn't go on a desperate search for his lost treasure. He didn't gather a posse to bring his son home. Instead, he did the one thing that can be the hardest thing to do in such a situation. He waited. The heartbroken dad in Jesus' parable patiently waited for God to write his own story as well as that of his hardhearted, rebellious, but nonetheless dearly loved offspring.

 Make It Personal

*Ask God for wisdom to know when to do something in the life
of someone you love and when to wait on Him to work.*

The Messiah

He first found his own brother Simon and told him,
"We have found the Messiah."

—JOHN 1:41

The Jews were waiting for God's Messiah but expected He would be a military hero sent to deliver them from political tyranny. When Jesus came, His weapons were humble service, love, and ultimately His death. The Jews, however, had been expecting pomp and circumstance. Because He came without fanfare, they couldn't buy it. They thought it scandalous that God's Anointed One would suffer, hang on a cross, and die.

All the Old Testament prophecies fulfilled by Jesus show God keeps His promises. He doesn't always do it in our way or time. Sometimes we have expectations of what Jesus should be like and what He should do. When He doesn't meet our expectations, we may be tempted to doubt He really is the Lord.

Christ's rule doesn't always lead to flamboyant victories or quick fixes. Sometimes He leads us through seasons of struggle, weakness, and hardship. But our hope and the message we proclaim is that Jesus is the Christ, God's Anointed One, who came to deliver His people from sin and death.

 Make It Personal

Has there ever been a time when Jesus didn't meet your
expectations? What did God teach you through that experience?

A Daily Allotment

"I am going to rain bread from heaven for you."

—EXODUS 16:4

When the children of Israel were in the wilderness, God brought them to a place where they had no provision. These two to three million Jews couldn't see where their next meal was coming from.

So God said, "I'm going to send manna." Each day (except for the Sabbath), they gathered this bread from heaven, getting what they needed for themselves and their families.

The prayer, "Give us today our daily bread," has in mind our physical needs. But it also relates to God's provision for our spiritual, emotional, mental, and relational needs. It's a prayer for sustenance, strength, grace, and wisdom. God sends those to us in daily portions and allotments.

We don't need grace today for the trials we'll face tomorrow. We don't need wisdom today for the problems we'll have next month. So, we're encouraged to ask God for what is sufficient for today, trusting that when tomorrow comes, He'll provide all that's needed.

 Make It Personal

Ask God to provide what you need now and
trust Him to provide the rest when needed.

Not an Add-On

A house is built by wisdom,
and it is established by understanding.
—PROVERBS 24:3

Today it's common for homes to be little more than physical structures where people sleep at night, take their showers in the morning, and then disperse in a hundred different directions. There's little shared life.

And that's the *best*-case scenario. At *worst*, our homes are in utter disarray, characterized by active hostility and oblivious neglect. They may be decorated to the nines, yet the relationships within the walls are seriously fractured—or at least emotionally distant and dishonest.

But home isn't an add-on to our "spiritual" life. It is part and parcel of our discipleship and our calling as children of God. We can't separate our home life from our Christian life without missing something that's critical to our fellowship with God and our usefulness to His mission in the world. When we minimize the importance of establishing and maintaining Christ-centered homes that put the gospel on display, we shortchange the enormous kingdom impact our life at home is supposed to have.

 Make It Personal

Ask God to show you ways that your home currently
reflects Him—and ways that it does not.

"*I Do*"

Therefore, if anyone is in Christ, he is a new creation.

—2 CORINTHIANS 5:17

When a man and woman stand before a minister to join their lives together, they affirm a series of vows, usually by saying "I do." At that moment, they make a full surrender of their lives to each other. They pledge to love each other, to be faithful to each other, and to serve each other.

However, once a couple says "I do"—once they come to that point of initial surrender—they begin a lifetime process of keeping those vows every day, for the rest of their lives. After the candles are blown out, the rice is thrown, and the rented tuxes are returned, they must begin to live out the implications of those vows in the nitty-gritty context of life—for better *and* for worse.

Likewise, in our relationship with the Lord, there's a point at which we say to Him, "I do." Now, on a daily, perpetual basis, we're called to live out that consecration by responding to the various circumstances and choices of life in obedience and surrender to His will.

 Make It Personal

How can you choose to say "I do" to the Lord every day?

Replace It with the Truth

"When the Spirit of truth comes,
he will guide you into all the truth."

—JOHN 16:13

Lies, by their very nature, are deceptive. We need the Lord to help us see that what we have been believing is not true. Once you identify the specific lies you have believed, what's next?

Name the lie and replace it with the truth. Satan is a powerful enemy. His primary weapon is deception. His lies are powerful. But there is something even more powerful than Satan's lies—and that is the truth. Once we identify the lies that have put us in bondage and repent of believing those lies, we have an effective weapon to overcome deception—the weapon of truth.

Each lie must be countered with the corresponding truth. Where we've listened to, dwelt on, believed, and acted on lies, we must begin to listen to, meditate on, believe, and act on the truth. That's how we will move from bondage to freedom, by the power of the Spirit of God. As Jesus declared, it is the truth that "will set you free" (John 8:32).

 Make It Personal

*What truths from God's Word can you meditate on
this week to replace any lies that you've been believing?*

Embracing Wisdom

Happy is a man who finds wisdom and who acquires
understanding, for she is more profitable than silver,
and her revenue is better than gold.

—PROVERBS 3:13–14

Wisdom is the ability to see all of life from God's perspective. It is more than knowledge; it's being able to take that knowledge and act accordingly. When we ask God to give us wisdom and discernment, we're acknowledging that we lack understanding and we need His wisdom.

This may be one of the reasons God delights to put us in situations and circumstances too great for us to handle. It's in these places that we are helpless on our own and we cry out to the Lord.

Scripture describes wisdom as precious, more valuable than either gold or silver. Wisdom is worth pursuing and is the source of true, enduring wealth.

When we embrace the wisdom of God, we find blessings beyond measure. Ultimately, true wisdom is found in Christ. When we abide in Him and are filled with His Spirit, God will make us wise!

 Make It Personal

What are you currently doing to become wiser?
How can you embrace the wisdom of God in your daily life?

A Clear Connection

"If you forgive others their offenses,
your heavenly Father will forgive you as well."
—MATTHEW 6:14

As a kind of PS to the Lord's Prayer, Jesus shows a clear connection between our willingness to forgive others and our ability to receive and experience God's forgiveness.

When we don't forgive, we affect our capacity to receive and experience God's grace and forgiveness. When we do so, we end up in prison ourselves. This explains in part why so many Christians live with chronic discouragement, depression, unresolved guilt, and anger.

Jesus isn't saying you'll lose your salvation or you can't get salvation until you're willing to forgive others. But He is saying that unforgiveness can keep us from experiencing the reality of God's grace and forgiveness.

In order to have that ongoing, open fellowship with God as believers, we need to follow the directive of 1 John 1:9: "If we confess our sins, he is faithful and righteous to forgive us our sins." In order to experience that forgiveness, we must forgive those who have sinned against us.

Make It Personal

How have you seen unforgiveness affect your fellowship with God? How have you seen it put people in "prison"?

A Kinsman-Redeemer

Blessed is the Lord, the God of Israel, because he
has visited and provided redemption for his people.

—LUKE 1:68

The book of Ruth tells of a widow named Naomi and her daughter-in-law, Ruth, who were left without a provider. Their situation was bleak. But rescue came through Boaz, a kinsman-redeemer.

A kinsman-redeemer had to fulfill three qualifications, all of which were fulfilled in Jesus. First, he had to be a relative. Jesus fulfilled this requirement when He took on flesh and at the cross became sin for us.

Second, a kinsman-redeemer had to have the means to redeem. Jesus redeemed us through His own blood. Finally, the kinsman-redeemer had to be willing to redeem. Aren't you glad Jesus wanted us?

Boaz fulfilled all three requirements and redeemed Naomi and Ruth; Jesus paid the price to save us from our sin. He is our nearest Kinsman. God's promised redemption was fulfilled in Him.

 Make It Personal

*Take time to worship Jesus and thank Him for being our
kinsman-redeemer and rescuing us from the destruction of sin.*

Not Even

Among you there must not be even a hint
of sexual immorality, or of any kind of impurity.
—EPHESIANS 5:3 NIV

Ours is obviously not the first period in history to experience the intense battle involved in maintaining a pure heart and walk. Listen to Paul, who urged the Ephesians to have not "even a hint" of sexual immorality.

To modern ears, that may sound antiquated, extreme, and not realistic. But consider the upside of pursuing a lifestyle of purity:

- Joy that comes from being fully surrendered to God.
- Freedom that comes from living inside His loving borders of protection.
- Depth of relationship with others that is possible when the barriers of impurity and impropriety are removed.
- Unity that takes place within marriages when honesty and transparency replace secrets.
- Opportunities to point others to Christ.

Surely it's worth any price to obtain and maintain a life that is pure and above reproach.

 Make It Personal

What are examples of ways we can hint at sexual immorality?
How can we guard against this in our lives?

The Evil of Ingratitude

For people will be . . . ungrateful, unholy, heartless,
unappeasable, slanderous, without self-control. . . .
Avoid such people.

—2 TIMOTHY 3:2–3, 5 ESV

Ingratitude steals it all—healthy relationships, humility, contentment, enjoyment, and the sweet walk with Christ that provides our only access to abundant life.

So, there is a good reason why, in his second letter to Timothy, Paul listed ingratitude right in the middle of such evil companions as abusiveness, heartlessness, brutishness, and treachery (2 Tim. 3:1–5 ESV). Because that's where it belongs. Ingratitude is no less heinous a sin than these other evil traits.

In fact, so powerful is the influence exerted by ingratitude that when we displace it with gratitude, we will likely find a multitude of other sins dislodged from our lives. Notice how Paul instructed the Ephesians, "Obscene and foolish talking or crude joking are not suitable, but rather giving thanks" (Eph. 5:4).

Left to ourselves, we do not naturally gravitate toward gratitude. Yet we can allow the Spirit to make gratitude the new default setting of our hearts.

 Make It Personal

How have you seen ingratitude "steal" from your life?
How can you instead make gratitude your default setting?

The Consequences of Unforgiveness

Don't you know that if you offer yourselves to someone as obedient slaves, you are slaves of that one you obey—either of sin leading to death or of obedience leading to righteousness?

—ROMANS 6:16

I f we choose the path of unforgiveness long enough, we become someone we neither intended nor wanted. We become bitter people.

The more we hold on to our hurts, anger, and bitterness, the more we become slaves to unforgiveness. And the longer we stay in that condition, the more difficult it becomes for those chains to be broken.

Bitterness grows in us when we fail to see the trouble and pain in our lives from God's point of view and when our *expectations* of what life should be diverge from our *reality*.

Life in a sinful, fallen world is painful. As Paul reminds us, "The whole creation has been groaning together with labor pains ... but we ourselves ... groan within ourselves, eagerly waiting for adoption, the redemption of our bodies" (Rom. 8:22–23).

Make It Personal

Is there a pattern of unforgiveness in your life? If so, cry out to the Lord and ask Him to help you change the pattern.

Willing to Hear

I call on you, God, because you will answer me;

listen closely to me; hear what I say.

—PSALM 17:6

You know what it's like to navigate through an automated phone system, spending several minutes concentrating on instructions such as "For billing questions, press 1." After pushing multiple buttons, you may have to hold for several more minutes while waiting to speak with a live human being.

Think about how many people you're waiting on right now. How much of your email is stuck in a friend's inbox, still un-opened? How many times have you left a voicemail, saying, "Please call me back," only to be ignored?

If it's so difficult to talk with customer service representa-tives or even friends, consider how amazing it is that the God of the universe is eager to talk with you at any time. Earthly failures to communicate should remind us of how amazing it is that God is willing to hear and answer our prayers. He has no automated phone system to send you in circles. He has no assistant who answers mail and runs interference. God is avail-able to you right now.

 Make It Personal

Thank the Lord that He's always available to hear
your prayers—and pour out your heart before Him.

The Importance of Truth

"I am the way, the truth, and the life.
No one comes to the Father except through me."

—JOHN 14:6

Anything that's out of alignment with Jesus isn't truth, no matter how true you think it is. Your attitude toward truth will be exactly the same as your attitude toward Jesus. If you reject the truth, you'll reject Jesus. If you love the truth, you'll love Jesus.

Our culture considers it intolerant to insist on a "fixed pitch" that everything must be tuned to. There's a tendency to pit truth against qualities such as love, mercy, and grace—and truth seems to lose out. But truth isn't incompatible with these things. God's truth is never at the expense of mercy, and His mercy is never at the expense of truth.

We don't have to apologize for saying Jesus is the truth. Those who know it are called to be faithful witnesses, pointing people to Him with grace and mercy. That day is coming when the one whose name is Faithful and True will return, and every knee will bow and every tongue confess that Jesus is exactly who He claimed to be.

Make It Personal

What are some voices of "truth" many people follow? What voice do you follow, and what difference does that make in how you live?

Away from Temptation

No one undergoing a trial should say, "I am being tempted
by God," since God is not tempted by evil, and he himself
doesn't tempt anyone.

—JAMES 1:13

"Do not bring us into temptation" (Matt. 6:13) is one of the most difficult phrases in the Lord's Prayer to understand. Does it mean that God sometimes tempts us to sin or He's somehow responsible if we fall into temptation?

God never tempts us to do evil. However, sometimes He places us in situations where our faith is tested. He does this to strengthen our faith and make us more dependent on Him.

When we pray Matthew 6:13, we're asking for help when temptation comes. We're also asking to have victory over temptation. And we're asking God to protect us from situations where we would likely be tempted.

The heart of this prayer is, "Lord, we want You to be magnified and Your name to be hallowed. As we walk through this life, help us realize that You won't lead us anywhere that You won't also give us the grace to deal with whatever we're going to face."

 Make It Personal

*Ask God to help you be on guard
against the dangers of temptation.*

His Sacrifice for Us

For Christ our Passover lamb has been sacrificed.

—1 CORINTHIANS 5:7

God came to Abraham and told him to take his son Isaac to sacrifice as a burnt offering. Abraham obeyed God. He got up early, cut wood for the offering, and headed out to make the sacrifice.

At the appointed place, Abraham put the wood on his son's back and took a knife and the fire to light the sacrifice. That's when Isaac said, "The fire and the wood are here, but where is the lamb for the burnt offering?" Abraham answered, "God himself will provide the lamb for the burnt offering, my son" (Gen. 22:7–8).

God did provide a substitute, foreshadowing that day when God would sacrifice His Son, the Lamb of God, who would die in our place.

For all eternity the Lamb will have a relationship with those He died to save (Rev. 7:17; 19:7, 9). If you don't have a relationship with the Lamb in this life, you won't have one with Him in eternity. But if you do know Him personally, the Lamb will be your Shepherd forever.

 Make It Personal

Take time to reflect on why Jesus' sacrifice was necessary.
Ask God to help you not take it for granted.

Ancient Realities and Modern Eyes

Whatever you do, do it from the heart,
as something done for the Lord and not for people.

—COLOSSIANS 3:23

In the world's eyes, women often derive their identity and status from paid work done outside of the home. This division between the private and public sphere has given rise to heated debates about the place of women and the meaning of home.

However, when Paul exhorted older women to train young women to be "workers at home" (Titus 2:5), he was living in a different setting than our current world. It could seem that Paul was diminishing women's worth and discouraging them from contributing to their church, community, or culture.

But Paul was progressive for his time and culture. He welcomed the participation and partnership of women in his ministry (Rom. 16:1–16) and never disparaged their contributions. Rather he encouraged them to utilize their skills and maximize their assets for the advance of God's kingdom.

 Make It Personal

What images come to mind when you think of being a "worker at home"? How does knowing Paul's perspective help your understanding?

We Are Weak but He Is Strong

The LORD sits enthroned over the flood.

—PSALM 29:10

People rightfully get scared in floods. It's possible to drown in a flood or to lose your home and personal possessions. When the waters recede, you're left to pick through the muck and slime of tarnished memories, unable to comprehend how your life could be in such utter ruin and chaos.

Floods are not to be taken lightly. But watch what your enthroned King does and can do— whatever form the flood takes in your life: "The LORD gives his people strength" (Ps. 29:11).

This statement implies we are weak—and we are. Every one of us faces many circumstances beyond our control in a world that often seems to be falling apart. But "my grace is sufficient for you," the Lord declares to us; "my power is perfected in weakness" (2 Cor. 12:9). That's why we, His people, can humbly, confidently affirm: "When I am weak, then I am strong" (v. 10).

Because He who reigns forever over the flood imparts His strength to those who trust Him with their weakness.

Make It Personal

Ask God to give you the strength you need
to overcome the challenges you face today.

Truth Encounter

Seek the LORD while he may be found;
call to him while he is near.
—ISAIAH 55:6

In the Old Testament, we clearly see God's desire to restore His wayward people. Consider, for example, the prophet Hosea. Hosea prophesied in the northern kingdom of Israel during a period of moral decline ending in destruction by Assyria in 722 BC. Hosea's family was a symbol of God's relationship with His people. His wife was a prostitute (representing spiritual adultery), and his children had prophetic names.

God sent Hosea to prophesy to Israel. Though they were God's chosen people, the nation was in a sad state of spiritual and moral decline. They replaced Him with idols, worldly pursuits, and earthly wealth. It was to these confused fellow countrymen that Hosea delivered repeated rebukes and appeals. If they didn't return to the Lord, he warned, judgment would surely come.

Even though Israel had wandered away from God, His desire was to restore them to Himself. And if we wander away, He desires the same thing for us.

 Make It Personal

Have you ever walked more closely with God than you are right now? What do you need to do to return to Him?

Death Brings Life

"Unless a grain of wheat falls to the ground and dies,
it remains by itself. But if it dies, it produces much fruit."

—JOHN 12:24

Jesus understood something that His disciples would not grasp until after His death, resurrection, and ascension back into heaven—something the Bible calls a "mystery." This mystery is that death brings life and that there can be no real life apart from our willingness to die. To help explain this principle, Jesus used an illustration from the world of farming.

As Jesus pointed out, if a grain of wheat does not fall into the ground and die, "it remains by itself." Our natural instinct is to hold on protectively to our own lives. When we refuse to shed that hard, outer shell called "self," no one can get close to us; no one can penetrate or enter into our life. Just as pride repulses God, so pride keeps others from getting close to us.

True Christian community is something few believers ever experience because it requires that each individual let go of "self" and pour out his life on behalf of others.

 Make It Personal

*Do you hold on to your "self," or can you let go
and let others get close?*

Holiness and Joy

I will shout for joy because of the works of your hands.

—PSALM 92:4

I was blessed to grow up in a home where holiness was emphasized and taken seriously while being presented as something wonderfully desirable. From earliest childhood, I remember thinking that holiness and joy were inseparably bound.

My dad longed to be "as pure as the driven snow" and challenged us to aspire to the same standard. He was deeply disturbed by sin—whether his own, ours, or others'. At the same time, he was a happy man and *enjoyed* his life in Christ.

Prior to his conversion in his mid-twenties, he had been a freewheeling gambler in mad pursuit of happiness and thrills. When God redeemed him, he no longer desired the earthly treasures with which he'd been trying to fill the empty places of his heart. Now he had found "the pearl of great price" he'd been lacking for so many years. He loved God's law and never considered holiness burdensome—he knew sin was the real burden, and he never got over the wonder that God had mercifully relieved him of that burden through Christ.

 Make It Personal

Are holiness and joy bound together in your life?
How can you more fully enjoy your life in Christ?

The End of the Story

"I am the Alpha and the Omega,
the beginning and the end."

—REVELATION 21:6

In Revelation, Christ refers to Himself as "the Alpha and Omega." This name tells us that everything we need—peace, joy, help, grace, love, kindness—is found in Jesus. If it's not found in Him, we don't need it.

In Christ, we have the wonderful assurance that our lives aren't left to chance. Every detail of our existence has been ordained by Him. When we're faced with a scary future, we can remember that Jesus is the first and the last, and we can go forward, knowing it's all wrapped up in Him.

To truly know Him is to be free from the cycle of worry that so many struggle with. Whatever our problems, He is there. He covers and surrounds us. Our trials, no matter how difficult, are not the end of the story. Jesus is!

We live in a fallen, messed-up world, and bad things do happen. But regardless of what happens to us here on earth, we can trust the Lord with our future. We know the end of the story—everlasting life with Him.

 Make It Personal

How does knowing Jesus as the Alpha and Omega encourage
you in any worries and trials you're currently facing?

Sweet Words

Death and life are in the power of the tongue,
and those who love it will eat its fruit.
—PROVERBS 18:21

Sit back and close your eyes. Recall a time when someone said words that really encouraged you. Perhaps it was your mom or dad who said, "I believe in you!" Or maybe a good friend uttered those needed words of affirmation, "Don't give up! You can do it." Or possibly a teacher's words were all you needed when she said, "You have a real gift in this area!"

Proverbs tells us, "Pleasant words are a honeycomb: sweet to the taste and health to the body" (16:24). Notice that we can't separate the body and soul. Sweet words can minister spiritual and physical blessing and health.

Honey is a natural sweetener that boosts energy. Likewise, words of encouragement boost our spirits. I'm so grateful for people who speak affirming, healing words into my life. But I don't want to just be the beneficiary of encouragement; I also want to be an encourager to others.

May we speak healing words that promote good health—words filled with grace, blessing, and hope.

 Make It Personal

Be intentional about speaking words that are
affirming and healing to those around you today.

A Way Out

[God] will not allow you to be tempted beyond what you are able, but with the temptation he will also provide the way out.

—1 CORINTHIANS 10:13

Think about a time when you were in a situation where you knew there was something you shouldn't do, somewhere you shouldn't go, or something you shouldn't be involved in.

You knew it, but you felt overwhelmed by the temptation. Is God responsible? Or is Satan so powerful you can't win? Temptation actually has its source in desires within our own hearts. The situation we were in brought those desires to the surface.

When it comes to our own sin, we're fully responsible. God doesn't tempt us, and Satan can't tempt us beyond what God allows him to do. But we also need to realize we can't resist temptation in our own strength.

God is able to keep us from falling into sin. And He always makes provision for us to resist temptation.

No matter what the circumstance, we need to recognize our need for God's protection, cry out to Him for grace, and cooperate with Him in resisting the evil one.

Make It Personal

Ask God to show you what practical steps you can take to avoid temptation and to stay clear of sin.

A Reflection of God

As through one trespass there is condemnation for everyone,
so also through one righteous act there is justification leading
to life for everyone.

—ROMANS 5:18

Robert Murray McCheyne, a nineteenth-century Scottish pastor, said, "The greatest need of my people is my personal holiness." That applies to more than preachers. The greatest need of your family, friends, and coworkers isn't your friendship or acts of service; it's not your abilities or financial provision. Their greatest need isn't even your verbal witness of your faith.

What they most need is to see in you a reflection of what God is like and of the transforming power of the gospel. Your life can create hunger and thirst for God in others' lives and can be a powerful instrument in the hand of the Holy Spirit to draw their hearts to Christ.

Why care about being holy? Why be willing to say no to your flesh and yes to God, day in and day out? Because the world desperately needs to see what God is like. And because your example may inspire someone who is watching you to choose the pathway of holiness.

 Make It Personal

Ask God to make your life one that will draw others to
Christ because of what they see through your example.

Hints and Hedges

For this is God's will, your sanctification:
that you keep away from sexual immorality.
—1 THESSALONIANS 4:3

Purity can sometimes feel like an unattainable standard. And in fact, it is—apart from the power of the Holy Spirit. But the very fact that Paul urges older women in Titus 2 to teach younger women to be pure suggests that purity can be *learned*.

In my life, I've found it helpful to implement some day-to-day strategies when it comes to sexual purity. I think of these practices as "hedges." Picture rows of manicured shrubbery people might place around their property, establishing a ring of privacy, a barrier to unwanted intruders. Hedges help keep things out, and they help keep things in. That's what these habits can do in your life.

And while these practices don't make us holy in themselves or render us less dependent on the Lord for the desire and power to be pure, they can help us as we wage war against the lure of the world and the cravings of our flesh. They contribute to our sanctification as the Holy Spirit motivates and animates our practical purity.

Make It Personal

How can "personal hedges" be helpful in the pursuit of holiness?
What are your hedges? Do you need to establish some new ones?

It's Just the Way I Am

The woman said, "The serpent deceived me, and I ate."

—GENESIS 3:13

"I can't help the way I am" could never be Eve's story. It wasn't any other person who accounted for the first woman's misery. Nor could Eve blame her environment—it was perfect.

Eve had no one and nothing outside herself to blame for the troubles she encountered. She made a simple, personal choice—there was no one but herself to blame. That choice placed her in bondage and brought untold misery to her life, her family, and every generation that was to follow.

The lie "I can't help the way I am" makes us into helpless victims of other people and outside circumstances. It leaves us without hope that we can ever be any different. Satan knows that if we believe we can't help the way we are, we will never change. The truth is we *do* have a choice. We can be changed by the power of God's Spirit. Once we know and embrace the truth, we can break free from the chains of our past, our circumstances, and even deeply ingrained habit patterns.

Make It Personal

Is there an area of life where you've thought "I can't help being that way"? Ask God to help you change through His power.

Consider the Consequences

The woman saw that the tree was good for food and delightful
to look at, and that it was desirable for obtaining wisdom.

—GENESIS 3:6

If it hadn't seemed so attractive, do you think Eve would have
fallen for Satan's offer? If that fruit had been crawling with
worms, would she have considered disobeying God? Of course
not. What makes Satan's offers so alluring and so deceptive is
that they look so enticing.

Eve didn't stop to evaluate what was really happening.
If she could have imagined the deadly consequences of her
choice—in her own life, in her relationship with God, in her
children, and in every human being that would ever live—
would she have listened to Satan's lie and disobeyed God?

But we have precisely the same problem. Very few Christians seriously consider the consequences of their choices. We
live our lives responding to the people, circumstances, and influences around us—adopting the latest fads, and embracing
the lifestyles and priorities of our friends. It feels so right; it
seems so innocent. But we end up angry, frustrated, trapped,
and overwhelmed. We have fallen for a lie.

 Make It Personal

*Ask the Lord to help you fully consider the consequences
before making any choices—both big and small.*

The Best Counselor

This also comes from the Lord of hosts;
he is wonderful in counsel and excellent in wisdom.

—ISAIAH 28:29 ESV

What makes Jesus such a Wonderful Counselor? *He knows people.* Jesus knows our innermost thoughts and longings. He knows us better than we know ourselves. He understands our needs.

He is able to diagnose our problems. He can help us understand the root issues that need to be dealt with.

He knows the right solution for our problems. He gives counsel that is tailored to our specific situation. It will always be consistent with His Word, and He knows whether we need encouragement, reproof, or practical instruction.

He knows what we need to hear, even if we don't want to hear it. He will tell us the truth about our real condition and the issues in our lives, if we'll listen to Him.

His counsel works. Think of the woman at the well, the thief on the cross, or the demonized man who lived in the tombs. Jesus gave each of them exactly the counsel they needed. And He counsels still today.

 Make It Personal

How has the counsel of Jesus helped you through a difficult time? Is there anything you need His counsel for today?

The Fear of the Lord

The fear of the LORD is the beginning of knowledge;
fools despise wisdom and discipline.

—PROVERBS 1:7

The fear of the Lord is the starting place for wisdom. All other types of knowledge are ultimately useless if they're not grounded in a knowledge of God and in a right relationship with Him. To fear God is to know Him, and to know Him is to fear Him.

Ultimately when we talk about the fear of the Lord, we're talking about that deep sense of reverence and awe that comes from realizing we are in the presence of true greatness. It is that conscious, constant sense of the presence of God—that He is in this place, that He sees, that He knows, that He is with us in this moment.

When we have this sense that we live, breathe, walk, and move in His presence, that awareness will affect every aspect of our lives. It will bring protection, as well as delight and blessing. And as we walk in the fear of the Lord, we will find the greatest joy and freedom possible.

 Make It Personal

What difference would it make in your life to have a constant, conscious awareness that you live in the presence of God?

Pray or Fall Prey

The Lord will rescue me from every evil work.

—2 TIMOTHY 4:18

How often have we fallen into sin because we never asked God to deliver us from it? We need deliverance from evil—not just once but again and again. The more you grow in your love for Christ, the more He will cause that love to surpass your love for sin. But there's never a time when we can afford to let down our guard. Until we're in heaven in the presence of Christ, we will never be immune to temptation or to the potential for falling.

In our warfare against sin and Satan, prayer is a key weapon. We need to develop a lifestyle of praying the Lord's Prayer, not just saying it in church aloud with the congregation. This prayer should be on our breath and in our consciousness all the time.

Pray before you get tempted. Pray when you're in the middle of temptation. And pray when you fall prey to the temptation. Prayer is key to protection, not only for ourselves but also for those we love and for the body of Christ collectively.

 Make It Personal

Are you crying out for God to deliver you from evil?
How can you develop a lifestyle of praying for protection?

A Spiritual Bath

> To the pure, everything is pure, but to those
> who are defiled and unbelieving nothing is pure.
>
> —TITUS 1:15

Christian purity stands in stark contrast to what is characteristic of the unbelieving world. Paul describes the latter in Titus 1:15. He goes on to say: "They claim to know God, but they deny him by their works. They are detestable, disobedient, and unfit for any good work" (v. 16).

These unbelievers are "enslaved by various passions and pleasures" (3:3). We see this everywhere we turn. It's hard to overstate how mainstream impurity has become in our culture.

Have we lost our capacity to be grieved by sin? Are we so accustomed to raunchiness, filth, and viciousness around us that we've become immune to its effects in our hearts?

Our world is awash in moral trash. And this isn't something we can simply blame on "the culture." We all need to take a mental and spiritual bath.

And that's exactly what Christianity offers. This is good news indeed.

 Make It Personal

*How do you think our culture has affected your attitude
toward purity? How can you protect yourself
from becoming desensitized to it?*

Confronting Ingratitude

Give thanks in everything;
for this is God's will for you in Christ Jesus.

—1 THESSALONIANS 5:18

There's something especially distasteful and repulsive about the sin of ingratitude when we see it in others—especially when *we're* the ones whose generosity or sacrifice has gone unrecognized. Jesus, for example, had every reason to be annoyed at those who had received everything they ever wanted from Him yet couldn't be bothered to say thank you!

And yet how often do we neglect to return thanks? Gradually, subtly, we become desensitized as layers of entitlement and resentment wrap themselves around our hearts.

It isn't hard for it to happen . . . even in the most precious of relationships.

Try this: Confront ingratitude and cultivate a thankful spirit in your closest relationship. For the next thirty days, purpose not to say anything negative about your loved one—not to them nor to anyone else about them! Then express at least one thing you appreciate about your loved one. Say it to them *and* to someone else.

 Make It Personal

Take this thirty-day challenge and ask God to
use it to cultivate a thankful spirit in your life.

Treasure Hunt

His mother treasured up all these things in her heart.

—LUKE 2:51 ESV

Two times when describing Mary, we are told that she "treasured up all these things, pondering them in her heart" (Luke 2:19, 51 ESV). The original word translated *treasured* means "to keep carefully; to preserve, keep safe, keep close." Amid the many responsibilities of being a wife and a mother, Mary took time to contemplate what was happening in her life and to meditate on what God had done.

The hurried, hectic, harried pace of our culture can be addictive and intoxicating. Many of us fill every waking moment with noise and activity. Email, voicemail, cellphones, music, and social media threaten to fill every bit of available space and to leave us emotionally and spiritually empty and shallow. If we are going to be instruments of His grace who reflect His light into the darkness around us, we must take time to be quiet—to be still—to ponder and reflect on who God is and what He is doing around us and in us.

 Make It Personal

Today, turn off your phone, social media,
or whatever fills your life with "noise," and
ponder what God is doing in and through you.

Getting Perspective

No discipline seems enjoyable at the time, but painful.
Later on, however, it yields the peaceful fruit of
righteousness to those who have been trained by it.

—HEBREWS 12:11

Hebrews 12 gives us perspective on the hardships we face as believers. It reminds us that God uses the experiences of our lives—*especially* the difficult ones—to do something special in us: to discipline us "for our benefit" (v. 10).

This is about as natural as a child looking forward to being disciplined by his parents! As this passage declares, we've all experienced pain in the process of being trained.

God's not implying that what has occurred in our lives is no big deal. He's not telling you to just shake it off, get a grip, grow up, and get on with it.

No, the teaching of Hebrews 12 should encourage us that God considers these matters weighty enough to require His special care. He wants to use these painful experiences for our spiritual training and maturity. They're part of His eternal purpose and plan to shape us into the image of Jesus, so He can be glorified through our lives.

 Make It Personal

*How has God used painful experiences
in your life to help you grow spiritually?*

Fallow Ground

"Break up your fallow ground, and sow not among thorns."
—JEREMIAH 4:3 ESV

Fallow ground—once plowed, but now lying waste—must be tilled with a sharp plow in order to make the soil ready for seed and, ultimately, fruitful and productive.

The condition of the Western church is remarkably similar to that of Israel when the prophet Jeremiah spoke the words in Jeremiah 4:3. In many ways we too have forsaken God and attempted to replace Him with other gods.

If Jeremiah were preaching now, he would scarcely need to alter his words! He might tell God's people today: return to a time when you obeyed His Word; accept God's mercy and forgive those who have wronged you; allow God to "plow up" the hardened ground of your hearts; and grieve over your sins.

Has there ever been a time when you walked more closely with God than you are right now? Take the words of Jeremiah to heart, and make seeking God your highest pursuit.

 Make It Personal

What do you think it means to "break up
your fallow ground" in your own life?

A Sweet Aroma

Thanks be to God, who . . . through us spreads
the aroma of the knowledge of him in every place.
—2 CORINTHIANS 2:14

The more I study Scripture, the more aware I am of my need for God to keep watch over my speech. My natural self wants to blurt out words. But the Holy Spirit reminds me that my words and life can be a sweet aroma of Christ.

When we speak words that are encouraging, wise, fitting, and true, it is because of His amazing grace. It is because He has opened our eyes and hearts to the truth. I love the first stanza of John Newton's "Amazing Grace":

Amazing grace—how sweet the sound,
That saved a wretch like me!
I once was lost but now am found,
Was blind but now I see.[22]

May you and I begin to sing and speak God's praises each day. May we honor Him with our words in such a way that people marvel, "Hallelujah, what a Savior!"

 Make It Personal

How can the words you speak be a sweet
aroma of Christ to those around you?

He Loves His Sheep

"I am the good shepherd. I know my own, and my own
know me. . . . I lay down my life for the sheep."
—JOHN 10:14–15

The Old Testament tells us about unfaithful human shepherds—religious leaders who were supposed to feed the sheep but fed themselves instead. They cared nothing for the sheep. By contrast, Jesus, the Good Shepherd, loves the sheep.

Unfaithful shepherds abandon the sheep when there's danger, but the Good Shepherd stays with the sheep no matter what. He never leaves them, especially when there's danger. There are times we may feel abandoned by God, but the truth is that He will never abandon us.

Unfaithful shepherds are self-seeking, but the Good Shepherd is self-sacrificing. Unfaithful shepherds come to steal, kill, and destroy, but the Good Shepherd came to give life.

Are you looking to Jesus to shepherd you? If so, He will always be your Shepherd—comforting, guiding, and providing—and you will echo the psalmist who says, "The LORD is my shepherd; I have what I need" (Ps. 23:1).

 Make It Personal

*How can you look to Jesus to shepherd
you throughout your day today?*

Our Deliverer

Who will rescue me from this body of death?
Thanks be to God through Jesus Christ our Lord!
—ROMANS 7:24–25

To be delivered from the evil one and to live a godly life requires constant vigilance. We need to guard our hearts and make constant choices to put off our old self and put on the new.

Do we really want to be completely delivered from sin, or do we just want relief from the consequences? We need to ask God to give us the desire to be completely delivered from *all* evil.

The good news is that deliverance is available. We don't have to succumb to sin. Christ can deliver us because He was assaulted by temptation and yet at every point said yes to the Father (Heb. 4:15).

The greatest strategy in resisting temptation is putting our eyes on Christ and realizing He has paid the price for our deliverance. He succeeded at obeying the will of the Father when He was under temptation, and He will deliver us. Whatever your struggle, the hope for deliverance is Christ.

 Make It Personal

How can you look to Christ to deliver you from sin
instead of struggling to win the battle in your own efforts?

A Breath of Fresh Air

Ascribe to the Lord the glory of his name.

—1 CHRONICLES 16:29

Few things are more attractive in a child of God than a grateful spirit. The opposite is also true; nothing makes a person more *unattractive* than the absence of a grateful spirit.

In every circumstance, I can choose to respond in one of two ways—I can whine or I can worship! And I can't worship without giving thanks. It just isn't possible.

When we choose the pathway of worship and giving thanks, especially in the midst of difficult circumstances, there's a fragrance, a radiance, that issues forth out of our lives to bless the Lord and others.

On the other hand, when we give in to whining, murmuring, and complaining, we end up on a destructive slide that ultimately leads to bitterness and broken relationships.

A grateful man or woman is a breath of fresh air in a world contaminated by bitterness and discontentment. The person whose gratitude is a by-product of and a response to the redeeming grace of God will showcase the gospel in a way that is winsome and compelling.

 Make It Personal

In difficult circumstances, do you tend to whine or to worship?
How can you make a deliberate choice to worship today?

It's All About Him

Who, existing in the form of God, did not consider
equality with God as something to be exploited.

—PHILIPPIANS 2:6

Very little is said of Mary after the birth of Jesus. Apparently, she was content to be identified as Jesus' mother. She was satisfied to be in the background, not well known herself, but making Him known.

The angelic messenger had said of her son, "He will be great" (Luke 1:32). Mary didn't see herself as worthy of God's favor: "He has looked with favor on the humble condition of his servant" (v. 48). Here was a woman who realized, "It's not about me; it's all about Him."

Women don't always get a lot of strokes for being wives and moms faithfully caring for their families. Culture presses women to do something "worthwhile." Even our own hearts long for appreciation for the sacrifices we make. But counter to culture's pressure, the woman God uses is humble; she follows in the steps of Jesus who "emptied himself, by assuming the form of a servant" (Phil. 2:7).

 Make It Personal

How does knowing that the Lord sees what you do
even when no one else does encourage you today?

No Need to Panic

You keep him in perfect peace whose mind is stayed on you,
because he trusts in you.

—ISAIAH 26:3 ESV

The night before Robert's first cancer surgery, I posted some thoughts on social media:

Here are three truths we're clinging to as we head into surgery tomorrow: (1) Anything that makes us need God is a blessing. (2) You can trust God to write your story. (3) Heaven rules!

The Lord blessed us with peace that day. And He has been blessing us that way ever since, the peace interrupted only by times when we forget or fail to believe that Heaven rules.

So, if we know that God has made His strength and peace available to us even in situations that feel unstable and uncertain, panic isn't our only option. Panic, in fact, makes no sense under these conditions.

Our God sits enthroned; our God is King forever (Ps. 29:10). And He can give us not only strength but also peace.

Make It Personal

What are some of the things that are causing you to panic right now? How can you submit them to Heaven's rule?

A Complete Change of Heart

Thomas responded to him, "My Lord and my God!"

—JOHN 20:28

In our culture, we're resistant to thinking of anyone being "lord" over us. We don't want someone telling us what to do. Yet Scripture's offer of salvation is never separated from the call to turn from sin and self and bow to Christ's authority.

"Lord" isn't just a title—it's a name that carries the right to rule. It represents a mandate to obey God and to declare with our hearts, lips, and lives, "Jesus is Lord!"

But there's something in the way—our sin. Confessing and calling on Jesus as Lord represents a complete change of mind and heart. It means repenting from doing what we want to do when we want to do it.

Jesus is our Lord and Savior; those titles are inseparable. Someone who professes to be a Christian but gives no credible evidence of following Christ as Lord can have no basis for assurance of salvation. Certainly change is slow. But someone who stays in that place and experiences no conviction of the Holy Spirit and no repentance likely doesn't have a saving relationship with Christ.

Make It Personal

As others observe your daily life, would they conclude that Jesus is your Lord? How can you surrender everything to Him today?

No Trifling Matter

In him we have redemption through his blood,
the forgiveness of our trespasses.

—EPHESIANS 1:7

I n his devotional, *My Utmost for His Highest*, Oswald Chambers reminds us that at the crux of forgiveness is the cross of Christ. There's no forgiveness possible apart from the cross—and the cross is no trifling matter.

"It is shallow nonsense to say that God forgives us because He is love. . . . The love of God means Calvary—nothing less; the love of God is spelt on the Cross, and nowhere else. The only ground on which God can forgive me is the Cross of my Lord."[23]

We somehow have the idea that God has forgiven us purely out of His kindness, just because He wanted to. Forgiveness is what we sort of expect from a God who wouldn't mind going out of His way to be nice to us. But it makes a huge difference when we realize the ground on which our forgiveness was procured. If we're to forgive others as God has forgiven us, we need to understand how He forgave us. Calvary required an agony we cannot fully comprehend.

 Make It Personal

*Have you ever been guilty of taking God's forgiveness
for granted? Today, reflect on what it meant
for Christ to forgive your sins.*

Instinctive Love

"Love your neighbor as yourself."
—MARK 12:31

How often have we heard someone say, "I've never liked myself," or "She just can't love herself"? According to Scripture, we do love ourselves—immensely. When Jesus tells us to love our neighbors as ourselves, He is saying we need to give others the same attention and care we naturally give ourselves.

If I get a toothache, I look for a way to get rid of it. If I didn't "love myself," I would ignore the pain. But when someone else has a toothache, it's easy to be indifferent. We naturally love ourselves; we don't naturally love others.

The same point is made in Ephesians, where Paul says husbands are to "love their wives as [they instinctively love] their own bodies. . . . For no one ever hates his own flesh but provides and cares for it" (5:28–29).

According to God's Word, we were created in the image of God, He loves us, and we are precious to Him. However, we don't bestow that worth on ourselves. Jesus taught that it is in losing our lives that we find our lives.

 Make It Personal

Ask God to give you opportunities today to love your neighbor
as yourself . . . and to show you practical ways to do it.

True Power

Now to him who is able to do above and beyond all that we ask
or think according to the power that works in us.

—EPHESIANS 3:20

At the end of the Lord's Prayer, we see this statement: "Yours is . . . the power." The power of God is incomprehensible, incomparable, and irresistible. There's nothing like it in all the universe. Jeremiah 32:27 says, "Look, I am the LORD, the God over every creature. Is anything too difficult for me?"

When we come to God and ask Him to meet our daily needs, for pardon for our sins, and for protection from evil, we will never tax His power. No matter what situation we may face, God has the power to protect us from it and help us through it.

God's power is sustaining power. In Him, all things hold together (Col. 1:17). It's His power that keeps us, guards us, and preserves us—and it will until the end.

God created us by His power, and it's that same power that will strengthen us, deliver us, and transform us. Through His power, even the coldest, hardest heart can be revived.

Make It Personal

How have you seen God's power at work in the world around you? How can you rely on it for whatever you face today?

You Are What You Eat

"I am the living bread that came down from heaven.
If anyone eats of this bread he will live forever."
—JOHN 6:51

Not everyone in the crowd was happy to hear Jesus' claim that He was the Bread of Life. Many were angered by His insistence that He's the only way to have life. But Jesus didn't back down. He never tames His claims for those who don't believe.

If you eat this Bread, you live forever. If you don't, you will die. The essence of sin is that we want to rely on something or someone other than Jesus. If we want to live, we must eat of Christ, which means that we come to Him and cease relying on ourselves.

You've heard it said, "You are what you eat." As we feed on Jesus in His Word, we're changed into His likeness. If you gorge on "junk food," you're not going to have much appetite for the true Bread of Life. Jesus and His Word will seem boring. Do you hunger for Jesus? To come to Him in faith is to recognize your desperate daily need for Him.

 Make It Personal

What are some "junk foods" that can dampen
your appetite for Christ? How can you turn
from those and "feed" on Christ instead?

Chosen by God

As you come to him, a living stone—
rejected by people but chosen and honored by God.

—1 PETER 2:4

Many people are desperately seeking affirmation; they're driven to gain the approval of others. It's as if they were trying to balance the scales of the negative input they have received from others.

But in most cases, no number of positive "strokes" can outweigh those negative, hurtful expressions that have led them to believe they're worthless. No amount of affirmation is enough. They can get a hundred compliments about how they look or what they've done, but let one person offer a criticism, and they're devastated. Why? Because they're letting others determine their worth.

There's a wonderful verse in 1 Peter that shows us how Jesus' sense of worth was determined, not by what others thought of Him—good or bad—but by the truth. Jesus was *rejected by men*—those He had created for Himself, those He loved and for whom He laid down His life. But that isn't what determined His value. He was *chosen by God*; that's what made Him precious; that's what determined His worth.

 Make It Personal

*Thank God for the high value He's placed upon you
and that you can find your self-worth in Him.*

Unbridled Gratitude

Where sin multiplied, grace multiplied even more.
—ROMANS 5:20

G race . . . gift . . . gratitude. The words are inseparable! And they should be inseparable in our hearts. Wherever you find *one*, you should also find the others.

Our gracious God generously and gladly bestows grace on us who deserve His judgment and wrath. Those who have received such generous grace respond to the Giver in glad gratitude.

In response to our abounding guilt, God poured out *super*-abounding grace. Should it not follow, then, that super-abounding grace ought to be met by *super-duper*-abounding gratitude?

Is the gratitude that flows out of your life as abounding as the grace that has flowed into your life? *Undeniable guilt* plus *undeserved grace* should equal *unbridled gratitude*.

For too many of us, deep, profound gratitude isn't something that shows up in our lives every day. How do we take what we know and make it what we live?

I say we start by making it our goal to have a heart that's as grateful toward God as the abounding grace He has poured into our life. That ought to keep us grateful for a long, long time.

Make It Personal

How can you make deep gratitude part of your everyday life? Start by thanking God right now for the grace He shows each day!

A Preview of Heaven

"In my Father's house are many rooms. If it were not so, would
I have told you that I am going to prepare a place for you?"

—JOHN 14:2

When we cultivate homes where others can grow and be nurtured, where they feel loved and cared for, we put the heart and character of God on display.

This connection may not be immediately obvious. But what God can do in the hearts of our family, working through the orderly, graceful, creative labors of our homemaking, is far more significant than what appears on the surface.

The welcoming atmosphere we provide, the errands we run, the care we provide, and the efforts we take—each of these daily actions reveals in miniature an aspect of God's nature. The often tedious and mundane tasks of homemaking become acts of worship, our ordinary movements works of art.

This is the goal of all our working at home—the previews of heaven we're able to provide to our family, neighbors, guests. With every act of planning and nurturing, we demonstrate realities that are supreme and ultimate. We create a taste for things above.

 Make It Personal

*How does the gospel embody homemaking? How can tending
well to your home point others to spiritual realities?*

Let Him Love You

When Jesus saw his mother and the disciple he loved standing
there, he said to his mother, "Woman, here is your son."
Then he said to the disciple, "Here is your mother."

—JOHN 19:26–27

Not only did Mary love her Son, she was dearly loved by
Jesus. In the final moments of His life, Jesus made sure
that His widowed mother would be cared for and that her
needs would be met. He provided means of grace for her within
the context of the family of God. She accepted His love and
provision for her needs.

As I minister all over the world, I find so many Christian
women who feel unloved and emotionally needy. When they
look to the things of this earth to fill their emotional void,
they invariably end up empty and disappointed. No one and
nothing can fill that God-sized vacuum. But in Jesus we have
One who knows and understands us, who loves us fervently,
and who cares for us and has provided for our needs.

The question is, will we believe His promise? Will we let
Him love us? Will we receive His provision?

 Make It Personal

How has God provided for your needs?
Thank Him for His past provision and that
He will provide whatever you need in the future.

A Powerful Legacy

Devote yourselves to prayer;
stay alert in it with thanksgiving.
—COLOSSIANS 4:2

Your heart may be breaking over a child or grandchild who is being held captive by Satan's lies. You cannot open his eyes; you cannot turn her heart.

What can you do? You can let God change you, even as you're longing for Him to change your child. You can pray and gather a few trusted confidants to join you.

You can trust that God is not only writing your story; He is also writing your child's story. And because of this, you can resist the temptation to pick up the pen and take over. You can wait patiently for the Lord to act in His time and His way. And you can demonstrate and declare that God is worthy of your worship and trust and that He is still good—even if your heart is breaking, even if your child's heart or circumstances never change.

This is the walk of faith that cherishes and honors the Lord above all other loves. And this is a powerful legacy you leave to those who are coming behind you.

 Make It Personal

*How can you declare the Lord's goodness today in a
hard situation where you're waiting on Him to work?*

Our Need for a Savior

"The Son of Man has come to seek and to save the lost."
—LUKE 19:10

News commentators spend countless hours debating what will bring change to our society, but we rarely hear any mention that our greatest need is salvation. Ever since the Fall, all of mankind has been in desperate need of deliverance. We need a Savior.

A savior rescues, heals, and preserves—and He has come. Our Savior is Jesus.

It's important to know your need of this Savior; if you don't, then you'll never embrace Him. When my childhood home burned when I was in high school, my family was deeply grateful for those who came to save us from the fire—we knew we needed to be rescued!

The wrath of God is a far worse fate than any earthly disaster. Jesus came to save us from divine judgment. Either you will have salvation through Jesus Christ, or you'll experience the eternal wrath and judgment of a holy God because of your sin.

There is salvation in no one but Jesus. If we want deliverance, there's no other place we can look.

 Make It Personal

Do you recall a time when you realized you needed to be rescued by Jesus? What showed you your need for a Savior?

The Choice to Forgive

Be kind and compassionate to one another, forgiving one
another, just as God also forgave you in Christ.

—EPHESIANS 4:32

Nowhere in Scripture will we come upon a secret formula for forgiveness. It's not a method to be learned as much as a truth to be lived. The concept of forgiveness isn't foreign to most of us. The problem is we simply haven't made the choice to forgive.

In urging you to choose the pathway of forgiveness, I don't intend to imply that what you've suffered isn't real. I don't want to minimize the experiences that have made a painful imprint on your soul. In fact, though some may insist you need to "forgive and forget," the truth is that forgiveness at its best requires you to face how badly you've been hurt.

But along the way, as we study God's Word, we discover this hard yet healing truth: whatever sin has been committed against you, the choice not to forgive is itself a serious sin. In fact, failing to forgive can often bring about problems in your life far worse and more long-term than the pain of the original offense.

 Make It Personal

*Is there someone you need to forgive? What steps can
you take today to choose the pathway of forgiveness?*

It Belongs to Him

Yours, LORD, is the kingdom,
and you are exalted as head over all.

—1 CHRONICLES 29:11

Yours, LORD, is the kingdom." When we say these words, we're declaring that God is the King here and now. He made everything, He owns everything, and He has the right to rule over it all.

As we make this affirmation, it means the kingdom isn't ours. We're not in control, and God has the right to do what He wants with our lives, our families, and our world.

It also means the kingdom doesn't belong to Satan or the rulers of this world, even though it may sometimes seem that wicked people are in control.

If we really believe the kingdom is God's, we will obey Him and surrender to Him as King. We will trust He is in control of all events in this world, as well as those of our own personal worlds. We will proclaim His kingdom, His reign, and His rule in every way possible.

When we know that His is the kingdom, we can live in hope and confidence of God's ultimate reign and rule over all creation.

 Make It Personal

*What difference should knowing this is God's kingdom
make in your family? In your workplace? In the world?*

Connected to the Head

He subjected everything under his feet and appointed
him as head over everything for the church.

—EPHESIANS 1:22

A head and a body: that's an important metaphor Paul uses to describe the relationship between Christ and believers. From a physiological standpoint, a head and a body are organically united. Just so, Jesus is organically, inseparably connected to His body, the Church. The Church isn't an institution; it's a living organism. The Church derives its life from its Head, Christ. We have no life apart from Him, and those who are not connected to Him are dead, spiritually speaking.

As the Head of the Church, Jesus is the "brain"—the control center for every function of His body. He rules over His Church. He knows what every member of the body needs, and He supplies those needs.

Paul says we must hold fast to Christ. If we have a right relationship with our Head, then we will have a right relationship with other members of the body. The body can't function unless the individual members are connected to each other and all the members together are connected to the Head.

 Make It Personal

What blessings do those in the body of Christ
receive from being connected to Christ, our Head?

Time to Evaluate

Their abundant joy and their extreme poverty
overflowed in a wealth of generosity on their part.

—2 CORINTHIANS 8:2

When I was young, God placed in my heart the desire to give everything I possibly can during my lifetime for the sake of Christ and His kingdom. I've always found this is the most joyous and secure way to live.

If we want to have the heart of Jesus, we should always be looking for opportunities to give spontaneously and extravagantly. Consider the specific needs in the body of Christ that God may allow us to help meet:

- Helping a family provide Christian education for their children.
- Ministering to the needs of a widow on a limited income.
- Supporting various ministries and missionaries, as well as the ministry of our own local churches.
- Making available an extra bedroom in our home for those who need a place to stay.

 Make It Personal

Ask God to reveal opportunities where you can share with others the blessings and resources He has entrusted to you.

A Grand and Glorious Goal

An excellent wife who can find?
She is far more precious than jewels.
—PROVERBS 31:10 ESV

The "excellent wife" in Proverbs 31 is perhaps the best known biblical example of a woman creating a taste of heaven in her home. This woman is servant-hearted and conscientiously cares for the needs of her family and home. Her life shines a spotlight on the God she fears and loves.

My mother embodied this ideal in many ways, as she cared for the seven of us children. The task of planning, managing, and corralling the hubbub of life and ministry in the DeMoss house was not for the fainthearted.

Yet my mother oversaw all this and more with remarkable grace. She served her family and her Savior through her devotion to our home. Countless people found Jesus in that home, having been extended the gracious hospitality and gospel witness my parents offered.

My mother worked hard to create an atmosphere in our home that reflected God's beauty, His order, and His merciful, welcoming heart. In so doing, she gave our hearts a taste for heaven.

Make It Personal

Think of someone you know who has created a home that is a reflection of the gospel. What makes you feel that way?

Sit Quietly

Whatever is true, whatever is honorable,
whatever is just, whatever is pure, whatever is lovely,
whatever is commendable . . . dwell on these things.

—PHILIPPIANS 4:8

In his book *The Seeking Heart*, Fenelon gives this wise counsel: "What you really need to do is sit quietly before God and your active and argumentative mind would soon be calmed. God can teach you to look at each matter with a simple, clear view."[24]

When my mind gets "active and argumentative," I'm not usually inclined to be calm and sit quietly before the Lord. Yet that's exactly what I need to do.

Philippians 4:8 tells us to think on the things that are virtuous and of good report. It's no secret that our thoughts reveal themselves in actions . . . and in words. So, if we want to speak words that are true, pure, lovely, etc., we need to fill our minds with those kinds of thoughts!

Our thoughts and words will be transformed as we spend time quietly before the Lord, letting Him show us His view, as we meditate on His Word.

 Make It Personal

Take time today to sit quietly in the Lord's presence.

To God Be the Glory

Ascribe to the LORD the glory due his name.

—PSALM 29:2

The purpose of every created thing is to give God the glory due His name. That's the end of all things, "that at the name of Jesus every knee will bow—in heaven and on earth and under the earth—and every tongue will confess that Jesus Christ is Lord, to the glory of God the Father" (Phil. 2:10–11).

To give God the glory means we have a high opinion of Him, that we think right thoughts about Him. It means we recognize His glorious presence and praise Him for the qualities that His acts reveal. It's to recognize where God is at work, where He is moving, and to praise Him for it.

Ultimately, we're to reflect God's glory to others around us. As His qualities are seen in our lives, He is glorified in us. As we display His ways, His beauty, His grace, and His deeds, then we become reflectors of His glory, much as the moon reflects the light of the sun. Our goal is to make Him known to the people of this world.

Make It Personal

*As others observe your life, what does it
reflect to the world about God?*

Your Price Tag

"For God so loved the world, that he gave his only Son, that whoever believes in him should not perish but have eternal life."

—JOHN 3:16 ESV

Our sense of worth is often determined by the opinions of others. Sometimes these are accurate and helpful. But not always.

If, for some reason, the people we're listening to are looking through a defective "lens," their vision will be distorted. Some of us have lived all our lives in an emotional prison because we have accepted what a false, "broken" mirror said.

It's conceivable that someone who didn't recognize or appreciate fine art would toss a masterpiece into the trash. Would that make the painting any less valuable? Not at all. The true worth would be seen when an art collector spotted the painting and said, "That is a priceless piece. I am willing to pay any amount to acquire it."

When God sent His only Son, Jesus, to bear our sins on the cross, He put a price tag on us—He declared the value of our souls to be greater than the value of the whole world. Whose opinion will you accept?

 Make It Personal

What distorted views of yourself have you believed?
How can you be set free by the truth of the cross?

Living Like We're Married

I also saw the holy city, the new Jerusalem,
coming down out of heaven from God,
prepared like a bride adorned for her husband.

—REVELATION 21:2

Just as a bridegroom woos a bride, Christ woos us. As a bridegroom rejoices when his proposal of marriage is accepted, Christ rejoices when we say yes to Him. As a bridegroom prepares a home for his wife, Christ prepares a place for us to live with Him.

As a groom pledges lifetime love to his bride, Christ says, "I will never leave you or abandon you" (Heb. 13:5). As the groom gives the bride his name, Christ has given us His name. As the groom assumes responsibility to provide for his bride, Christ provides us with everything we need.

Our divine Bridegroom delights in being with His bride. He shares His life with her for the long term. He wants an exclusive, faithful relationship with her. If we allow worldly attractions to pull our hearts away, we commit spiritual adultery against our Bridegroom. It may be tempting to live as though we're single, but if we belong to Jesus, we're already married!

 Make It Personal

Thank God for Christ, our perfect Bridegroom,
who fulfills all our needs and will never abandon us.

Sin Destroys

For you are not a God who delights in wickedness;

evil cannot dwell with you.

—PSALM 5:4

S in destroys our fellowship with God. We can sing praise choruses loudly enough to be heard in the next county; we can join sell-out crowds in cheering for God at concerts and conferences; we can applaud speakers who stir our emotions; we can have mystical spiritual experiences. But none of that will get us one iota closer to God if we are ignoring or cherishing sin in our hearts.

"Who among us can dwell with a consuming fire?" the prophet asked. "The one who lives righteously" (Isa. 33:14–15). Intimacy with God is reserved for those who are holy: "For the LORD is righteous; he loves righteous deeds. The upright will see his face" (Ps. 11:7).

Do you see the destruction that sin causes in your life? If you are a child of God, sin keeps you from the intimate relationship God has made possible. Let it be your heart's desire to actively pursue a holy life and grow to be more like the One who has saved you.

 Make It Personal

Is there any sin in your life keeping you from an intimate relationship with God? Ask Him to give you victory in those areas.

God's Faithful Love

You must return to your God. Maintain love and justice,
and always put your hope in God.

—HOSEA 12:6

G od's unfathomable love for us moves Him to draw us
back to Him when we've strayed. It was His love for
Israel, in fact, that caused them to want to return to Him. It
wasn't that they suddenly felt love for Him again, or that they
somehow remembered how wonderful it was to live with an
awareness of God's love. It was that God *caused* them to desire
that love relationship again.

He enabled His people to see not only how wrong they
had been and why His discipline was necessary but also that
He would welcome their return because He had never ceased
loving them.

Perhaps your own heart is hungering for intimacy with
God—an intimacy that you haven't enjoyed for a long time or
perhaps have never known. That very desire is God-initiated.
He wants you back! Why?

Because He loves you and knows that you cannot experience all He has for you in your present condition.

 Make It Personal

*Write a prayer thanking God for His faithful love and for His desire
to restore His people when they have wandered away from Him.*

He'll Always Be There

The Rock—his work is perfect; all his ways are just.
A faithful God, without bias, he is righteous and true.

—DEUTERONOMY 32:4

Certainly there are times when God's relentless holiness feels more like a burden than a blessing. We find ourselves almost wishing that His flawless example and righteous requirements weren't always so rock-solid and unbending.

And yet what divine mercy, that even when our human natures might shortsightedly wish for some wiggle room inside His absolute standard of perfection, we can always be sure that God is holy and He is faithful. His holiness is more unshakable than the Rock of Gibraltar. While everyone else around us is subject to instability and change, He is always the same.

This steadfastness of God isn't something to bristle at and quaver under. Rather it's a gift, the "blessed assurance" that no matter how unreliable those around us may be, no matter how unstable our own footing, or how often or far we may fall, God will always be there, ever true, ever trustworthy.

God is ever true, ever trustworthy, faithful, and holy. Let us be grateful.

 Make It Personal

List ways you can thank the Lord for His steadfastness
and unchanging faithfulness in your life.

God Alone

The scribes and the Pharisees began to think to themselves,
"Who is this man who speaks blasphemies?
Who can forgive sins but God alone?"

—LUKE 5:21

Remember the time in Jesus' ministry when the men brought their friend to be healed, lowering him through the roof because the crowd was so large? Jesus said to the paralyzed man, "Your sins are forgiven," to which the Pharisees protested, "Who is this man who speaks blasphemies?"

There was a lot wrong with their attitude but not with their question. *Who can forgive sins but God alone?* No one. This is important to remember, especially when all the regret, shame, and guilt leads you to say, "I just can't forgive myself."

Perhaps you're having a hard time getting past a decision that cost you a good job. Or a moment where you failed to keep one of your children safe. It could be any of a million things.

You may try to forgive yourself, but that will not lead to healing. Nowhere in the Scripture does God instruct us to deal with heartache this way. He urges us to receive *His* forgiveness.

Make It Personal

Are there any areas in life where you're struggling to forgive yourself? Instead, take them to God and receive His forgiveness.

Creation in Control

How countless are your works, Lord!
In wisdom you have made them all.

—PSALM 104:24

Psalm 104 describes the world when it was fresh and new and in submission to God. We see a definite, unquestioned hierarchy in which God acts, initiates, directs, sets boundaries, supervises, and lovingly rules over His creation. The creation looks to Him, waits for Him, bows before Him, surrenders to His control, and does as He directs.

The oceans stay within the boundaries He has established. The grass and the trees grow according to God's direction and provide nourishment for man and animals. The sun and moon keep their appointed seasons; the animals get up when God tells them to get up and they lie down when God directs them to do so.

What's the result? "The earth is satisfied" (v. 13); "they are satisfied with good things" (v. 28). To surrender to the Creator's control is not onerous or burdensome; it is, in fact, the place of blessing and peace. There's no evidence in this passage of any stress or strain. Because the creation isn't vying with the Creator for control.

🌿 Make It Personal

Are you vying with God today over control of some area of your life? How would surrendering to His will bring you blessing and peace?

Bowing to Our King

He has a name written on his robe and on his thigh:
King of Kings and Lord of Lords.
—REVELATION 19:16

One of my favorite chapters in God's Word is Revelation 19. It's an amazing picture of our coming King. No longer will Jesus wear a crown of thorns. He will be wearing the crown God gave Him when He was exalted as the King of Kings (v. 12).

But that's not the end of the story. Satan and all those who resist God's reign wage war against Jesus. Eventually, those who lead rebellions against Christ are "thrown alive into the lake of fire" (v. 20). There is total devastation and ruin for all who refuse to bow before Jesus.

In the end, King Jesus triumphs. He will have the final word over all other kings, over every human being, and over this entire world that He is redeeming and making new.

So, will we let Jesus have His rightful place as King? If we resist His rule in our lives, we will lose. Those who willingly, gladly, wholeheartedly bow before Him will share in His ultimate, eternal triumph.

Make It Personal

Are there any areas of life where
you're trying to be your own king?

A Pure Legacy

May your whole spirit, soul, and body be kept sound
and blameless at the coming of our Lord Jesus Christ.
—1 THESSALONIANS 5:23

I have a friend whose parents moved out of the house where they'd lived for fifty years. My friend spent a month sorting through a lifetime of their accumulated "stuff"—correspondence, financial data, photos, etc. "It was a complete record of their lives," my friend reflected.

After poring through this massive collection, this son observed, "There wasn't one single thing in my parents' belongings inconsistent with their relationship with Christ!"

How would you fare if someone were to go through the record of your life—all your possessions, journals, correspondence, emails, a record of your internet activity?

What if the person could also review a photographic replay of the choices you've made when you thought no one was watching? Add to that a script of your thought life . . . your attitudes . . . your secret motives. A commitment to be holy and pure is a commitment to be clean through and through.

 Make It Personal

Is everything in your life "record" consistent with your profession of Christ? If not, what do you need to do for that to be true?

Forever and Ever

He will reign forever and ever.

—REVELATION 11:15

The fact that God is forever means He is unchanging. He was here in the beginning, He's been here ever since, and He'll be here long after everything He's created is gone. In that whole time span, He never will have changed.

The Scriptures describe several aspects of God that will endure forever. They include His name (Ps. 72:17), His righteousness (Ps. 111:3), His faithfulness (Ps. 117:2), His Word (Isa. 40:8), His glory (Ps. 104:31), His counsel (Ps. 33:11), His reign (Ps. 45:6), and His steadfast love (Ps. 106:1). These aspects of God endure past our sins and our failures.

Because the Lord is forever, He will outlast every problem we have, every pain we bear, and every stress we carry. When we've exhausted our own endurance, strength, and power, His has only just begun to be expressed to us and through us.

Because He is forever, we can cry out to Him, "Lord, I'm failing. I can't hang on. Help me cling to Your power and glory that endure for all eternity."

Make It Personal

How does knowing that God is forever affect your perspective on your current struggles as well as what's happening in the world?

The King's Choice

When Rehoboam had established his sovereignty
and royal power, he abandoned the law of the LORD—
he and all Israel with him.

—2 CHRONICLES 12:1

The inclination of our hearts toward pride or humility becomes evident when God brings to our attention something in our lives that isn't pleasing to Him. The way we respond in moments of conviction reveals the true condition of our heart. This is illustrated in the life of Rehoboam, king of Israel.

Rehoboam inherited the throne from his father, Solomon. Rehoboam's heart was filled with sin and self. He had led the nation far away from God. The Lord raised up an enemy to punish Rehoboam for his rebellion. God wanted him to understand why the nation was under siege, so He sent a prophet to explain.

Read what happened next: "The leaders of Israel and the king humbled themselves and said, 'The LORD is righteous.'" The Lord responded, "They have humbled themselves; I will not destroy them but will grant them a little deliverance" (2 Chron. 12:6–7).

Because Rehoboam chose to demonstrate humility before God, the whole nation benefited.

🌿 Make It Personal

How do you normally respond when you are confronted with sin?
What does that reveal about the condition of your heart?

The Amen

"Write to the angel of the church in Laodicea:
Thus says the Amen, the faithful and true witness."

—REVELATION 3:14

Whatever you need, whatever your season of life, whatever your circumstance, whatever your challenge, you will find all you need in the name of Jesus. He is worthy of all your trust and obedience, which is what the believers in the church at Laodicea had forgotten.

In Revelation there are letters to seven churches, and the one to Laodicea is the final letter. This church was in the worst spiritual condition of all seven, and Jesus has firm words for them. He begins by reminding those believers who He is (Rev. 3:14). Jesus is the Amen, which means that He is constant and unchanging. This name fits Him perfectly. In fact, in its truest sense, it couldn't apply to anyone else.

He's the one who searches and inspects hearts. He knows the truth; He knows our true condition. He is about to tell the Laodicean church the truth about themselves, which is quite different from their perception. What about you? Do you trust His assessment of your true condition?

Make It Personal

Ask Jesus to reveal the true condition of your heart—and then for the wisdom and grace to live in a way that glorifies Him.

He Stooped Down

[Jesus] emptied himself by assuming the form of a servant.

—PHILIPPIANS 2:7

We've been chosen as servants of the Lord—to carry out His purposes in the world. But we've failed to be the servants we ought to be. So often we would rather be served than serve. We're reluctant to lay down our lives when it's inconvenient or costly.

Yes, we have failed, but Jesus is the righteous substitute for the failed servant. He succeeded where we have failed.

Isaiah 52:13 tells us, "See, my servant will be successful; he will be raised and lifted up and greatly exalted." God's Servant stooped down. He obeyed the Father and came to earth to serve fallen creatures who should have been the servants.

The exalted King became the humble Servant! He set aside His crown to serve us. If He hadn't done so, we would have no hope. But He did come, and He served. He stooped down and washed the feet of those who should have been servants in order to raise us up. Shall we not with grateful hearts forever delight to serve Him in turn?

 Make It Personal

How can you follow Jesus' example today and put aside your own wants and needs in order to serve others?

Eye Problems

The LORD God is a sun and shield.
The LORD grants favor and honor;
he does not withhold the good
from those who live with integrity.

—PSALM 84:11

Several months ago, one of my eyes became extremely irritated and I began to have problems wearing my contact lens. My eye doctor discovered the lens had been damaged and to restore my vision, it had to be replaced with a new one.

What we believe about God is crucial because it affects what we believe about everything else. A damaged view of God will distort the way we see everything around us. Frequently we fail to realize that what is causing the irritation and turmoil within our souls is not the people or the circumstances we think are annoying us; rather the problem is that we are seeing things through a damaged lens.

One of the areas that is particularly impacted by our view of God is our view of ourselves. If we do not see Him as He really is—if we believe things about Him that are not true—invariably, we will have a distorted view of ourselves.

 Make It Personal

*Take time to reflect on what you think about God—
and how you see yourself. Is it correct or distorted?*

Extreme Holiness

"You are to be holy to me because I, the LORD, am holy."
—LEVITICUS 20:26

The congregation of the Gustaf Adolph Evangelical Lutheran Church, located in a small town in northern Maine, learned just how dangerous a little bit of impurity can be. On April 27, 2003, the church council gathered after services to discuss the installation of a new heater. Several people stopped by the kitchen to grab a cup of coffee on the way into the meeting. Within hours more than a dozen were gravely ill, and within days one man had died.

Investigators discovered a man with a vendetta had dropped a handful of powdered arsenic in the church's coffee urn. No one had noticed the small amount of poison—until its consequences became apparent. Like the bit of leaven that leavens a whole lump of dough, tolerating "just a little sin" in our lives can be deadly.

A commitment to be holy is a commitment to be clean through and through—to have no unholy part. True holiness starts on the inside—with our thoughts, attitudes, values, and motives—those innermost parts of our hearts that only God can see.

 Make It Personal

What does God see in your heart?
Ask Him to give you a passion to live a life of true holiness.

Joy and Relief

How joyful is a person whom
the LORD does not charge with iniquity.
—PSALM 32:2

Read the opening verses of Psalm 32, and you can almost hear the joy and relief returning to David's spirit after he confessed his sin to God. When he finally let go of his pride, humbled himself, and got honest with God and others about his sin, heaven-sent relief poured over him. The weight of his iniquity was lifted, and his sin was carried away.

That can be your experience too. As Psalm 32 indicates, God is willing to cover (with the blood of Christ) every sin that we are willing to "uncover" before Him. If David could experience the freedom and joy of a restored relationship with God after committing such great sin, you can know it too!

Simply begin with the matter at hand—whatever sin God may be convicting you of, whether "large" or "small." Remember no sin is so large that God cannot forgive it, and no sin is so small that you can afford to keep it hidden.

 Make It Personal

Do you need to be honest with God about some sin in your life?
Pause right now to confess it to Him.

A Good Report

Whoever spreads slander is a fool.

—PROVERBS 10:18

Although it happened decades ago, it seems like yesterday I was unjustly slandered and my reputation and pride hurt. Although devastated at the time, I can look back and see how God used that incident to mature me in several areas. One valuable lesson I learned was the damage we do when we spread an "evil report."

There have been times when I've put another Christian in a bad light by repeating needless information. As a result, I've had to ask forgiveness. Having to humble myself and deal with those issues has taught me to be more careful about what I say about others.

If we approach God in humility, He will convict us when our words don't please Him. Ask, "Is this a good report of this person? Have I verified the facts? Are my words kind and necessary?"

Philippians 4:8 is a good test for both our thoughts and our words: "Whatever is true, whatever is honorable, whatever is just, whatever is pure, whatever is lovely, whatever is commendable ... dwell on these things."

 Make It Personal

Ask the Lord to help you be wise when speaking of others.

Open and Exposed

If we walk in the light as he himself is in the light,
we have fellowship with one another.

—1 JOHN 1:7

In 1 John, the apostle explains that our relationship with God is inseparably linked to our relationship with other believers. Brokenness in the life of a believer has both a vertical and a horizontal dimension—it goes two ways.

First, a broken person walks in transparent honesty and humility before God. That's what it means to "walk in the light." Our lives are open and exposed before the eyes of Him who knows and sees all. Walking in the light means there is nothing between my soul and my Savior.

However, it's not enough that we be humble and broken before God. Invariably, our relationship with God is reflected in our relationships with others. A person who has been broken before God will also be humble and broken before others. One writer has likened our lives to a house with a roof and walls.[25] For our hearts to be revived, the roof must come off (brokenness toward God) and the walls must come down (brokenness toward man).

Make It Personal

*Ask the Lord to help you be humble
and broken before Him and others.*

Amen!

> "For Yours is the kingdom and the power
> and the glory forever. Amen."
>
> —MATTHEW 6:13 NKJV

*A*men is more than just a word on the end of a prayer. It's a direct transliteration of a Hebrew word that means "firmness" or "truth." It refers to something reliable, true, and absolutely certain.

When we say "amen," we're saying we're in wholehearted agreement that what has just been said is the truth or we're affirming it's in accordance with God's will.

When we pray the last line of the Lord's Prayer, we're saying yes to all of it. Yes, Lord, I want Your name to be hallowed. I want Your kingdom to come. I want Your will to be done above everything else.

Yes, I need daily bread, and I believe You will supply it. I need forgiveness and the grace to forgive others as You have pardoned me through Jesus Christ. Yes, I need help against temptation. I need to be delivered from evil. I acknowledge that all the kingdom, all the power, and all the glory belong to You forever.

Make It Personal

Can you truly in your heart say "amen" to each part of the Lord's Prayer? Which parts do you need to surrender to God?

Scripture Verses

DATE	VERSE(S)	DATE	VERSE(S)
January 1	Genesis 1:3	January 27	Philippians 4:19
January 2	Psalm 139:16	January 28	James 4:7
January 3	1 Corinthians 6:19–20	January 29	1 Peter 1:16
January 4	Proverbs 10:20	January 30	Psalm 119:50
January 5	Luke 11:1	January 31	Psalm 103:2
January 6	John 5:37–38	February 1	Daniel 2:23
January 7	Titus 2:10	February 2	James 4:10
January 8	Hebrews 4:13	February 3	Genesis 3:5
January 9	2 Timothy 3:16	February 4	Proverbs 16:23
January 10	Isaiah 41:10	February 5	Matthew 20:28
January 11	Psalm 103:12	February 6	Psalm 43:5
January 12	Colossians 3:2	February 7	Matthew 5:7
January 13	Proverbs 4:23	February 8	John 17:1
January 14	Matthew 5:3	February 9	Psalm 35:18
January 15	2 Peter 3:16	February 10	Matthew 16:25
January 16	Ephesians 1:4	February 11	Jeremiah 3:1
January 17	2 Peter 1:3	February 12	Psalm 2:12
January 18	Habakkuk 1:12	February 13	Ephesians 5:20
January 19	Romans 12:5	February 14	Genesis 32:24
January 20	Psalm 25:4	February 15	Matthew 19:26
January 21	Matthew 6:26	February 16	Exodus 14:13–14
January 22	Proverbs 15:1	February 17	Hosea 10:12
January 23	Psalm 119:105	February 18	Isaiah 9:6
January 24	1 John 1:6	February 19	1 Timothy 2:1
January 25	Psalm 119:9	February 20	Titus 2:1
January 26	John 15:9	February 21	Daniel 4:26
		February 22	Matthew 7:24

DATE	VERSE(S)	DATE	VERSE(S)
February 23	John 6:63	March 27	1 Peter 2:5
February 24	Habakkuk 3:17–18	March 28	Lamentations 3:22–23
February 25	Job 34:21		
February 26	James 4:8	March 29	2 Timothy 4:2
February 27	Ephesians 5:27	March 30	Genesis 3:8
February 28	Titus 2:7	March 31	Psalm 96:9
February 29	Luke 1:28–29	April 1	Hebrews 12:14
March 1	Jude 1:16	April 2	2 Corinthians 5:7
March 2	Romans 5:8	April 3	Proverbs 14:1
March 3	Luke 15:2	April 4	John 3:10
March 4	Hebrews 10:19, 22	April 5	John 6:35
March 5	Psalm 103:19	April 6	Matthew 17:27
March 6	Titus 2:2	April 7	Malachi 3:6
March 7	Philippians 3:12	April 8	Titus 3:1–2
March 8	Proverbs 11:13	April 9	Luke 1:46–48
March 9	Romans 3:10	April 10	Revelation 7:12
March 10	Psalm 24:8	April 11	Psalm 139:1
March 11	Titus 1:7–8	April 12	Acts 9:36
March 12	Isaiah 29:13	April 13	John 8:36
March 13	Matthew 1:20	April 14	2 Thessalonians 3:16
March 14	Titus 2:11–12		
March 15	1 John 1:5	April 15	Matthew 16:24
March 16	1 John 3:20	April 16	Proverbs 31:28
March 17	Luke 6:37	April 17	1 Corinthians 7:7
March 18	John 18:37	April 18	Psalm 115:3
March 19	Daniel 4:34	April 19	Romans 1:21
March 20	Exodus 33:11	April 20	Hosea 6:3
March 21	Titus 1:11	April 21	Philippians 2:3
March 22	John 13:35	April 22	1 Thessalonians 5:11
March 23	Psalm 45:11		
March 24	Psalm 33:13–14	April 23	Daniel 11:32
March 25	Habakkuk 1:3	April 24	Daniel 10:11
March 26	Psalm 46:1	April 25	Ephesians 4:2

DATE	VERSE(S)	DATE	VERSE(S)
April 26	Luke 1:38	May 27	John 13:7
April 27	Hebrews 13:15	May 28	1 John 2:1
April 28	John 12:46	May 29	Genesis 3:20
April 29	Ephesians 4:1	May 30	Daniel 4:27
April 30	Isaiah 6:5	May 31	John 19:25
May 1	Isaiah 12:2	June 1	Romans 6:18
May 2	Luke 9:23	June 2	Colossians 1:14
May 3	Proverbs 31:26	June 3	Deuteronomy 16:17
May 4	John 2:5		
May 5	Habakkuk 1:5	June 4	Daniel 1:2
May 6	Psalm 119:18	June 5	Luke 2:35
May 7	Proverbs 16:9	June 6	2 Corinthians 3:18
May 8	Proverbs 14:12		
May 9	Revelation 7:17	June 7	Psalm 51:17
May 10	1 Corinthians 13:12	June 8	Psalm 25:20
		June 9	Romans 4:25
May 11	Psalm 141:3	June 10	Titus 2:5
May 12	1 Peter 1:15	June 11	Ephesians 1:11
May 13	Isaiah 7:14	June 12	Luke 1:34
May 14	Psalm 119:11	June 13	1 Peter 3:18
May 15	Psalm 13:5	June 14	Psalm 85:6
May 16	Colossians 1:13	June 15	Exodus 6:6
May 17	Mark 8:35	June 16	2 Chronicles 20:12
May 18	Revelation 1:17–18		
		June 17	Ecclesiastes 4:9–10
May 19	Psalm 119:97		
May 20	Hebrews 13:18	June 18	Psalm 11:7
May 21	Luke 4:43	June 19	Habakkuk 1:2
May 22	Psalm 37:34	June 20	Proverbs 31:12
May 23	Luke 12:2	June 21	Galatians 2:20
May 24	Philppians 2:4	June 22	2 Chronicles 20:6
May 25	Luke 1:45	June 23	Mark 12:30
May 26	1 Timothy 6:6	June 24	Revelation 5:6
		June 25	Matthew 6:33

DATE	VERSE(S)	DATE	VERSE(S)
June 26	Job 1:1	July 28	James 1:15
June 27	Hebrews 12:15	July 29	Romans 8:28
June 28	John 12:25	July 30	Psalm 101:3
June 29	Colossians 3:13	July 31	Colossians 4:6
June 30	Genesis 3:1	August 1	Psalm 105:17
July 1	Matthew 6:21	August 2	Philippians 4:4
July 2	John 5:30	August 3	Matthew 7:7
July 3	Esther 2:8	August 4	John 11:25
July 4	John 8:32	August 5	Genesis 45:5
July 5	James 3:5	August 6	Jeremiah 31:3
July 6	Psalm 139:23	August 7	Song of Songs 4:11
July 7	Psalm 118:1		
July 8	Isaiah 42:1	August 8	Mark 14:3
July 9	Proverbs 15:4	August 9	Proverbs 21:23
July 10	Deuteronomy 33:27	August 10	Isaiah 57:15
July 11	Psalm 72:11	August 11	Ephesians 5:31–32
July 12	Isaiah 61:1	August 12	Romans 8:2
July 13	Philippians 2:13	August 13	John 7:37
July 14	Genesis 1:1	August 14	Daniel 1:9
July 15	Habakkuk 2:4	August 15	Ephesians 4:31
July 16	John 8:12	August 16	2 Chronicles 7:14
July 17	Ruth 2:3	August 17	Isaiah 6:3
July 18	Proverbs 15:28	August 18	Daniel 1:8
July 19	Revelation 1:8	August 19	John 1:29
July 20	Matthew 6:10	August 20	Proverbs 30:8–9
July 21	Genesis 3:12	August 21	1 Thessalonians 4:18
July 22	Proverbs 10:19	August 22	2 Corinthians 8:9
July 23	Proverbs 11:2	August 23	John 8:44
July 24	1 Peter 2:24	August 24	Jeremiah 17:5
July 25	John 10:10	August 25	Isaiah 11:2
July 26	Genesis 39:2	August 26	Matthew 6:11
July 27	Revelation 19:7		

DATE	VERSE(S)	DATE	VERSE(S)
August 27	Ephesians 4:29	September 27	Proverbs 25:12
August 28	Jeremiah 29:11	September 28	Matthew 6:12
August 29	John 11:35	September 29	Matthew 1:23
August 30	Proverbs 16:24	September 30	Daniel 1:1
August 31	Galatians 5:22–23	October 1	Revelation 21:5
September 1	1 Corinthians 1:27	October 2	Psalm 22:26
September 2	1 Corinthians 15:57	October 3	Psalm 69:32
		October 4	James 1:17
September 3	Daniel 1:20	October 5	2 Timothy 2:15
September 4	Titus 2:3–4	October 6	Hebrews 7:27
September 5	Matthew 6:34	October 7	Psalm 32:1
September 6	Psalm 139:6	October 8	2 Peter 2:19
September 7	Joel 3:16	October 9	Psalm 29:11
September 8	Romans 12:2	October 10	Philippians 4:6–7
September 9	Exodus 3:6	October 11	Romans 8:1
September 10	Romans 6:23	October 12	Romans 12:1
September 11	Psalm 29:4–5	October 13	Hosea 11:3–4
September 12	John 16:33	October 14	Luke 15:20
September 13	Titus 2:14	October 15	John 1:41
September 14	Daniel 2:20	October 16	Exodus 16:4
September 15	2 Corinthians 12:10	October 17	Proverbs 24:3
		October 18	2 Corinthians 5:17
September 16	Colossians 2:13	October 19	John 16:13
September 17	Luke 1:31	October 20	Proverbs 3:13–14
September 18	Matthew 18:21	October 21	Matthew 6:14
September 19	Luke 17:4	October 22	Luke 1:68
September 20	Hebrews 1:8	October 23	Ephesians 5:3
September 21	Psalm 19:14	October 24	2 Timothy 3:2–3, 5
September 22	Psalm 57:2	October 25	Romans 6:16
September 23	Daniel 2:21	October 26	Psalm 17:6
September 24	Romans 8:31	October 27	John 14:6
September 25	1 Corinthians 1:25	October 28	James 1:13
September 26	1 Peter 5:6	October 29	1 Corinthians 5:7

DATE	VERSE(S)	DATE	VERSE(S)
October 30	Colossians 3:23	November 30	1 Peter 2:4
October 31	Psalm 29:10	December 1	Romans 5:20
November 1	Isaiah 55:6	December 2	John 14:2
November 2	John 12:24	December 3	John 19:26–27
November 3	Psalm 92:4	December 4	Colossians 4:2
November 4	Revelation 21:6	December 5	Luke 19:10
November 5	Proverbs 18:21	December 6	Ephesians 4:32
November 6	1 Corinthians 10:13	December 7	1 Chronicles 29:11
		December 8	Ephesians 1:22
November 7	Romans 5:18	December 9	2 Corinthians 8:2
November 8	1 Thessalonians 4:3	December 10	Proverbs 31:10
November 9	Genesis 3:13	December 11	Philippians 4:8
November 10	Genesis 3:6	December 12	Psalm 29:2
November 11	Isaiah 28:29	December 13	John 3:16
November 12	Proverbs 1:7	December 14	Revelation 21:2
November 13	2 Timothy 4:18	December 15	Psalm 5:4
November 14	Titus 1:15	December 16	Hosea 12:6
November 15	1 Thessalonians 5:18	December 17	Deuteronomy 32:4
		December 18	Luke 5:21
November 16	Luke 2:51	December 19	Psalm 104:24
November 17	Hebrews 12:11	December 20	Revelation 19:16
November 18	Jeremiah 4:3	December 21	1 Thessalonians 5:23
November 19	2 Corinthians 2:14		
		December 22	Revelation 11:15
November 20	John 10:14–15	December 23	2 Chronicles 12:1
November 21	Romans 7:24–25	December 24	Revelation 3:14
November 22	1 Chronicles 16:29	December 25	Philippians 2:7
November 23	Philippians 2:6	December 26	Psalm 84:11
November 24	Isaiah 26:3	December 27	Leviticus 20:26
November 25	John 20:28	December 28	Psalm 32:2
November 26	Ephesians 1:7	December 29	Proverbs 10:18
November 27	Mark 12:31	December 30	1 John 1:7
November 28	Ephesians 3:20	December 31	Matthew 6:13
November 29	John 6:51		

Notes

1. John Bunyan, *Grace Abounding to the Chief of Sinners* (Boston: Ginn and Company, 1910), 116.

2. Donald S. Whitney, *Spiritual Disciplines for the Christian Life* (Colorado Springs: NavPress, 1991), 38

3. James M. Gray, *How to Master the English Bible* (Edinburgh: Oliphant, Anderson & Ferrier, 1907), 53.

4. John Burton, "Holy Bible, Book Divine," *Youth's Monitor in Verse*, 1803.

5. Matthew Henry, *Matthew Henry's Commentary on the Whole Bible: Complete and Unabridged in One Volume*, Regency Reference Library (Grand Rapids, MI: Zondervan, 1961), Matthew XI.

6. John Piper, "As We Forgive Our Debtors" (message), March 20, 1994, www.desiringgod.org/library/sermons/94/032094.html.

7. *Memoirs of Jonathan Edwards*, Works of Jonathan Edwards, vol. 1 (Edinburgh: Banner of Truth Trust, 1974), xiv.

8. A. W. Tozer, *I Call It Heresy* (Harrisburg, PA: Christian Publications, 1974), 63.

9. William Barclay, *The Lord's Prayer* (Louisville, KY: Westminister John Knox Press, 1998), 49–50.

10. Betty Scott Stam, 1925, quoted in Elisabeth Elliot, *Quest for Love* (Grand Rapids, MI: Revell, 1996), 131.

11. *Smooth Stones Taken from Ancient Brooks*, comp. Charles H. Spurgeon (Morgan, PA: Soli Deo Gloria, 1996), 93.

12. Darlene Deibler Rose, *Evidence Not Seen* (San Francisco: Harper & Row, 1988), 143.

13. From a message called "The Maximum Man" by Dr. Adrian Rogers, preached at a Maximum Manhood Conference at Bellevue Baptist Church, Memphis, TN, on October 10, 1985.

14. Augustus M. Toplady, "Rock of Ages," 1776.

15. "Wyoming Woman Accused of Starting South Dakota Wildfire," *Black Hills Pioneer*, October 2, 2000, www.bhpioneer.com/ wyoming-woman-accused-of-starting-jasper-fire/article_ 96203203-ecad-5780-86d2-6ed609eee661.html.

16. Cesar Soriano, "Vow of Silence Ends in Torrent," *USA Today*, Arlington, VA, September 6, 2001.

17. UTU News, Volume 27, November 1995, Number 11, https:// smart-union.org/wp-content/uploads/2022/02/November-2005- SMART-Transportation-Newsletter.pdf.

18. This story was featured in the devotional *Our Daily Bread* on December 31, 1998. The anecdote was likely based on a sentence by Mary Geraldine Taylor, *Borden of Yale* (Philadelphia: China Inland Mission, 1926), 260.

19. Jonathan Edwards, *Memoirs of Jonathan Edwards, The Works of Jonathan Edwards*, vol. 1 (Edinburgh: The Banner of Truth, 1976), xlvi.

20. Fanny Crosby, *Fanny Crosby's Life-Story* (New York: Every Where Publishing Company, 1903), 13. Emphasis added.

21. Charles H. Spurgeon, *Evening by Evening* (Alachua, FL: Bridge-Logos, 2005), December 1.

22. John Newton, "Amazing Grace," 1779.

23. Oswald Chambers, *My Utmost for His Highest* (United Kingdom: Oswald Chambers Publications Association, Ltd., 1927), November 19.

24. Fenelon, *The Seeking Heart* (Jacksonville: Christian Books Publishing House, 1992), 111.

25. Norman Grubb, *Continuous Revival* (Fort Washington, PA: Christian Literature Crusade, 1997), 15.

Source List

Adorned: Living Out the Beauty of the Gospel Together
1/7, 2/20, 2/22, 2/28, 3/6, 3/11, 3/14, 3/21, 3/22, 3/29, 4/3, 4/4, 4/8, 4/12, 4/16, 4/22, 4/25, 5/3, 5/22, 5/29, 6/5, 6/10, 6/13, 6/17, 6/20, 7/1, 7/27, 8/7, 8/11, 8/12, 8/15, 8/21, 8/27, 8/31, 9/4, 9/8, 9/13, 10/17, 10/23, 10/30, 11/8, 11/14, 12/2, 12/10

Brokenness: The Heart God Revives
1/14, 2/2, 2/26, 4/30, 6/7, 6/23, 6/28, 7/6, 7/23, 8/10, 8/17, 9/11, 9/26, 11/2, 12/30

Choosing Forgiveness: Moving from Hurt to Hope
1/11, 2/7, 2/15, 3/17, 4/1, 5/16, 6/27, 6/29, 7/4, 9/16, 9/19, 9/24, 10/1, 10/25, 11/17, 11/26, 12/6, 12/18

Choosing Gratitude: Your Journey to Joy
1/31, 2/1, 2/6, 2/9, 2/13, 2/19, 2/24, 3/1, 4/10, 4/19, 4/27, 5/24, 9/2, 9/15, 10/4, 10/10, 10/24, 11/15, 11/22, 12/1, 12/17

Heaven Rules: Take courage. Take comfort. Our God is in control.
2/21, 3/5, 3/19, 3/28, 4/18, 4/23, 4/24, 5/1, 5/27, 5/30, 6/4, 6/11, 6/22, 8/14, 8/18, 9/3, 9/14, 9/23, 9/30, 10/9, 10/31, 11/24

Holiness: The Heart God Purifies
1/16, 1/29, 2/11, 2/27, 3/31, 4/13, 5/12, 6/18, 7/28, 11/3, 11/7, 12/15, 12/21, 12/27

Lies Women Believe: And the Truth that Sets Them Free
1/17, 2/3, 3/2, 3/26, 5/8, 6/8, 6/30, 7/25, 7/30, 8/23, 9/10, 10/8, 10/19, 11/9, 11/10, 11/27, 11/30, 12/13, 12/26

The Lord's Prayer: A 30-Day Devotional
1/5, 1/19, 2/8, 3/4, 3/24, 4/29, 5/21, 6/25, 7/2, 7/11, 7/20, 8/3, 8/20, 8/26, 9/5, 9/18, 9/28, 10/7, 10/16, 10/21, 10/28, 11/6, 11/13, 11/21, 11/28, 12/7, 12/12, 12/22, 12/31

My Personal Petitions Prayer Journal
1/13, 1/26, 2/23, 4/2, 4/21, 6/1, 7/7, 9/21, 10/20, 11/12

A Place of Quiet Rest: Finding Intimacy with God Through a Daily Devotional Life

1/1, 1/6, 1/9, 1/12, 1/15, 1/20, 1/25, 1/30, 2/14, 3/12, 3/20, 3/30, 4/11, 5/6, 5/10, 5/14, 5/19, 6/6, 6/16, 6/21, 8/6, 8/13, 9/9

Portrait of a Woman Used by God: Lessons from the Life of Mary of Nazareth

2/29, 3/13, 4/9, 4/26, 5/4, 5/25, 5/31, 6/12, 8/16, 9/1, 9/17, 9/22, 9/25, 10/2, 10/5, 11/16, 11/23, 12/3

The Power of Words

1/4, 1/22, 2/4, 3/8, 4/7, 5/11, 5/20, 7/5, 7/9, 7/18, 7/22, 7/31, 8/9, 8/30, 9/27, 11/5, 11/19, 12/11, 12/29

Seeking Him: Experiencing the Joy of Personal Revival

1/8, 1/24, 2/17, 2/25, 3/15, 4/20, 5/23, 6/14, 8/24, 10/3, 10/13, 11/1, 11/18, 12/16, 12/23, 12/28

Singled Out for Him: Embracing the Gift, the Blessings, and the Challenges of Singleness

3/7, 4/17, 5/26, 6/3, 8/8, 8/22, 12/9

Surrender: The Heart God Controls

1/3, 1/28, 2/10, 4/15, 5/2, 5/17, 7/14, 10/12, 10/18, 12/19

The Wonder of His Name: 32 Life-Changing Names of Jesus

1/23, 2/5, 2/12, 2/18, 3/3, 3/10, 3/18, 3/23, 3/27, 4/5, 4/14, 4/28, 5/9, 5/13, 5/18, 5/28, 6/2, 6/9, 6/15, 6/24, 7/8, 7/12, 7/16, 7/19, 8/4, 8/19, 8/25, 8/29, 9/7, 9/12, 9/20, 9/29, 10/6, 10/11, 10/15, 10/22, 10/27, 10/29, 11/4, 11/11, 11/20, 11/25, 11/29, 12/5, 12/8, 12/14, 12/20, 12/24, 12/25

Worries, Woes & Worship: Moving from Fear to Faith

1/18, 3/9, 3/25, 4/6, 5/5, 5/15, 6/19, 7/15, 8/2, 9/6, 10/26

You Can Trust God to Write Your Story: Embracing the Mysteries of Providence

1/2, 1/10, 1/21, 1/27, 2/16, 3/16, 5/7, 6/26, 7/3, 7/10, 7/13, 7/17, 7/21, 7/24, 7/26, 7/29, 8/1, 8/5, 8/28, 10/14, 12/4